D0712638

MINORITIES IN PHOENIX

MINORITIES IN PHOENIX

A PROFILE OF MEXICAN AMERICAN,

CHINESE AMERICAN, AND

AFRICAN AMERICAN COMMUNITIES,

1860 - 1992

BRADFORD LUCKINGHAM

THE UNIVERSITY OF ARIZONA PRESS
Tucson & London

The University of Arizona Press
Copyright © 1994
Arizona Board of Regents
All rights reserved

∞ This book is printed on acid-free, archival-quality paper.
Manufactured in the United States of America

99 98 97 96 95 94   6   5   4   3   2   1

Library of Congress Cataloging-in-Publication Data

Luckingham, Bradford.
    Minorities in Phoenix : a profile of Mexican American, Chinese
American, and African American communities, 1860-1992 /
Bradford Luckingham.
        p.   cm.
    Includes index.
    ISBN 0-8165-1457-7 (acid-free paper)
    1. Minorities—Arizona—Phoenix—History.   2. Phoenix
(Ariz.)—Ethnic relations.   3. Phoenix (Ariz.)—Race relations.
I. Title.
F819.P57L82 1994
979.1'73004—dc20   94-8103
                                                                  CIP

British Library Cataloging-in-Publication Data
A catalogue record for this book is available from the British Library.

TO HATTIE AND HER PARENTS

CONTENTS

MAPS

TABLES

PREFACE

In recent years historians have revealed much about minority group members as integral parts of vital communities rather than picturing them only as passive victims of Anglo American oppression. This inclusion represents a new and deserving emphasis, one that shows minority group members as playing active roles in American history, attempting and often succeeding in shaping their own destiny despite the barriers of prejudice, discrimination, and exploitation. The new emphasis has been a positive development in historical writing, but the formidable barriers of prejudice, discrimination, and exploitation that have existed continue to need attention from historians.

Life for minority groups in Phoenix has historically been difficult but promising. Over time, the struggle for equity resulted in gains being made, but progress was never easy. Unfortunately, little attention has been given to the historical experience of Mexican Americans, Chinese Americans, and African Americans in the nation's ninth largest city, but past neglect is giving way to new awareness. This book is a beginning, covering the experience of three important minority communities in Phoenix from their origins in the late nineteenth century to the present. It profiles the general history of each group, emphasizing the problems as well as the progress the group experienced. A variety of sources, ranging from newspaper files to statistical data to oral accounts, has been utilized in an attempt to provide both an internal and external view of the groups involved. Also, an attempt has been made to compare the Phoenix experience with that of other cities in the region and the nation.

I wish to thank all the historians, librarians, and students who have helped me in my work. Special appreciation is due several institutions and the able people who staff them: the Arizona Historical Society, the Arizona State Department of Library Archives and Public Records, the Phoenix Museum of History, the Salt River Project Archives, and the Hayden Library, Arizona State University. The Arizona Collection and the Arizona Historical Foundation, both located in the Hayden Library, proved indispensable.

I also want to thank all those involved in the Phoenix Chinatown project for their support and cooperation. Portions of Part 2 first appeared in *First Street and Madison: Historical Archaeology of the Second Phoenix Chinatown,* a report prepared for the City of Phoenix, Pueblo Grande Museum, by Dames and Moore Intermountain Cultural Resource Services, Phoenix, Arizona, 1992.

I am also deeply indebted to Edward Oetting, Chris Marin, Susie Sato, Evelyn Cooper, Cindy Myers, Melanie Sturgeon, Dennis Preisler, Larry Guillow, Jay Antle, Pat Moore, Michael Lawson, Carolyn Sol, Michael Konig, Michael Kotlanger, S.J. and the late Geoffrey Mawn. I also wish to acknowledge the support of the Arizona State University History Department, the Arizona State University College of Liberal Arts and Sciences, and the Arizona State University Faculty Research Grants Program. To James Dybdahl, Senior Word Processor, Humanities Computing Facility, I am also indebted.

Finally, I wish to thank my wife, Barbara, for her aid and encouragement.

Brad Luckingham

MINORITIES IN PHOENIX

INTRODUCTION ALWAYS THE STRUGGLE

In 1990, Phoenix ranked as the ninth largest city in the United States. Historically, the population of the Arizona capital has been largely Anglo, with small groups of people of color making up the difference. In the early years of the city's history, Mexicans accounted for half the population, but they quickly lost ground to Anglos, who progressively outnumbered them. During most of the twentieth century, Mexicans remained the largest minority group in Phoenix, making up about 15 percent of the total population; blacks continued to make up about 5 percent; and Chinese, about 1 percent. In recent years each group has experienced a surge in numbers, gaining in representation but remaining small within the total population (see Table I.1). For these minority groups the past has been a struggle for equity.[1]

The struggle has not been unique to Phoenix. Although the experience differed from region to region, from city to city, it always involved struggle. Historians rightly point out that the struggle has been heroic as well as tragic. Variations in the level of racism and responses to it over time and place are evident. All types of conditions existed: Mexican Americans seemed better off in Tucson than in Phoenix; Chinese Americans seemed worse off in Los Angeles than in Phoenix; African Americans seemed better off in Seattle than in Phoenix; and so on. The responses to racism by various groups also differed. Minority group populations varied in size and minority group problems varied in intensity from city to city, but they did exist, and minority group leaders and members acted in positive ways rather than as passive victims of negative racial attitudes

Table I.1. Phoenix Population Statistics, 1870–1990

Year	Total	Mexican Americans	Chinese Americans	African Americans
1870	240	124	—	3
1880	1,708	772	110	5
1890	3,152	—	—	—
1900	5,544	802	91	150
1910	11,134	1,100	110	328
1920	29,053	2,323	130	1,075
1930	48,118	7,293	227	2,366
1940	65,414	9,740	431	4,263
1950	106,818	16,000	448	5,217
1960	439,170	61,460	1,092	20,919
1970	584,303	81,239	1,483	27,896
1980	789,704	116,875	2,493	37,672
1990	983,403	176,139	4,254	51,053

SOURCE: U.S. Census of Population, 1870–1990.

and actions. They created viable communities and they worked diligently to shape their own lives despite the barriers of prejudice and exploitation. They actively fought segregation, discrimination, and oppression at whatever level they existed. Over time, the struggle for equity bore fruit and many succeeded in achieving their goals. Struggle proved integral to the total experience of minority group members in the urban West; for many of them, the struggle goes on.[2]

From the beginning, the struggle existed. During the Spanish and Mexican periods, Anglo Americans began to enter the towns of present-day Texas, New Mexico, Arizona, and California. During and after the Mexican War of conquest, Anglos increasingly found their way to the towns, fast becoming the urban centers of the American Southwest. They joined local Mexicans in the further development of Santa Fe, Albuquerque, Tucson, Los Angeles, San Diego, and other communities. With the coming of the railroads, the relationship between the two groups deteriorated. More Anglos than Mexicans arrived and Anglo population gains increased. As the oasis towns developed during the late nineteenth century, they became more attractive to Anglo elements, and as Anglos assumed power in the regional centers of the Southwest, they utilized the Mexican population to help them realize their goals, including economic growth, political control, and social and cultural prominence. Having achieved a dominant position in each community, the Anglos acquired more wealth, influence, and prestige, and from these positions of strength dictated the terms of the ethnic arrangement, which invariably found the majority of Mexicans and Mexican Americans living on the "wrong side of the tracks." For them, upward mobility proved elusive and poverty remained a problem. Although their situation was bleak north of the border, Mexicans kept coming because it usually meant economic improvement over what was available in Mexico; indeed, during the years 1900 to 1930—the migration era—more than a million Mexicans moved into the American West, many of them to the emerging cities.[3]

Economic deprivation, political domination, and ethnocentric Anglo social and cultural attitudes and actions, along with a preference for living together, encouraged the majority of Mexicans and Mexican Americans to reside in their own neighborhoods, or *barrios*, in the urban centers. A sense of ethnic identity and cultural awareness, along with patterns of discrimination and segregation, inspired barrio development. Within them, a vibrant family and community life emerged, providing Spanish-speaking residents with many of their basic needs. A small middle class served the largely working-class population, establishing a variety of businesses; in time, churches, schools, mutual-aid societies, newspapers, and other institutions appeared. The many organizations prior to 1930 represented numerous interests, from the protective to the social. Many of them included nationalistic and patriotic themes, for most barrio residents before 1930 were wedded to their language and their culture, and they still considered Mexico home; they hoped to return once they acquired sufficient savings. They often visited "home," and while in the United States they lived a "Mexican" life as much as possible; they especially enjoyed participating in Mexican national holiday celebrations such as Diez Seis de Septiembre and Cinco de Mayo.[4]

Over the years, despite the barriers of prejudice and exploitation, the attractions of America had their impact, especially in the minds of Mexican Americans, and the 1930s were the beginning years of the Mexican American era—a period that lasted until the 1960s. Feelings of cultural nationalism remained but lessened, and many middle-class Mexican Americans began to identify more with America than with Mexico. Educated and acculturated, they increasingly directed their attention to assimilation into the dominant society. The Great Depression of the 1930s, however, did not help smooth the way for the Mexican Americans, nor did it help their image in the eyes of dejected Anglos. Many Mexicans and Mexican Americans returned to Mexico voluntarily and involuntarily during the decade. Influential Anglo American leaders and groups encouraged them to leave; repatriation efforts reflected the strong anti-Mexican feeling of Anglos in the United States. Nevertheless, the acculturation and assimilation movement among Mexican Americans continued.[5]

For those Mexican Americans who remained in the urban centers during and after the Great Depression, new times brought new hope. World War II proved to be a major turning point in Mexican American history. During the 1940s, more than ever before, the American Dream displaced the dream of returning to Mexico. Mexican Americans especially began to escalate their struggle for the rights and opportunities enjoyed by first-class citizens in the United States. The war experience inspired Mexican American veterans and their supporters to challenge their second-class status. Mexican Americans fought with distinction in the armed services, and at home they worked in defense plants and at military installations. Despite ugly racial encounters in Los Angeles and elsewhere, the war proved to be a catalyst in the Mexican American struggle for equality and dignity. The G.I. Bill gave veterans new educational opportunities, job possibilities, and housing benefits. Mexican American American Legion posts and other veterans groups joined with established Mexican American voluntary associations in the struggle for civil rights. Largely a middle-class Mexican American movement in the 1940s and 1950s, the overall goal was an integrated society with equal rights for all, but also freedom for all to retain their cultural heritage. By the end of the 1950s, modest progress had been achieved in areas ranging from school desegregation to professional attainment, but it was slow and hard.[6]

The civil rights struggle continued at a more aggressive pace, and more gains were made in the 1960s and 1970s—the Chicano era—inspiring ethnic pride and bolstering a sense of identity and accomplishment. Although falling far short of parity with Anglo ratings, improvements in educational opportunities, occupational and residential mobility patterns, and political participation helped open up and expand the Mexican American middle class in the urban centers. Chicanos sought economic and political justice, along with bicultural accommodation, and their organized, determined efforts brought some success. More economic and political influence, along with a sense of social and cultural awareness, allowed more militant Chicanos to evolve into mainstream participants without forgetting their original goals of helping oppressed Mexican Americans, but the experience proved difficult and often transformed them. By the 1980s many in the "Hispanic" middle class no longer actively pursued solutions to the persistent problems in the poor Mexican and Mexican American barrios of the urban Southwest. Whether new leadership would work on finding solutions remained to be seen. As in the past, the Mexican American population continued to express diversity. Unity occurred on occasion for particular causes, but disparate elements often went their own way, each with their own agendas.[7]

Chinese Americans also engaged in a long struggle for equity. The first significant arrival of Chinese in the United States occurred during the California gold rush in the late 1840s and early 1850s. Mostly Cantonese, they entered the port of San Francisco from the province of Guangdong in southeastern China. Unrest in that province had created political and economic havoc, and many residents sought opportunity elsewhere, including California. Paying their own way or exchanging their labor for passage to San Francisco, they sought a source of income. Sojourners, they wanted to accumulate enough money to return home to China and live out their lives with their families.[8]

From the beginning, Chinese newcomers felt unwelcome in California and other parts of the American West. Following gold rushes to Nevada, Oregon, Montana, Colorado, and other strike points, they met discrimination and persecution. Chinese also helped build the western portions of transcontinental railroads during the period. When the mines played out and the railroads were completed, those who did not return to China often drifted into emerging towns and cities in the region, where they also found prejudice and oppression. By 1880 more than 100,000 Chinese, mostly males, were living in the United States, most of them in California and other parts of the American West. Some of them were merchants and artisans, but the great majority were unskilled workers. Like the Mexicans, the Chinese helped fill the region's need for an abundant supply of cheap labor. Chinese merchants, artisans, and unskilled workers contributed to the economic development of the region; they built Chinatowns in San Francisco and other urban centers, and they pioneered in the rural, agricultural areas of the West.[9]

The reception given Chinese in the American West was dismal. Objections to their presence led to the Chinese exclusion movement, a successful attempt to keep them out of the country. Anti-Chinese spokesmen characterized them as unassimilable and undesirable additions to American society; labor leaders accused them of depressing wages and being willing to work under any conditions, causing unemployment and creating hardship in the white worker population. Violence erupted; in 1871, for example, nineteen Chinese died in Los Angeles riots. Labor unions and other white working-class groups cried "the Chinese must go," and politicians got the message. Congress finally acted in 1882 by passing exclusionary legislation. The Chinese Exclusion Act of 1882 excluded Chinese laborers for ten years. The law was the first immigration law in American history to bar a specific nationality. Exempted were Chinese merchants, their wives and children, and other "select" groups such as students and travelers.[10]

The exclusion of Chinese laborers did not end prejudice and oppression against Chinese already in America. Verbal and physical abuse, along with local laws, continued to make life difficult for them. Anti-Chinese individuals and groups kept demanding tighter restrictions, and Congress responded; legislation in 1892, 1902, and 1904 legally extended the exclusion of Chinese laborers indefinitely. Unwelcome in America, Chinese in the urban centers turned to Chinatowns for economic and cultural security, for comfort and safety. A familiar neighborhood helped Chinese immigrants to survive in unfriendly larger cities, just as it did other proscribed ethnic groups. Few of the mostly male Chinese wished to stay forever in America; they yearned to return "home" to China. Being sojourners, and denied participation in an egalitarian society in America, they found refuge in Chinatown and its offerings. Living in Chinatown and harboring the hope of returning to China made it easier for them to retain and cherish their cultural heritage. They remained more interested in China than the United States; the 1911 Chinese Revolution, for example, captured their attention. San Francisco's Chinatown evolved into the most significant of America's Chinatowns, and it set the tone for others in cities throughout the country, including the Southwest.[11]

Chinatowns contained tightly knit communities. Residents built impressive *joss* houses (temples) and established boarding houses, grocery stores, specialty shops, and other businesses, including restaurants and laundries. Opium dens and gambling establishments also opened, many of them underground. Chinese often lived as well as worked in these places of business and pleasure. Chinese religious traditions, holidays, language, food, music, philosophy, medicine, reading, and games (such as chess and mah jong) remained popular; a Chinese mode of life prevailed as much as possible.

Anti-Chinese attitudes and actions only caused Chinese to draw closer together. Clan/regional associations and activities helped. The Chinese Consolidated Benevolent Association in San Francisco, known widely as the Chinese Six Companies, set the example, speaking for the general interests of Chinese America and Chinese Americans, but numerous subordinate clan/regional associations throughout urban America enjoyed considerable local autonomy. These organizations, based on familial lineage and/or territorial ties (including village dialects) in China, offered aid and protection and generally took care of their own members as much as possible in the Chinatowns of America. As in the case of Mexicans and other immigrant groups, Chinese newcomers reflected the chain migration process, in which concentrations from a specific place or family reunited in a specific place in the United States; for example, the Ong clan in Phoenix is from the district of Hoiping in the province of Guangdong in southeastern China.[12]

Chinese immigration to the United States declined during the years of exclusion. Smuggling and other means of entry continued, but the Chinese population dropped from 107,000 in 1880 to 77,000 in 1940 as many of the sojourner population died or returned to China. Moreover, the percentage of Chinese urban dwellers increased from 76 to 91 percent in 1940. During the 1920s and 1930s, American-born Chinese acculturated more than in the past. English-speaking Chinese Americans replaced Chinese sojourners and sought the American Dream.

Racial prejudice and discrimination continued to confront Chinese Americans, however, and they made few substantial gains. The Great Depression was hard on them, but their tradition of taking care of their own helped. Segregated in many places and oppressed in many ways, they nevertheless endured and persevered. They operated small businesses in which whites did not compete, such as laundries, groceries, and restaurants. They created them by borrowing money from their associations; Chinese American capital financed large business ventures as well. The rise of a Chinese American entrepreneur class inspired the formation of Chinese American Chambers of Commerce and other organizations to support Chinese American businesses and businessmen.

Most Chinese business ventures remained small. To succeed they required long hours of operation, low profit margins, and low wages. Family members often worked seven days a week, fifty-two weeks a year to survive and educate their children. Hard work and education became the keys to success for Chinese families, and as Chinese American children received educations they accepted American ways and American dreams. In 1870 only 1 percent of the Chinese population was American-born, but that figure rose to 52 percent by 1940. Over time, more children were influenced by American institutions and ideas. Americanization of Chinese individuals and organizations encouraged them to increase their participation in mainstream American life. Chinese American business and professional people led the way. A few became prominent, but for the great majority prejudice and discrimination remained barriers.[13]

The struggle for entry into mainstream American life continued, and some success was recorded. Chinatowns began to decline and even disappear, especially in smaller urban centers. As for Mexican Americans, World War II was a turning point for Chinese Americans. Thousands of them served gallantly in the armed forces, and others worked diligently in war-related plants and shipyards. China became an ally of the United States in World War II, and in 1943 the United States government repealed the Chinese immigration exclusion laws as well as many naturalization barriers. Chinese patriotism during the war and Chinese achievement in education and other areas of American life improved on past images held by the general population, and many new doors opened to mainstream America, including occupational and residential mobility. Following the war, Chinese Americans held anti-Communist views and opposed the Communist takeover of China. Chinese American organizations expressed their commitment to Chiang Kai-shek's Nationalist government in Taiwan and their gratitude to the United States for supporting it.

Chinese Americans in the United States also continued to take care of their own, although most of them benefited from postwar progress and prosperity. The sojourner mentality no longer existed as Chinese Americans considered the United States their home. Prejudice and discrimination remained but in subtler forms. Although many Chinese Americans eventually succeeded in entering the mainstream, they retained an interest in Chinese culture and traditions. Their organizations reflected a knowledge of Chinese history and heritage. Significant economic progress also occurred in the 1950s and 1960s, especially in the business and professional ranks. The number of young Chinese American males and females going to college increased considerably as the years passed; by 1970 observers were marveling at their success. Critics quickly pointed out, however, that not all Chinese Americans were progressing or prospering; unskilled Chinese and Chinese American laborers still suffered from low pay and poor working conditions, and most Chinese and Chinese American businesses remained small.

A quota system after 1943 had set limits on Chinese entry, but more liberal immigration laws passed by 1965 encouraged more Chinese to come to the United States. A large number of the newcomers were women, bringing the male-female ratio closer to parity by 1970. The new immigrants came from many parts of China and Asia and tended to settle in major cities; by this time, more occupational and residential areas included Chinese Americans. Educated and affluent, many of them differed from immigrants of the past; others were poor and uneducated. Class and cultural differences created progress and problems. Benefiting from the civil rights movement and new economic opportunities, younger Chinese Americans had less difficulty integrating into mainstream society, but they remained an identifiable group with a distinct, though by no means homogeneous, subculture. In the 1970s and 1980s, while common values persisted among Chinese Americans, diversity existed.[14]

African Americans also sought equity in the American West. As elsewhere in the country, their efforts often fell short, but the struggle brought gains. Progressively entering the region from points east during the last half of the nineteenth century, African Americans settled in San Francisco, Los Angeles, Portland, Seattle, Denver, Phoenix, and other Western cities. They sought economic and social betterment in an environment offering more occupational and educational mobility than could be found in the Northern and Southern regions of the country, but despite success there was no escaping American attitudes and actions. As time passed, black urbanites in the American West found problems similar to those they had left behind. Prejudice, discrimination, and segregation, although less evident in some places than others, eventually confined the majority of African Americans to second-class status. Prevented from integrating into white-dominated societies, African Americans created their own communities within the larger cities.[15]

Unwelcome in the mainstream, African Americans established their own physical and institutional neighborhoods. Denied entry into the white-dominated world of the urban centers and excluded from their offerings, they forged viable, vibrant worlds of their own. Most of the residents of an African American community were unskilled laborers, service workers or domestic servants, but a small middle class provided leadership. Made up of small businessmen, skilled artisans, and professionals, it served the black population and itself. The black middle class not only provided internal leadership but contained leaders who acted as spokesmen in contacts between the African American community and the larger city.

A sense of ethnic identity and cultural awareness, along with patterns of discrimination and segregation, inspired black community development. Churches became centers of African American life; through them black families and friends met amidst amity and affability, and black clergy and lay people planned special events, including protests. The black church as a cultural association not only filled the needs of its members for spiritual security but also served as a social rallying point, a center of group life. It conducted many activities—spiritual, educational, charitable, recreational, and political in their purpose. Church-related benevolent societies proved especially useful in serving the needs of the black population. Black fraternal lodges, business organizations, social and cultural clubs, and other voluntary associations also contributed to a sense of identity, stability, and order in the black communities of the American West. Black schools and the black press helped educate and inform black residents. By the 1920s, African American communities were well established throughout the region.[16]

During the Great Depression, African Americans suffered severe hardships in the cities. High unemployment rates and fierce competition for private and public aid retarded their ongoing efforts to achieve first-class status in urban America. World War II, however, proved to be a major turning point for African Americans, as it did for Mexican Americans and Chinese Americans. During the war they served bravely in the armed services and on the home front; military posts and defense plants hired them, and they were able to benefit from better wages and working conditions. During and following the conflict, African Americans in Western cities made gains, but not without a struggle. Black veterans, determined to acquire first-class status as Americans at home, utilized the G.I. Bill and joined organizations to achieve economic opportunities and equal rights. The National Association for the Advancement of Colored People, the National Urban League, and other determined groups led the way. In the 1940s and 1950s, considerable progress was made, especially in the area of school integration, and in the 1960s a variety of leaders and groups, exuding black pride and power, inspired a massive movement for change, resulting in the passage of laws forbidding discrimination in employment, housing, voting, and public accommodations. The struggle was far from easy; it brought forth violence and chaos on occasion, but it also brought forth additional justice and freedom for many African Americans and others in need of equity.[17]

Improvements in cultural, educational, employment, and housing opportunities, along with increased political influence at the polls, continued into the 1970s and 1980s, but problems persisted. African Americans participated in the mainstream more than ever, and the expansion of the African American middle class was notable, but parity with white Americans remained elusive. Observers noticed that at times class interests proved more compelling than minority loyalty. As in the past, economic, political, and social attitudes and actions differed among African American classes, as they did among other groups making up the urban mosaic. The progress and prosperity of the black middle class increased the differences between it and the less fortunate classes, especially the so-called underclass left behind in the problem-plagued poorer neighborhoods. As in the Mexican American and Chinese American communities, class divisions contributed to the fragmentation of the African American community, leaving it by the 1990s as diverse and complicated as the others. For many, the struggle continues.[18]

For Mexican Americans, Chinese Americans, and African Americans the struggle has been endless. The history of their experience in Phoenix, Arizona, is told in the pages that follow. Coming from every direction to Anglo-dominated early Phoenix, minority group members sought equity and opportunity. Over the years progress was made, but problems persisted. And problems remain. In this account the author has tried to focus on the external and internal forces involved in the history of minority group life in Phoenix. Although the Phoenix experience is unique in and of itself because of its personal nature, it is also seen as a reflection of the historical record in many other urban centers of the region and the nation.

PART 1   THE MEXICAN AMERICANS

1 COMMUNITY DEVELOPMENT TO 1930

In 1598 the Spaniard Juan de Oñate reached the south bank of the Rio Grande several miles below the future town of El Paso. There, nine years before the settlement of Jamestown in Virginia and twenty-two years before the settlement of Plymouth in Massachusetts, Oñate took formal possession of the province of New Mexico for Spain. Friendly natives then led the expedition along the river to a ford above the mountain narrows of the Rio Grande, and the caravan proceeded northward to establish settlements in New Mexico. Oñate called the passageway El Paso del Norte, or Pass of the North.[1]

Santa Fe was founded in 1610, and there followed the emergence of Albuquerque, Tucson, Santa Barbara, Los Angeles, San Diego, and other communities during the Spanish period. Mexico won its independence from Spain in 1821, and in 1846 war broke out between the United States and Mexico. Following that conflict Anglos (white people of non-Hispanic descent) increasingly found their way to the towns, now the urban centers of the American Southwest. After the conquest, they joined local Mexicans in the further development of the growing oases. Although a joint effort created Phoenix in the 1860s, Anglos soon dominated the Arizona settlement.[2]

From about A.D. 300 to 1400, a people known as the Hohokam, the modern Pima word meaning "those who have disappeared," occupied the Salt River valley in central Arizona, the present site of metropolitan Phoenix. The Hohokam were agriculturists who built canals and diverted water from the Salt River to irrigate their fields. They settled villages, cultivated crops, and lived in harmony with the desert environment. The Salt River provided a year-round water supply, and this invaluable resource, along with the rich soil and semitropical climate of the area, allowed the farmers to flourish. For unknown reasons, around 1400 the Hohokam occupation of the Salt River valley ended. Explanations for the failure of the Hohokam to survive include a great drought, a gigantic earthquake, a decimating disease, marauding invaders, declining soil fertility due to alkalinity, and excessive irrigation that caused a higher water table and waterlogging of agricultural land. The disappearance of the Hohokam remains a mystery, but the archaeology of their canal and village civilization is still present.[3]

Although other Indian tribes lived around the Salt River valley, it remained unoccupied for several centuries following the departure of the Hohokam. While the Spanish explored much of the Southwest and developed Santa Fe, Albuquerque, Tucson, Santa Barbara, Los Angeles, and other towns, the future site of Phoenix was left undisturbed. Even after the United States acquired the area in 1848, following the Mexican War, few Americans expressed an interest in the Salt River valley. Gold seekers rushing to strikes in California and Arizona in the 1850s and 1860s also avoided the place. Thus, by the end of the Civil War, the location of Phoenix, which was to become the ninth largest city in the United States, continued to contain only the canal remnants and residential ruins of the ancient Hohokam.[4]

In September 1865 the United States Army established Camp McDowell to protect the residents of Prescott, Wickenburg, and other central Arizona mining settlements from hostile Indians. The soldiers stationed at the remote post, located twenty miles northeast of the Salt River valley, had difficulty raising food for themselves and feed for their horses. The residents of the mining communities experienced the same problem. The high cost of bringing in foodstuffs from California or Mexico compounded their predicament. To meet the needs of the military and civilian population of the region, the Salt River valley agricultural settlement of Phoenix emerged.[5]

From the beginning, Mexican Americans played an influential role in the development of Phoenix, especially in agricultural work. In 1867 Mexican workers helped John Smith (later called John Y.T. Smith) harvest hay along the Salt River for Camp McDowell. That same year John William (Jack) Swilling, husband of Trinidad Escalante and promoter of the first modern irrigation operation in the Salt River valley, worked with

Anglos and Mexicans in clearing out old Hohokam Indian canals, digging new ones, and planting crops for nearby military posts and mining
camps. In 1870 the valley contained 240 residents, 124 of them Mexican.
In that year the population selected a townsite near the geographical center of the valley. Realizing that they were revitalizing the land of an ancient people, they named it Phoenix, in their view a fitting symbol of life
rising anew from the remains of the past. Mexicans helped survey and
clear the Phoenix townsite.[6]

The labor and expertise of Mexicans proved essential to the success of
early irrigation operations in the valley. Most of the canal (*acequia*) construction was done by them, and they usually served as *zanjeros* (ditch
overseers). They also made a contribution as small farmers and farm
workers. In addition, Mexicans constructed many of the buildings in
early Phoenix; adobe brick proved practical and useful in the desert. As
the young urban center emerged, Mexican laborers cleared and maintained streets, built utility systems, and helped provide other services.
Mexican entrepreneurs achieved success by establishing small businesses,
and some individuals became prominent in the larger business community, including Jesús Otero, J. M. Montano, Jesús Contreras, Miguel
Peralta, and J. M. Castanedas. Several Mexican businessmen formed
partnerships with Anglos and served both populations. While Mexican
businessmen provided goods for the Mexican and Anglo populations,
Jesús Melendez, F. T. Davila, and other newspaper editors kept Phoenix
Mexicans informed.[7]

Mexicans took part in politics in early Phoenix both as voters and as
candidates. They preferred to vote Democratic, but they belonged to both
political parties. A number of them won election to minor offices in Phoenix and Maricopa County, but Anglos predominated as officeholders.
Mexicans had been influential in politics since the beginning, and because
of their numbers they could make a difference in election outcomes. Any
Anglo candidate had to take the Mexican vote into consideration; in
turn, patronage jobs in government service and public projects served as
rewards for those who voted for the victor. For Mexican leaders, being
able to deliver the vote assured political stature and attention from political parties and candidates. Perhaps the most important Mexican politician in the 1870s and 1880s was Henry Garfias, who served as town
marshal of Phoenix for many years. Born in California, Garfias came
to Phoenix in 1874 as a twenty-three-year-old law officer. He became
known almost immediately as the fastest gun in the territory. "He was

brave and conscientious and never failed in his duty no matter how much danger menaced him," an observer later recalled.[8]

At the same time, among Anglos the Mexican population developed a reputation for "bad behavior." Local Anglo newspapers carried numerous notices of unlawful activity on the part of Mexicans. In 1873 an Anglo vigilante committee consisting of "most of the citizens of the town" lynched Ramon Cordova and Mariano Tisanado, two Mexicans accused of robbery. Later in the decade another "law and order committee" hanged robbery suspect Joaquin Barba. Such incidents, an observer noted, encouraged the departure of "bad" Mexicans and other "undesirables" from the area, but it did not harm the reputation of Phoenix, which continued to be generally regarded as a "peaceable and law-abiding town." In turn, some Mexicans left Phoenix because of their fear of angry ethnocentric Anglos.[9]

As more Anglos arrived, the proportion of Mexicans in the Phoenix population declined. "The Indian is now a nuisance and the Sonoran a decided annoyance," remarked a correspondent in an 1872 article about the budding town, "but both are sure to disappear before civilization as snow before the noonday sun." Phoenix "is markedly an American town," noted a reporter in 1877, and "the Spanish element is fast-taking a back seat." A year later another observer declared that "every house in town is crowded with its human dwellers and even that part of it occupied by the Mexicans is being encroached upon by the whites."[10]

Unlike many other Southwestern towns, Phoenix did not exist through Spanish or Mexican periods. It was founded largely by Anglos for Anglos, and they were determined to transplant familiar cultural patterns to their new home in Arizona. As soon as possible, buildings of fired brick, wood, and stone, including schools and churches, replaced the Mexican adobe structures constructed in the early years, in order to give the town more of an "American" look. Adobe was considered too "Mexican" for most Anglos; as one of them put it, "it may be very appropriately styled as Greasian, when we consider its origin." Anglos also abhorred Mexican neighborhoods. As the *Phoenix Herald* declared in 1879:

> It is a disgrace to a civilized community to be compelled to witness the nuisances created by our Mexican residents. They do their washing and cooking on the sidewalks, and all manner of filth is thrown into the ditches. They have no outhouses, and the stench arising from the numerous adobe holes is simply fearful. When an epidemic breaks out and we lose a dear friend or relative then some action will be taken. Some portions of our town surpass that of the Chinese quarters in San Francisco for filth and stench.[11]

At the end of the 1870s, a visitor called the large two-story fired-brick school, where Anglo culture and Anglo children predominated, one of the "chief adornments" of Phoenix. The first churches erected represented the Protestant faith. While the Methodist Episcopal Church South and the First Presbyterian Church served most religious needs of the Anglos in Phoenix during the 1870s, a Catholic priest arrived from the town of Florence once every few months to conduct services in the home of Jesús Otero, a local merchant. A small adobe structure, the first building of La Imaculada Concepción de Santa Maria, or St. Mary's Catholic Church, was eventually erected in 1881 on east Monroe Street on land donated by Otero, Miguel Peralta, and Carlos Perrazzo, an Italian merchant.[12]

Otero and other Mexican leaders planned the church, and Mexican workers built it; a festive dedication drew a large number of proud participants to its opening. Religious services were offered on a regular basis, and church members celebrated holy days and holidays. The Mexicans loved to celebrate, especially Diez y Seis de Septiembre, or Mexican Independence Day. Mexico's Independence Day, September 16, commemorates that day in 1810 when the priest Miguel Hidalgo y Costilla gave an inspiring speech that began the Mexicans' quest for independence, which lasted until 1821. Each year the Junta Patriotica Mexicana and other organizations in Phoenix sponsored the gala event.

In 1881 the Mexican neighborhood located along east Monroe Street hosted the celebration and offered fireworks, bonfires, dancing, singing, drinking, and other diversions to the community. Local Mexican leaders, standing on platforms draped with the national colors of Mexico and the United States and displaying portraits of Miguel Hidalgo y Costilla and George Washington, read the Declaration of Independence and gave patriotic speeches, while the Yucatec Hose Company No. 2, an all-Mexican fire company, and the Mexican Military Company, along with proud Mexican groups and individuals on horseback, paraded to the music of Mexican bands. The celebration always culminated in a grand ball. East Monroe Street, often called by the press the "Sonora corner of Phoenix," was located in the northern part of town and contained a concentration of Mexican houses and businesses (see Map 1.1). Other Mexican neighborhoods existed in the southern parts of Phoenix. Another popular occasion, the Fiesta de San Juan, annually offered fireworks, dancing, brass bands, games, bull and cock fighting, chicken pulling, shooting contests with live pigeons, and so on. Another traditional fiesta, Our Lady of Guadalupe, also drew enthusiastic participants.[13]

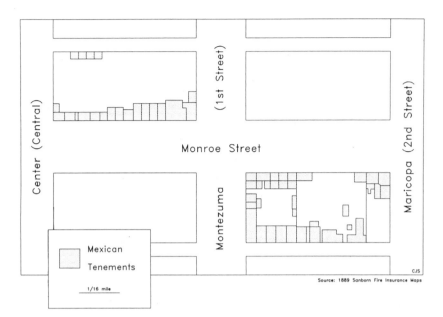

MAP 1.1 Heart of the East Monroe Street Mexican Neighborhood, 1889

Jesús Otero, Miguel Peralta, and a few other successful Mexican merchants operated on a large scale and served Mexicans and other members
of the larger community; by 1879, Peralta's impressive general store on
the corner of Washington and Center streets, according to the *Salt River
Herald,* carried a line of goods "complete in all respects." He lived in a
house at the rear of his store. Otero moved into a new house on Adams
Street, one of the finest in town, in 1888. Brother of Miguel Otero, future
governor of territorial New Mexico, he sent his three boys to college
in Santa Clara, California. Otero, Peralta, and others experienced good
and bad business days but usually found time to promote political and
cultural life in the Mexican community. Small businessmen and skilled
Mexican artisans also found a place in Phoenix, as did unskilled Mexicans. "Our unskilled ranks are filled by Mexicans who work for one
dollar and one dollar and a half per day," noted a Phoenix promoter
in 1878. Low wages prevailed, but observers considered them better
than what was available in Mexico. The Mexican population of Phoenix
"consists chiefly of immigrants from Sonora, attracted by the opportu-

nities for more profitable employment than at home." As one reporter noted in 1888:

> Forty-six Mexicans with their families arrived in Phoenix this morning from Altar, Sonora. The whole company counting men, women and children numbered over one hundred, and all came on foot, "packing" their luggage themselves. There was not a horse, mule or burro in the outfit. They are loud in their complaints against the Sonoran government, where they say it is impossible for poor people to make a decent living on account of the impositions of the rich.[14]

Organizations within the Mexican American community remained varied, ranging from the Mexican Literary Society to the Mutual Benevolent Society of the Latin American Races. Cultural and social associations proved extremely beneficial to those who participated, for Mexicans and other minority groups often were shut out of the larger community dominated by Anglo Americans. The newspaper *La Guardia*, established in 1881 by Jose Garcia, was the first of several Spanish-language publications that included *El Progresso* (1883) and *La Verdad de Phoenix* (1888). When Mexican theater and musical groups came to town, they drew appreciative audiences, as did traveling Mexican circuses. And when Mexicans in need sought help, local charitable groups cooperated in meeting their requests. Political clubs also aided Mexicans in their quest for attention from Anglo politicians. Despite charges that Democrats and Republicans "manipulate the Mexican vote," patronage jobs provided a welcome source of income for party workers. Ethnocentric Anglo Americans in Phoenix gave very little away. Their attitude and actions reflected their feelings of superiority. As an onlooker declared in 1888:

> The walks of the street contain a motley crowd. On the curbstones were groups of Mexicans, with their dusky features and wearing their favorite sombreros; numbers of Indians were moving listlessly, bedecked with bright and gaudy colors, with long, black hair, without any covering on their heads. The Chinaman has his share in the motley crowd, in his native costumes, sprightly on his feet, and ever on the alert. The African, with features unlike any other, varies the type of nationalities and last, the Caucasian, with bright and cheery face, is more the type of manhood than all the rest together.[15]

"Treacherous greasers" were especially denounced by the local press, which gave considerable space to their violent exploits. Phoenix judges commented that more Mexicans appeared in court than all the other residents together. At times Mexican fiestas became "rascally gatherings," according to the *Gazette,* and it urged something be done; "the Mexican fiesta is an institution that is a disgrace to any civilized community," it noted in 1890. Reports like the following were common: "Sonora Town Saturday nights keep our police officers in healthy exercise. Saturday night last no less than four different fights took place in the space of two hours." Mexicans, called by one Anglo spokesman "the scum and dregs of Sonora," were often arrested for being "drunk and disorderly," but Anglos arrested for the same offense always seemed to be given less jail time than the Mexicans.

The Anglo American community also resented attempts by Mexican Americans to make Phoenix and Arizona society more bilingual. As the editor of a local paper put it, "With all due deference to our Spanish-speaking population, the *Herald* is not in favor of printing the Governor's message in the Spanish language. This is an English-speaking country; our laws are printed in the English language and in no other, and our courts are conducted in the English language and in no other." When an Arizona legislator in 1893 suggested making it "necessary" for teachers in public schools to pass an examination in Spanish and teach Spanish to their pupils, the public and the press quickly attacked him. Many residents preferred the existing law, which stated that "all schools must be taught in the English language." A number of them complained that such requirements would be too expensive, too difficult, and too unrewarding. "Why not try to teach the Mexicans English instead of trying to make Mexicans of the Americans," asked a critic. A newspaper stated its case:

> Being American schools and the territory fast growing away from the Mexicans, what good would result to the scholars from their knowledge of the Spanish language gained at the sacrifice of the English studies. Those who may desire to learn Spanish have the opportunity offered by the private Spanish schools of the territory. When it is remembered that the majority, almost, of those children who attend public schools never find the opportunity to get beyond a common school education and every hour spent in studies that are not practical in the extreme are that many hours lost to them. The study of the Spanish language would simply rob them of that much knowledge of the English. It is not a necessity, rather an accomplishment and as such should be given only to those who may desire it.[16]

Anglo Americans often questioned the loyalty of Mexican Americans. During the Spanish-American War, for example, patriotic Mexicans did everything possible to prove their allegiance. Some joined the service;

a number of them fought with Theodore Roosevelt's Rough Riders in Cuba. At home, in public and private meetings, leaders declared that the Mexican American community in Phoenix favored the United States over Spain. For example, in April 1898, Pedro G. de la Lama, Asuncian Sanchez, Julio Marron, Manuel Garcia, and other Mexican American leaders addressed the loyalty issue. The Mexican Band played patriotic songs in front of the court house and attracted a large crowd of local citizens. After several spirited speeches, the Mexican Americans resolved to "heartily endorse the action of the United States in declaring that Spanish rule in the island of Cuba must end." As "citizens of the United States," they pledged their "lives and sacred honor to the cause of the American government" and pledged their "services in any manner that they may be called for in upholding the national honor in support of the government and flag of the United States."

Phoenix boosters failed to appreciate the positive role Mexican Americans played in the war effort, but as they promoted tourism in the city, they realized their value as attractions. "Here in Phoenix there are only enough Mexicans and Indians to make picturesque the poorer quarter of the city," the *Arizona Republican* asserted in 1899. The "Mexican settlements in the vicinity of the Catholic Church and on the south side of the city have no longer their former prominence but are sufficiently in evidence to be of great interest to Eastern visitors who, having traveled so far to escape the monotony of modern ways of living, are naturally more interested in the picturesque remnants of the past than in present improvements and embellishments."[17]

Unruly Mexicans, however, remained a problem, according to Anglo American promoters. Volatile, violent male Mexicans persisted in making headlines. In June 1900 the *Republican* detailed another Mexican brawl. "Yesterday was San Juan Day and the local Greasers celebrated the occasion with much eclat and mescal," it declared. "Near Broadway ranch, southwest of Phoenix, several hundred Mexicans congregated and created a great commotion with their cock fights and their caballeros, which consist in reaching down from the backs of horses and pulling heads from roosters partially buried in the ground." Late in the afternoon, "a fight ensued and knives, rocks and clubs were freely used. Several participants were injured, but none died. Only half a dozen Greasers were arrested."[18]

Active, ambitious Mexican American leaders also caused disruption in their own organizations. Even the Junta Patriotica Mexicana was accused in September 1900 by Mexican Consul Leon W. Navarro of being more interested in politics than in celebrating Mexican Independence Day. Navarro also accused Spanish-language newspaper editors Pedro G. de la Lama, Asuncian Sanchez, and Pedro Salazar of being too political and too removed from Mexico. Rivals within Mexican organizations experienced difficulty agreeing on common goals; jealousy often inflamed the competition between adversaries. Pedro G. de la Lama, an immigrant from Mexico who arrived in Phoenix in 1893, acquired a reputation as a volatile, violent individual. At the same time, when tragedy called for a united effort, the Mexican American community responded. In March 1902, for example, Phoenix Mexicans, under request from Consul Navarro, started collecting contributions for the relief of victims of the Chalpancingo earthquake, a disaster in the state of Guerrero, Mexico.[19]

Memories of home did inspire Phoenix Mexicans to rejoice in their heritage. Phoenix was not that far from Mexico, especially Sonora, and there was much traveling and visiting back and forth. Many Mexicans hoped to eventually return to Mexico permanently once they achieved success in Arizona. Many of them tolerated the intolerance of Anglos because they expected to leave. Cultural conservatives, Phoenix Mexicans felt a strong bond to their homeland, and they often celebrated their Mexican heritage. Fiestas Patrias (Mexican Independence Day) in September remained a major event of the year. The Phoenix lodge Sociedad Zaragoza gave an annual ball in May in celebration of Cinco de Mayo, the anniversary of the day General Ignacio Zaragoza defeated the French at Puebla, Mexico, on May 5, 1862. The Alianza Hispano-Americana, a mutual-aid and fraternal insurance society founded in Tucson in 1894, listed sixty members in Phoenix by the turn of the century. It urged Mexicans to work hard and be proud, and it sponsored a number of historically oriented celebrations. The Phoenix chapter was established in 1898 and in 1905 hosted a convention drawing delegates from Arizona, New Mexico, and California.[20]

During the 1880s, Phoenix enhanced its standing as an urban center by securing a railroad and becoming the capital of Arizona Territory. In July 1887, a twenty-six-mile branch line of the Southern Pacific, called the Maricopa and Phoenix, was completed north to the town, thus connecting it to the outside world. In January 1889 the importance of Phoenix was recognized by the legislature when it removed the capital from Prescott to Phoenix; the move proved to be permanent. The coming of the railroad and the acquisition of the capital, along with the agricultural and commercial progress of the place, pleased local promoters and outside investors, and they boosted Phoenix as "the future metropolis of Arizona."

In February 1895 another branch railroad, the Santa Fe, Prescott and Phoenix, connected with the Santa Fe main line running across northern Arizona; thus the city enjoyed access to two transcontinental lines. Mexicans supported both railroads and helped build them. The railroads, however, brought more Anglos than ever before to Phoenix, increasing their influence. Local Anglos proudly agreed with an observer when he called Phoenix "a progressive American city" without the "sleepy semi-Mexican features of the more ancient towns of the Southwest." Often shut out of the larger community, Mexicans created their own social and cultural life centered around family relations, association activities, and religious services at St. Mary's Catholic Church. The Mexican community became more distant; although there had never been many, now fewer business partnerships, mixed marriages, and mutual celebrations occurred. Patterns of discrimination and segregation, along with a sense of ethnic identity and cultural awareness, encouraged the development of the Phoenix Mexican community, whose population had grown from 772 in 1880 to 1,100 in 1910.[21]

Most of the Anglos lived on the north side of town. Following the "great flood of 1891," when the Salt River overflowed its banks and reached Washington Street, few real estate promoters undertook residential development in the southern parts of the city. Anglos who could afford it were encouraged to live on higher ground, away from potential flood damage. They lived in the additions north of Washington, while poorer neighborhoods containing economically and socially disadvantaged groups became more apparent in the lower areas of south Phoenix. There, along with the railroads, factories, warehouses, and stockyards, the depressed areas of the "Garden City of Arizona" emerged. Most of the Mexicans lived in the southern parts of the city, south of Washington between Seventh Street and Seventeenth Avenue (see Map 1.2). Salt River valley growers found many of their farm workers in the neighborhoods. They proved to be inexpensive and efficient workers; as one Phoenix promotion pamphlet put it, "Mexicans make excellent day laborers."

As Table 1.1 indicates, the Mexican population remained at the lower end of the occupational ladder in Phoenix, as elsewhere. A small middle class existed, but most of the Mexican males labored as unskilled or semi-skilled workers, while the great majority of Mexican females were domestic and service workers. Although the figures from the unpublished manuscript census schedules used in this study are not adjusted upward,

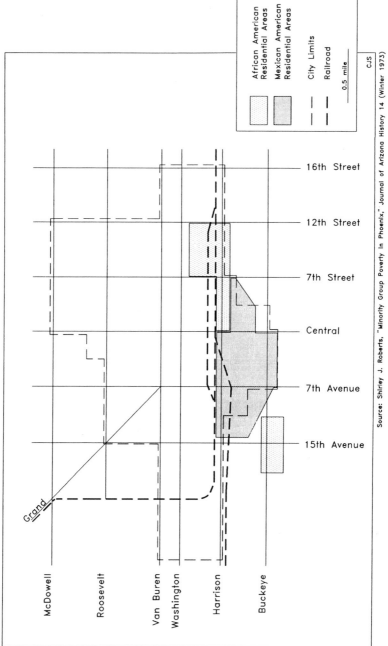

Source: Shirley J. Roberts, "Minority Group Poverty in Phoenix," Journal of Arizona History 14 (Winter 1973)

MAP 1.2 Minority Neighborhoods in Phoenix, 1911

African American
Residential Areas

Mexican American
Residential Areas

City Limits

Railroad

0.5 mile

CJS

16th Street

12th Street

7th Street

Central

7th Avenue

15th Avenue

McDowell

Roosevelt

Van Buren

Washington

Harrison

Buckeye

Grand

Table 1.1. Occupational Structure for Spanish-Surnamed
            Population, 1870–1900^a

Occupations	1870	1880	1900
Unskilled	60	103	170
Semiskilled	17	38	24
Skilled	—	7	51
Farming/Ranching	30	30	9
Mercantile	1	6	30
Professional	—	3	6
Totals	108	187	290

SOURCE: Federal manuscript census schedules, 1870, 1880, 1900.
^aSpanish-surnamed populations derived from place of birth for individuals or par-
ents, and surname, since manuscripts do not delineate Spanish-surnamed from
white (W) category.

Oscar J. Martinez, Lawrence A. Cardoso, Albert Camarillo, and other
historians have noted that period population figures for Mexicans are
underenumerated by as much as 40 percent.[22]

The Mexicans south of Washington Street lost much of what little
political power they had in August 1913, when the structure of the Phoenix government changed from a mayor–city council to a city manager–
city commission system. Unlike the ward system under the old city charter, in which council members were elected from each ward, the new
charter required all commission members to be elected at-large. "Progressive" reformers claimed that the ward system unnecessarily faction-
alized the city; under the new charter elected officials would be account-
able to the entire electorate, not a section of it. At the same time,
advocates knew that by eliminating the ward system, they eliminated the
political influence of the less affluent, less numerous part of the population residing in south Phoenix, especially minority groups. Under the old
structure, the city was divided into four wards, the lines being Central
Avenue and Washington Street, with the northeast quadrant being ward
1 and the remaining three numbered counter-clockwise. Thus wards 3
and 4 were located in south Phoenix, while the more affluent, more populous wards 1 and 2 were located north of Washington Street. As R. L.
Dyer, secretary of the Phoenix Good Government League, noted at a

meeting in February 1914, "the third and fourth wards are composed of people who do not meet the high ideals of those here present." Under the new charter, elected at-large officials from the predominantly Anglo north side would replace those who had represented the less affluent, less numerous residents of the south side wards in the past. As a result, it was felt by dominant interests, the government of Phoenix would be in the hands of the "right people."[23]

The Mexican Revolution erupted in November 1910 and local Spanish-language newspapers kept interested Phoenix Mexicans informed. The Protective League of Political Refugees and other organizations, including the Sociedad Mutualista Benito Juarez and the Sociedad Mutualista Porfirio Diaz, were formed in the city. They welcomed many newcomers from Mexico, but not all Mexicans who fled to Phoenix were appreciated. The *Republican* complained that "many outlaws and anarchists" had taken refuge in the city and were responsible for the violence and bloodshed at the 1912 Independence Day celebration. The newspaper called for an end to Mexican Independence Day celebrations in Phoenix. According to reports, a "small-sized riot" broke out at the rear of the Central Hotel bar on September 16. Participants had been drinking and fighting, and while the police arrested some of those involved, Phoenix Police Chief A. J. Moore and two police officers, along with an Anglo citizen, were shot and stabbed by unidentified Mexicans. Arrests continued and order was finally restored. The violence brought an end to the celebration, including cancellation of the grand ball. The riot and its aftermath clearly indicated that the growing Phoenix population was not entirely united regarding the Mexican Revolution.

In August 1915 considerable anxiety arose in Phoenix over the "Plan de San Diego," a paper confiscated from a Mexican arrested on the border. Calling for a general uprising of border Mexicans to regain territory lost as a result of the Mexican War and its aftermath, the plan, "if successfully worked out would restore to Mexico the states of California, Arizona, New Mexico and Texas." Hardly a major "brown scare," with nothing coming of it, the plan nevertheless caused rumors to spread among some Anglos. According to one rumor, Mexicans had "signed an oath to kill Anglos when the outbreak should come." According to another, six hundred Mexicans were "drilling daily" southwest of the nearby town of Glendale, near the Agua Fria River. As it turned out, the only body of Mexicans southwest of Glendale near the Agua Fria River "were members of a camp engaged in the peaceful occupation of ditch digging." Still another rumor made the frightening charge that "a small force of Mexicans was on the way from Mexico to blow up the Roosevelt Dam." Phoenix Mexican leaders loudly proclaimed their anger at such rumors and protested. The *Republican* also asked that the rumors be put to rest; it called them "foolish," and declared that "Mexicans in Phoenix and other large towns are loyal."[24]

In Arizona and Phoenix, the struggle for progress continued. The Kinney, or Eighty-Percent, Bill was passed by an initiative vote of Arizonans in November 1914. It stated that no firm employing more than five people could hire fewer than 80 percent citizens. The measure was ruled unconstitutional by a federal court in San Francisco. In February 1915, Phoenix Mexican leaders led a protest against a new bill being considered in the Arizona Legislature; called the Kinney-Claypool Bill, it was a re-action to the recent court action. If passed, it would have excluded all non-English-speaking men from employment in hazardous occupations, an obvious threat to Mexicans who spoke only Spanish. Large crowds of Mexicans in and out of Phoenix complained that the bill was unfair, and eventually it was defeated. Mexican individuals and organizations played crucial roles in preventing its passage, especially Pedro G. de la Lama and the Liga Protectora Latina (LPL). Headquartered in Phoenix and presided over by de la Lama, the LPL soon had lodges throughout the state. The organization attracted hundreds of members in Phoenix and thousands throughout Arizona and beyond. Established in February 1915 to oppose the Kinney-Claypool Bill, it came out against such "radical measures" and supported "only such candidates for office as are friendly to the Mexican people."

In Phoenix and elsewhere the lodges served as employment bureaus, benevolent societies, and insurance agencies. They provided medical aid to sick members, funeral expenses to deceased brethren, and financial benefits to survivors. The LPL placed great emphasis on the need for education and political action. It pushed for bilingual education in the primary grades and for night schools for adults. It also recognized that Mexicans should acquire a knowledge of English for their own good. The organization published *La Justicia,* a weekly newspaper devoted to its goals. In May 1916, for example, it protested the execution of four Mexicans at the state prison at Florence, pointing out that the great majority of executions at the prison involved Mexicans. As one observer noted, "In the last year alone, only Mexicans have been hanged." In 1920 the LPL had over three hundred members in the Phoenix lodge. Unfortunately, during the 1920s a struggle for control of the organization took place, and membership and services declined.[25]

Internal problems also caused conflict in the religious organizations of Phoenix. A new St. Mary's Catholic Church was completed and dedicated in 1915 on the same site as the old one on Monroe between Third and Fourth streets. Mexican Catholics played a substantial role in its construction but soon found themselves segregated at its services. The church and Father Novatus Benzing seemed to be a church and a priest for Anglo Catholics. As one observer declared in June 1915, "Since the attempt on the part of the local Catholic authorities to segregate the Mexican worshippers in the basement chapel, reserving the upstairs for the other members of the congregation, the movement to build a separate church for Mexicans of the faith has steadily acquired impetus." The recently formed Mexican Catholic Society secured 1,500 signatures on a petition in which Spanish-speaking Catholics complained that they had only St. Mary's Catholic Church to attend and that, "as English is spoken there," few of them received "the full benefits of the services." They also believed that the basement arrangement was the result of Anglo demands in exchange for financial contributions to the building of the new edifice. Moreover, in the Southwest, not only did many Catholic clerics support quotas on Mexican immigration to ensure a higher Anglo population percentage in the region; they also worked diligently to keep the ranks of Mexican priests small.

The Mexicans' desire to have Spanish services upstairs at St. Mary's was rejected by the Anglo priests. In the old church the masses had been said in Latin, but the sermons had been in Spanish or English at different hours. In the completed new church, Mexicans wanted to continue the same type of arrangement rather than worshipping in the basement. Anglo priests, speaking for Anglo Catholics, were adamant; Father Novatus Benzing, who noted time and again the "poverty" and the "ignorance" of the Mexicans, illustrated the prejudice involved when he declared that English and English only would be used upstairs. The cultural bias expressed was blatant; as Benzing put it, "As all the world knows, Mexicans tenaciously adhere to their own language and customs, and will not amalgamate; not even those who are born and raised right here. Nor will the American people put up with the untidiness of the majority of Mexican peons that continually come up from Mexico."

Upon appealing to Bishop Henry Granjon in Tucson, A. R. Redondo, Dr. Lorenzo Boido, and other members of the Mexican Catholic Society received permission to establish a parish and erect a church of their own. Mexican Catholics began collecting funds for the new structure at church fairs, socials, dances, dinners, plays, and other events, but it would be years before they realized their goal. A succession of delays, along with Catholic Church financial demands for the construction of a new structure, retarded the movement. Bishop Granjon had granted permission for a Mexican Catholic Church in Phoenix subject to strict compliance with Section IX of the diocesan statutes, which stated that before the Mexican Catholic Society began erecting a church, "one-half of the total amount needed shall be on hand, one-half of the balance shall be reliably subscribed, leaving an indebtedness of one-fourth of the total amount."

Until the church for Mexicans was completed, they continued to attend mass in the basement of St. Mary's or at St. Anthony's Chapel, a small structure opened in 1925 on Seventh Street between Yavapai and Maricopa. Finally, in 1928, the new Mexican church was finished under the guidance of Father Antimo Nebreda, a dedicated Mexican priest. Located at Washington and Ninth streets, it became known as Immaculate Heart of Mary Catholic Church. In the meantime, the Mexican Presbyterian Church, the Mexican Methodist Church, the Mexican Baptist Church, and other Mexican churches appealed to those of different religious persuasions.

For thirteen years, 1915 to 1928, Mexican families endured the "basement" experience at St. Mary's. Masses, weddings, baptisms, funerals, and other church functions remained in the basement for them. Mexican American Adam Diaz later recalled attending services at St. Mary's as a child; especially vivid was his first communion. The Mexican children waited in the basement for the bishop from Tucson to finish serving the Anglo children upstairs; they could hear the lovely organ music. The wait seemed eternal to Diaz, but eventually the bishop came down and quickly gave the Mexicans communion. The Mexican children were then taken upstairs to leave. "That's when we saw the beautiful tables of food that the nuns had laid out, but they wouldn't let us stay or take part. It was for the Anglos." Mrs. Diaz took the Mexican children home and gave them refreshments, but the episode upset the parents, who became more determined to overcome the discrimination and segregation they and their families were experiencing.[26]

Progress and problems followed Mexicans in Phoenix. During World War I, Phoenix Mexicans served the nation well. "The Mexican Americans," noted an officer of the Liga Protectora Latina, "are ready to serve, with their substance in blood and money and labor, to show their appreciation of the hospitality of the United States." As he viewed it, "No other class of people have stood by the government of the United States more wholeheartedly in this war than the Mexican Americans." They furnished their quota of men, bought their allotment of Liberty bonds, and gave all they could to war effort organization. Mexican American women, he continued, "were untiring in their work for the Red Cross and gave up their sons, husbands and sweethearts with the same fortitude displayed by all other patriotic women."[27]

Phoenix booster groups, taking advantage of the National Reclamation Act of 1902, supported the federal government in the construction of nearby Roosevelt Dam, completed in 1911. This and similar endeavors brought vital stability to the water supply, allowed irrigation control, and assured agricultural growth, and as the Salt River valley prospered, so did Phoenix. The population of the city reached 11,134 in 1910, and the following decade it almost tripled to 29,053. During World War I especially, Phoenix and the valley enjoyed boom times. Cotton production became the leading industry, and a "cotton craze" erupted. Unfortunately, a "cotton bust" occurred during the postwar years, causing much suffering in the area.

Local boosters during the period worked hard to attract new residents and visitors, and affluent Anglo Americans were clearly preferred. For example, the ethnocentric chamber of commerce did not try to hide that feeling. A representative of the chamber recorded in a 1920 city directory: "Phoenix is a modern town of forty thousand people and the best kind of people too. A very small percentage of Mexicans, Negroes or foreigners." But the cotton boom demanded large numbers of field workers, and when World War I created a labor shortage in the valley, cotton growers became desperate. They turned their labor recruitment problems over to the Arizona Cotton Growers' Association (ACGA). From 1917 to 1920, the ACGA recruited thousands of farm workers from Mexico. Low pay and poor working conditions caused some protest, but despite abuses the workers received a better deal in the Salt River valley than they did in Mexico. The Mexican Revolution caused violent chaos and massive unemployment south of the border, and experiencing little economic opportunity at home, Mexicans came in droves to the central Arizona oasis to participate in the "cotton craze." As long as the cotton growers were doing well and expanding, the workers benefited, but when the cotton market failed in 1920, hard times arrived. Many of the growers went bankrupt, business in general declined, and Mexican farm workers became destitute and their situation increasingly intolerable. The cotton bust caused a short-lived depression in the valley, and relations between Anglo growers and Mexican laborers quickly deteriorated.[28]

Many valley growers simply set their cotton pickers adrift, often without pay. Thousands of unemployed Mexicans, stranded and desperate, sought help from the ACGA, but it failed to respond to the crisis quickly enough. Local newspapers reported that Mexicans, most without shelter, were "starving, literally starving." Soup kitchens and bread lines formed in and about Phoenix. Jails filled with "Mexican vagrants." The Liga Protectora Latina and other Mexican American organizations did what they could to publicize the bleak situation, alleviate the suffering, and promote constructive change, but their efforts fell short. For not paying the Mexican nationals and for not repatriating those who could not find work, the ACGA was severely criticized, especially by the Mexican press. In March 1921 a Mexico City paper asserted that "Mexicans were dying of hunger in Phoenix and were treated as if they were animals." Another Mexico City paper charged that the ACGA treated Mexican workers "worse than Negroes."

Finally, the reluctant ACGA, in an agreement with Mexican officials, promised to pay workers the money owed them and to pay for the transportation of thousands of workers back to Mexico, but it proved once again to be slow in keeping its commitment. Many Mexicans tried to make the journey back to Mexico on their own. Those who managed to reach the border were described as being in "miserable and deplorable condition, deceived by the promises of the cotton growers of Arizona." One outside observer, citing the situation as "an example of man's inhumanity to man," declared that the "shameful treatment of the Mexican cotton picker in the Salt River valley surpasses in heartlessness anything that has occurred in Arizona since its organization as a territory 57 years ago." In the end, the ACGA failed to adequately uphold its end of the agreement, and Mexico eventually paid for the repatriation of thousands of unemployed Mexican workers left stranded in the Salt River valley, but the crisis lasted for months and had a lasting effect on relations between Mexico and Arizona.[29]

During the cotton boom and bust, more Mexicans settled in the barrios of south Phoenix. Rather than returning to Mexico, they remained in the Arizona city, seeking any kind of available employment and living in some of the poorest neighborhoods. On the south side most Mexicans concentrated in the area south of Washington extending from Seventh Avenue to Twenty-fourth Street. Certain sections contained better homes, but generally Mexicans could afford only substandard housing. Upward mobility proved elusive, and poverty remained a problem, but a number of institutions and associations helped residents meet their needs.

As Phoenix developed into Arizona's largest city, Mexicans made up the largest minority group, increasing from 2,323 in 1920 to 7,293 (15.2 percent of the population) in 1930. More "Mexican" churches, schools, parks, and voluntary associations appeared to support Mexican neighborhoods; for example, Immaculate Heart of Mary Catholic Church, Grant School, and Grant Park became community centers. Celebrations of Las Posadas, a Mexican Christmas tradition, and El Dia de los Muertos, or the Day of the Dead, in October attracted appreciative participants. The Mexican community cultivated a cultural identity and a cultural agenda. Most important was the family, the protective bastion of Mexican culture. Families and friends interacted at birthday parties, dances, weddings, baptisms, and funerals. Mexican musical and theatrical performances, horse races, and other forms of entertainment drew enthusiastic audiences. Spanish-language newspapers and periodicals continued to inform and instruct. The popular Junta Patriotica Mexicana retained a sense of the past and called for an awareness of Mexican cultural heritage by sponsoring bigger than ever Mexican Independence Day celebrations. Although most Anglos found the celebration of Mexican Independence Day acceptable, many of them preferred to "Americanize" Spanish-speaking foreigners, and this conviction led to the founding in 1921 of Friendly House, an important institution in the history of Mexican life in Phoenix.[30]

During World War I and the postwar years, a national movement to "Americanize" foreign-born newcomers swept the nation. In the Southwest this meant primarily Spanish-speaking individuals from Mexico, and in the Arizona capital the Phoenix Americanization Committee worked diligently to establish educational courses that included classes in English and civics, which were the foundation of all Americanization programs. Most members of the Mexican population in Phoenix, with their close cultural ties to nearby Mexico, were not interested in learning English and civics, but the Anglo-inspired movement to Americanize them persisted. Phoenix schools emphasized the teaching of English and civics to Mexican students, and older Mexicans were encouraged to participate in adult education classes also emphasizing the Americanization theme. The Phoenix Americanization Committee, which consisted of representatives, including Mexicans, from a variety of local organizations, never missed an opportunity to encourage patriotism toward the United States among the foreign born. "One flag, one language, one country—America," declared one Americanization program organizer. Rarely mentioned were such issues as discrimination and segregation.

Moreover, some Phoenicians felt that Americanization should be

forced upon individuals if necessary. The *Republican,* for example, declared that it was "to be applied systematically to those who are willing
to learn and to be forced upon those who are apathetic." The *Republican*
and many of its readers felt threatened by many of the forces that created
the national "red scare" of the post–World War I years. With Americans
feeling threatened by the spread of communism in Russia and Europe
and seeing "reds" everywhere in the United States, self-proclaimed pro-
tectors of the nation sounded the rallying cry of "One Hundred Percent
Americanism" in city after city, including Phoenix. Foreigners, with their
radical ideas and alien ways, it was said, had to be watched carefully.
Those who would not become "good Americans" and thus "loyal citizens" were suspect. In Arizona, it was said, many of "them" had chosen
to join or sympathize with such radical "anti-American" groups as the
Industrial Workers of the World, a labor union that had militantly but
unsuccessfully tried for several years to organize Mexican and other mine
workers in the state.[31]

Other Phoenicians, however, disagreed that among immigrants "there
must be a cutting loose, a forgetfulness of all national ties." They made
it clear that it was not their intent to "destroy the immigrant culture
nor to force unwilling foreign-born residents to become citizens." As
one Phoenix Americanization Committee member put it, "the man who
would cease to love the language he learned at his mother's knee, or
the country of his birth would indeed make a poor citizen of any country." And, he added, "citizenship which was obtained under compulsion
would be a detriment to all concerned." In the end, his attitude reflected
that held by most members of the influential committee.

Americanization classes were held in selected schools and churches in
Phoenix, but some committee members wanted to establish a separate
facility to promote the program. Led by Carrie Green, a former teacher
and social worker, and a driving force in the movement, the committee
began using in 1921 a small house located on west Sherman Street in a
south Phoenix Mexican neighborhood. The facility became known as
Friendly House, and in it Green conducted classes in English, civics, hygiene, and home economics. The philosophy that guided Green and the
Friendly House programs assumed that "immigrants should be loyal to
the United States but should be encouraged to preserve and take pride in
their native culture as well."

The institution also served as an employment bureau and a relief
agency. Called a community house in Phoenix, it fulfilled many of the
functions of a traditional urban settlement house. Referred to "as the

American Home in a foreign section," Friendly House moved directly across from the original facility to larger quarters on south First Avenue in 1927, where under the direction of Carrie Green it continued as a "gathering place for foreigners" and an "Americanization Center for Mexicans." Friendly House served a useful purpose throughout the decade, and the attempt by more ardent assimilationists to deny the Mexican population their cultural identity failed; moreover, the attempt did not help the Mexican population because the basic economic and social problems facing the Mexican community in Anglo-dominated Phoenix remained in place.[32]

During the 1920s, Anglo Phoenix often expressed its dissatisfaction with the Mexican immigrant. Death and disease rates appeared to be disproportionately high in Mexican neighborhoods, and the dependence of Mexicans on folk medicine upset the Anglo medical community. "Study in hygiene will be one of the mainstays of Grant School," announced the *Republican* in September 1920, "as past experience has taught that ignorance of body hygiene has been the cause of most ills among the Mexicans." A survey of Phoenix, including minority neighborhoods, during the Spanish influenza epidemic in 1918–1919, found that many influenza cases remained "unattended and poverty stricken." Many of the most serious cases were Mexicans, Dr. Frederick T. Fahlen pointed out, because the "crowded conditions in which the poorer class of Mexicans live and their low disease-resisting power on account of improper nourishment make them more susceptible to the disease than persons living under more favorable circumstances." Those who did not resist were taken to the Women's Club emergency hospital, where they were treated by volunteer Anglo doctors and nurses. Most Mexicans, as they had in the past, relied on folk healers and folk medicine.[33]

Despite the goals of the Americanization movement, some Anglo leaders felt that too many Mexicans were simply unable or unwilling to adapt adequately to Anglo culture, with its English language requirements. They declared that Arizona was "handicapped by an appalling percentage of illiteracy due, in a large measure, to the steadily increasing number of its foreign born population." In calling for immigration restrictions, they asserted that "the need for labor is overemphasized—we don't need unskilled, ignorant, non-English speaking people." Yet Mexicans remained the primary source of cheap labor in Arizona and the Southwest. Economic pressure excluded them from the quotas of immigration acts in 1921 and 1924.

In times of crisis, such as World War I, the need for Mexican laborers became critical. In providing the labor force, they contributed to the war effort. Dwight Heard and other Phoenix growers pleaded with the United States government to exempt Mexicans from the immigration laws of 1917 because they feared a farm labor shortage. Wanting to enhance food production and provide against a probable shortage of farm labor, Secretary of Labor W. B. Wilson issued orders for the temporary admission to the United States of Mexican agricultural workers and their exemption from literacy tests, per capita taxes, and other restrictions of the 1917 immigration laws. The news pleased Heard and other local growers.[34]

While Mexican merchants, professionals, and skilled artisans helped maintain a small middle class, the bulk of the Mexican population provided a source of cheap labor. Mexican men and women filled the ranks of service workers and farm workers in the Phoenix area. "The Mexican has been Arizona's chore boy," declared a national magazine in 1929. "In the last decade Arizona's population has increased faster than that of any other state. To the increasing arrival of Mexicans this is partly due, and in Arizona's rise from a wilderness to a more populous, prosperous place. Most of the manual work has been done by Mexicans." Yet, noted the magazine, "useful as they are economically, their steady increase presents a sociological riddle." Arizona's Mexicans and Indians "have retarded the state's progress." From "laboring classes in New York or Wisconsin often sprung our best minds; but few recruits for leadership in finance, education, or the professions come from the Mexican or Indian population of our Southwest." Finally, it concluded, "Most of Arizona's cultured class, such as her lawyers, doctors, journalists, and engineers, are still imported from elsewhere in the United States."[35]

As in the case of other groups, some Mexicans also participated in the irregular economy. Bootlegging, gambling, and drug dealing, especially in marijuana, proved profitable but dangerous endeavors for a number of Mexicans. Val Aguilar, known as the Marihuana King of Phoenix in 1919, did a good business with Mexicans and Anglos. Called the "national flower of Mexico," marijuana helped Phoenix become known as "the dope headquarters of the Pacific slope," according to the *Republican*. The city became the federal drug law enforcement headquarters in Arizona in 1922 as reports of widespread use of "morphine, cocaine, and heroin" continued, much of it being consigned to Phoenix from Nogales and other Mexican border towns. Throughout the 1920s and 1930s,

Phoenix retained a reputation as an "open and notorious" town. In 1935, for example, private investigator W. D. Chesterfield asserted that the Silver Dollar, located at 411 East Madison Street,

> is indeed a vicious Mexican establishment, a contact for illicit narcotic peddlers. Mexican marijuana peddlers are selling the narcotic for two dollars and fifty cents for an ordinary tobacco tin, such as Prince Albert is sold in; while the cigarettes are selling for five cents each or fifty cents per dozen. This place has for its patrons Mexicans, Negroes, Whites, and other nationalities and while it is classed as a Mexican establishment the doors are open to all regardless of race or color. Mexican boys noticeably from the rural sectors have been noted in the place as well as Mexican girls. Prostitutes have been noted in the place. It is also evident that this place is bootlegging illicit liquor. The place is also a hangout for crooks.[36]

At the same time, the Anglo-dominated police force often arrested Mexican suspects without sufficient evidence, and charges of police brutality were frequent, often with deadly acts involved. In September 1929, for example, when four Anglo police officers were acquitted of first-degree murder in connection with the killing of a Mexican youth named Jose Bustamante, Phoenix Mexican Consul Manual Payno expressed outrage and mailed formal protests to Arizona Attorney General K. B. Peterson and to Mexican Ambassador Manuel C. Tellez in Washington. Payno claimed that the Mexican youth had not been sufficiently warned before the overreacting police shot him, but pleas for a reversal of the decision failed.[37]

2   DEPRESSION, WAR, AND PEACE, 1930-1960

In 1940, Mexicans remained the largest minority group in Phoenix, with a population of 9,740, up from 7,293 in 1930 and 2,323 in 1920. Mexicans continued to make up about 15 percent of the population, although the 1930s had been a difficult decade for them in Phoenix. When the Great Depression arrived in the Arizona capital, minority group members often suffered the most; by October 1933, 59 percent of the Mexican population, 51 percent of the blacks, and 11 percent of the Anglos in Phoenix were on relief. A heritage of poverty and a language problem, along with a lack of education and ambition, according to many Anglo observers, allowed Mexicans little mobility, and the Great Depression only made matters worse.

Life proved especially difficult in the poorer neighborhoods of south Phoenix; in 1940 most of the city's Mexicans and Mexican Americans still lived in and beyond that section of the city. Over the years a sense of ethnic identity and cultural awareness, along with patterns of discrimination and segregation, had encouraged minority enclave development. Cheap housing and the availability of employment also drew Mexicans and blacks to the southern parts of Phoenix. Low income jobs, including farm work, could be acquired. For example, buses often carried neighborhood residents to the fields to work. In the 1930s adverse economic conditions had brought even more difficult times.[1]

During the decade, the Mexican population concentrated in two areas. The poorest neighborhoods were located between Sixteenth and Twenty-fourth streets, from Washington Street south to the Salt River.

The area contained blocks of shacks in the vicinity of the railroad tracks where many destitute Mexicans lived. A second area housing mostly Mexicans was south of Washington between Second and Seventh avenues (see Map 2.1). Cuatro Milpas, Little Hollywood, El Campito, Green Valley, Golden Gate, and other barrios contained homes and yards, stores and shops, churches and chapels, schools and societies, and other Mexican community necessities. Adequate housing existed, but low incomes forced residents of the poorer neighborhoods to accept substandard housing. They often built their own homes, with whatever material was available. In barrio yards animal stock and vegetable gardens helped sustain poor families. Golden Gate Settlement House, East Madison Settlement House, and other neighborhood centers were organized in the early 1930s to assist those in need, but they often were inadequate.[2]

Barrio residents lived a life separate from Anglo Phoenix. The Mexican community provided a sense of welcome, while the Anglo community made Mexicans and Mexican Americans unwelcome; as one observer put it, throughout Anglo Phoenix signs warned, "No Mexicans Allowed." Or when Mexicans were allowed, they were restricted to certain days: Mexican day at local swimming pools; Mexican night at the Riverside Ballroom; the *Arizona Republican*'s picnic for "Mexican kiddies" only. As one observer later recalled, "Discrimination went from the church, parks, schools, hotels, theaters—the whole spectrum of rights was permeated with discrimination." Over the years, along with the discrimination and segregation imposed by the larger population, the combination of cheap land and housing, nonexistent or weak building codes, shared language and folk customs, ties to family and friends, and the need for an identity with the homeland and a bridge to American society drew residents to Phoenix's barrios. In many ways the barrios offered a cultural and geographic environment reminiscent of Sonora. They offered a refuge from the critical outside world, a sense of security, and a means of survival.

The physical condition of some barrios, however, was appalling; one area was described as "a foul slum, the like of which can probably not be found elsewhere in the United States." Often called Little Hollywood, it "is free from the land-overcrowding so characteristic of slums in Eastern cities." The "shacks and shanties have plenty of room around them," but "room-overcrowding is prevalent, often equalling or surpassing the congestion found in Eastern tenements. Open-pit privies are the rule. Sanitation does not exist. It is a miracle that this area of shacks has not produced an epidemic of major proportions."[3]

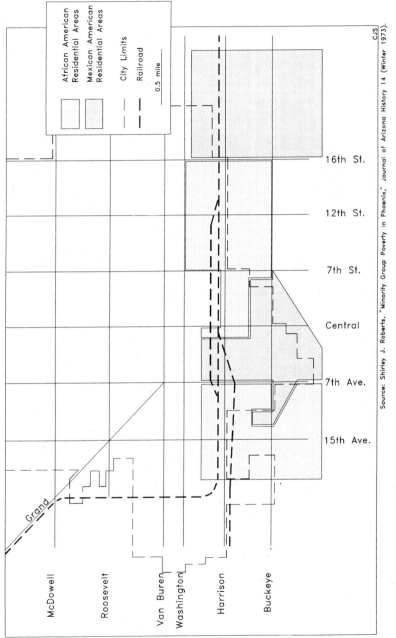

MAP 2.1 Minority Neighborhoods in Phoenix, 1940

African American
Residential Areas

Mexican American
Residential Areas

City Limits

Railroad

0.5 mile

16th St.

12th St.

7th St.

Central

7th Ave.

15th Ave.

McDowell

Roosevelt

Van Buren

Washington

Harrison

Buckeye

Grand

Source: Shirley J. Roberts, "Minority Group Poverty in Phoenix," Journal of Arizona History 14 (Winter 1973).

CJS

During the 1930s, Father Emmett McLoughlin became a hero to many people in south Phoenix. In north Phoenix, however, few residents could figure him out. His first assignment as a Catholic priest brought him from California to St. Mary's Church in Phoenix in June 1934. Upon arrival, he became deeply involved in his duties and in the history of St. Mary's Church. He learned that the original congregation had been almost entirely Mexican and that the present structure had replaced a small adobe chapel in 1915 and become a "double church" accommodating Anglos above and Mexicans in the lower church.

> The Mexican Roman Catholics whose parents had built the old adobe and who themselves had contributed to the new edifice were relegated to the basement. By the time I reached Phoenix, the Mexicans had built their own church a half-mile away. But, among the people and some sympathetic priests, the bitter memory still persisted of the Spanish-speaking priest standing in front of the church directing the worshippers: Mexicans abajo!—"All Mexicans downstairs!"

Latin was the language used for both services, and only the sermon was in English or Spanish. Many Anglos recalled that it seemed logical and proper to have sermons in English and Spanish, but Father McLoughlin felt they had missed the point.

The new priest also found the poorer neighborhoods of south Phoenix in desperate need of attention, especially the black neighborhoods. Moreover, according to Father McLoughlin, the residents of the poorer areas were "the rejects of a lusty, sprawling, boasting cow- and-cotton town that was trying hard to become a city." Phoenix "was trying to compete for the tourist trade with Miami Beach, San Diego, Tucson." It "was trying to bolster the social status of its citizens by shunting across the tracks the immigrants from Oklahoma, Arkansas, and Texas and by veneering itself with the gloss of a symphony orchestra, a Little Theater, and necklace of resort hotels."

> Phoenix did not know—or pretended not to know—that it had slums. But in them lived the Negroes, the Mexicans, the "white trash." There, in 1935, were prostitutes and outlaws, the glass-eyed victims of denatured alcohol, and the innocent children of minority groups, forced by the "better element" to be born and to live in the slums.[4]

In the late 1930s, Placida Garcia Smith became a supporter of Father McLoughlin in the drive for public housing projects in Phoenix. Noting the deplorable conditions in the poorer neighborhoods, she declared in

1938 that "the greatest thing we could do to relieve the situation would be to inaugurate a slum clearance program. By providing clean homes for underprivileged families, we can give them a foundation on which they can raise themselves and their children to a better standard of living." The developments were the Marcos de Niza Project for Mexicans and the Matthew Henson Project for blacks, both located in south Phoenix, and the Frank Luke, Jr. Project for Anglos, located in east Phoenix. In 1931, Garcia Smith had replaced Carrie Green as director of Friendly House. A native of Colorado and a college graduate, she had done volunteer work at Friendly House upon her arrival in Phoenix. A dedicated teacher, she was determined to carry on the Americanization programs associated with Friendly House, but the unemployed were desperate for relief in the form of food, clothing, and jobs. The institution became a center of Mexican life during the decade when it became the chief relief agency "for all Spanish-speaking residents."[5]

Friendly House was also involved in "repatriation" during the 1930s. Many Mexicans returned to Mexico of their own accord, but others were encouraged or forced to return. The economic distress of the Great Depression, along with increased anti-Mexican sentiment, inspired this "back to Mexico" movement, and Friendly House assisted in local repatriation efforts. In 1933, for example, Garcia Smith reported that during the previous six-month period, 130 Mexican families had been repatriated through Friendly House. Garcia Smith later regretted her organization's participation and her own role in the repatriation effort, believing that the process showed little regard for the Mexican people; after all, when their labor was needed, Mexicans were encouraged to come to Arizona, but when it was not, they were expelled. In Arizona both Mexicans and Mexican Americans were repatriated, voluntarily and involuntarily. At times Mexican Americans blamed Mexican immigrants for increasing Anglo discrimination against them; they also resented Anglos for not differentiating between Mexicans and Mexican Americans.

When not assisting in the repatriation or deportation of Mexicans to Mexico, Garcia Smith and her Friendly House staff provided food and clothing to the Mexican needy. The service proved to be critical, for despite city of Phoenix allocations, outside funds were limited; in 1932, for example, Friendly House was the only agency "for Mexican people" to receive financial aid from the Phoenix Community Chest. Friendly House also provided the Anglo community with trained Mexican domestic workers; by the end of the decade it had achieved a reputation for providing efficient and reliable help. For the Mexican workers, who were mostly female, this exposure to "American" culture in the homes of north Phoenix Anglo families was seen as a positive experience.

By 1933 federal funds and programs became available, and Friendly House increased its services. Since the government required citizenship for individuals to be eligible for relief programs, more English and other Americanization courses were offered. Day care nurseries for Mexican children and projects for Mexican "musicians and actors" were started. Garcia Smith's aggressive promotional work made Friendly House a widely admired community asset during the Great Depression. In September 1935 the *Republican* described it as "an institution devoted to the economic and social welfare of Spanish-American citizens of Phoenix."[6]

Federal funds and programs were welcome in the Phoenix area. A New Deal official in the Southwest noted that relief, however inadequate it might have been for Anglos, did not involve any lowering of living standards for African Americans or Mexican Americans. For them, she declared, "it made possible in many, many cases, a better standard of living." Wages were so low that they were better off on relief. This fact of life disturbed Anglo employers, "particularly farmers and housewives because of the difficulty in hiring help at the ridiculously low wages they offered." The flow of Mexican nationals northward stopped in the 1930s, and low wages and poor working conditions discouraged unemployed local residents from working in the cotton fields; in October 1937, for example, the Arizona Cotton Growers' Association demanded that the Works Progress Administration (WPA), a New Deal agency, "drop all able-bodied workers from its rolls in order that the cotton crop may be harvested." Desperate for cotton pickers, local growers advertised and attracted migrants from Oklahoma and Texas. They promised the migrants good wages and working conditions but rarely delivered what they promised.[7]

Mexicans who remained in the United States during the Great Depression became more focused on their rights or lack of rights as Mexican Americans. They may have dreamed of returning to Mexico, but the American Dream also appealed to them. The longer they lived in the United States, the more they acculturated; for example, English language use increased. In Phoenix, as in other Southwestern cities, the emerging Mexican American era would see not only an appreciation of cultural heritage and economic progress but also a striving for first-class citizenship in the United States. Unfulfilled goals called for more political involvement and participation, and new Mexican American organizations came into being intent on influencing change.

In the meantime, mutual-aid societies such as Sociedad Mutualista Benito Juarez, Sociedad Mutualista Porfirio Diaz, Lenadores del Mundo (Woodmen of the World), and the Alianza Hispano Americana continued to help the needy, as did the Catholic and Protestant churches. And the Mexican Chamber of Commerce, created in 1937, worked to further Mexican American businesses and businessmen. Despite hard times, the Junta Patriotica Mexicana persisted in sponsoring Mexican Independence Day celebrations; in 1938 more than five thousand Mexicans participated in the festivities at Riverside Park. The revival of the Fiestas Patrias (Mexican Independence Day celebrations) during hard times was helped considerably by the newspaper *El Sol*. Started by the Jesús Franco family in the early 1930s, it began promoting the Fiestas Patrias tradition in 1934 and helped the festival renew itself as a source of pride for the Mexican American community.[8]

At times, celebrations brought tragedy. Personal feuds occasionally caused violent acts to occur. In 1939, for example, Gregorio Moreno, president of Alianza Hispano Americana and an editorial writer for *El Mensajero,* a local Spanish-language newspaper, was shot and wounded seriously near Sixth and Madison streets; the shot was fired from a passing automobile. Police arrested Jesús Franco, the chairman of the 1939 Mexican Independence Day celebration and editor of *El Sol.* Apparently both men were in a "bitter feud" over who would serve as queen of the September holiday. Acquitted at the October trial, Franco insisted he only fired in self-defense when he saw Moreno crouch and reach toward a rear pocket "as though to produce a weapon."[9]

The Latin American Club of Arizona, founded by Luis Cordova in Phoenix in 1932, was especially active in politics. During the decade local chapters emerged throughout Arizona, and they often met in convention, usually in Phoenix, and endorsed political candidates who supported the interests of Mexican Americans. In Phoenix, Cordova and other Latin American Club leaders led voter registration drives to help motivate politicians to come to meetings and listen to requests. Minor political appointments, government jobs, and other benefits resulted. Moreover, as in the past, there continued to be no love lost between minority groups, which competed for what little was available to them. In 1935, for example, the Latin American Club of Arizona presented a resolution to the Phoenix City Commission asking that blacks be excluded from using

Southside Park at Second Avenue and Grant Street, a largely Mexican neighborhood.

Luis Cordova, a Southern Pacific railroad worker, was an acknowledged leader of the Mexican American community. As founder and organizer of the Latin American Club, he represented an influential voting bloc. Endorsement of successful Anglo political candidates led to patronage positions for Mexican Americans, although they remained few in number. The organization also backed Mexican American candidates, notably James Carreon, the first Spanish-language representative in the Arizona State Legislature from the Phoenix area. Most of the Mexican people in Phoenix were laborers, and they had no problem supporting a leader and an organization that could relate to them and their needs. Although gains were made, there was little doubt that second-class status remained for many Mexican Americans. As Val Cordova, one of several sons of Luis Cordova who would graduate from college, later recalled: "Here in Phoenix, up to World War II, we could not live where we wanted to. In some areas they would not rent or sell to a Mexican American. At the Fox Theater, you had to sit upstairs. At the Studio Theater, in downtown Phoenix, you couldn't even get in. At the public parks, such as, for example, University Park—which was founded and maintained with city tax dollars which we all paid—a Mexican American was not permitted." [10]

Another influential organization appeared in the city in 1941 when Phoenix Council #110 of LULAC, the League of United Latin American Citizens, entered the scene. LULAC, a national organization, emphasized education, and its purpose was "to make useful citizens of its members— citizens that are proud of their race—and to eliminate the problem of discrimination against the Latin race." Local leadership was provided by Placida Garcia Smith, Pedro Guerrera, Gabriel Peralta, and Daniel Grijalva. LULAC often honored city and state politicians for their efforts on behalf of the Mexican American community. Like many other Mexican American organizations of the period, LULAC wanted not only an integrated society with equal rights for all but also freedom for all to retain their cultural heritage.[11]

Phoenix Mexican Americans also served in the armed forces during World War II and distinguished themselves in combat. Spanish-language newspapers carried accounts of their valiant exploits. A Phoenix Congressional Medal of Honor winner, Silvestre S. Herrera, inspired many Mexican Americans in and out of the Arizona capital. On the home front, Alianza Hispano Americana, Lenadores del Mundo, LULAC, and other Mexican American organizations sold and bought war bonds; collected rubber, paper, and metal; harvested cotton; led cigarette drives; and engaged in other war effort activities. They participated in freedom parades and patriotic rallies. They hosted dinners, dances, parties, and other social gatherings for Mexican American servicemen and Latin American cadets who trained at nearby military installations and air bases; many of the latter lived with local families while in training. Mexican Catholic and Protestant churches also played an important role in the community during the conflict; family sacrifices encouraged more religious involvement in the churches as places of prayer and hope. The churches sponsored many war effort events and programs. Most important, new job opportunities opened up for Mexican Americans because of the war. They helped build and work in military facilities and defense plants in the Phoenix area.[12]

World War II was a turning point for the Mexican American community in Phoenix. Following the conflict, veterans returned home determined to make gains. The G.I. Bill, for example, offered them new educational opportunities, job possibilities, and housing benefits. Mexican American American Legion posts and other veterans groups joined with established Mexican American voluntary associations in the struggle for first-class citizenship, and some progress was made, especially in the area of housing for returning servicemen. In 1946, for example, Tony F. Soza American Legion Post 41 led the way in securing final construction of the Harry Cordova Project for Mexican American veterans. Originally built in 1943 to house war workers, it expanded into the Harry Cordova Project (Cordova was a Phoenix soldier who died in World War II). Anglo property owners in the neighborhood complained to Phoenix authorities that the admittance of Mexican Americans into the area would lower property values and increase crime, but the American Legion post and related veterans groups pressured residents and Phoenix politicians into accepting construction of the project.[13]

Overall, however, progress was slow. Most Mexican Americans in Phoenix continued to labor in the bottom ranks of the work force. Their representation in the skilled trades was minimal and they made up less than 1 percent of the area's professionals. The economic position of the typical Mexican American worker had improved, noted a study in 1950, "but only slightly." The "door of economic opportunity and social acceptance was still, on the whole, closed to the greater number of Mexican

Americans." Upward mobility remained low, leaving many poor Mexicans and Mexican Americans with no choice but to live in the substandard housing offered in the barrios or the city's segregated projects.[14]

Local financial institutions continued to contribute to poor housing conditions by refusing to extend loans to members of minority groups. Many of those who owned their own homes had built the dwellings themselves; as a result, houses in Phoenix barrios often appeared to be of substandard construction, and many "shacks" were evident. As one observer declared, "Low income families [were] not able to accumulate money with which to buy a house—if they built a house at all, they built it with the sweat of their brow." Federal policies and loans also failed to encourage decent single-family housing development in poor neighborhoods; the government preferred to invest in new suburban house construction.[15]

In the more affluent Anglo neighborhoods, however, Hispanics were discouraged from buying homes. In December 1947, for example, Amadeo M. Suarez, an Arizona native, World War II veteran, and professor at the American Institute of Foreign Trade, tried to purchase a home in Melrose Manor on north Seventh Avenue but was rejected on "racial grounds." The racial restriction, which was common at the time, stated:

> No lot or tract, or any part thereof, shall be leased, let, occupied, sold or transferred to anyone other than to members of the white or Caucasian race except those of Spanish or Mexican ancestry, and this exclusion shall include those having perceptible strains of Mexican, Spanish, Asiatic, Negro or Indian blood.

Viewed generally, an observer reported, the housing conditions of the residentially segregated Mexican Americans "are deplorable."

Other restrictions irked Mexican Americans, especially veterans. One injustice was the Arizona literacy law, enacted by the state legislature in 1913, which made passing a literacy test a voting requirement. To register, a person had to read a portion of the U.S. Constitution in English to prove eligibility to vote. The United States Congress outlawed such literacy tests in 1965, but the Arizona law was not repealed by the state legislature until 1972, nearly sixty years after its inception. Manuel Pena, Jr., a future member of the Arizona Legislature, remembered when he and other Mexican American veterans returned from World War II to the Phoenix area and decided they wanted to exercise their right to vote without obstruction. "Very few people registered to vote at that time," Pena recalled. "We got involved in voter registration and attempted to teach people to read the preamble to the Constitution." Pena and future Phoenix Councilman Adam Diaz later said it was common for political reactionaries to show up at the polls and mount "challenges" to those waiting to vote. "Many of our people, very innocent, just walked off," Diaz recalled. "They were kind of intimidated."

The practice increased in the early 1960s; if right-wing conservatives had some concern over whether someone was able to read or write, they would hand the person a large index-style "Constitution card" displaying excerpts from the document to see if he or she could meet the requirement to read or write English. The literacy voting requirement passed in 1913 stated:

> Every citizen of the United States and every citizen of Mexico who shall have elected to become a citizen of the United States . . . who, not being prevented by physical disability from so doing, is able to read the Constitution of the United States in the English language in such a manner as to show he is neither prompted nor reciting from memory, and to write his name, shall be deemed to be an elector of the state of Arizona.[16]

Segregated schooling also persisted following World War II, largely because of cultural and residential factors. In the rural communities of the valley, where Mexican Americans and Anglos were most likely to share the schools available, "language deficiencies" often provided a reason for segregation. Although unofficial, the practice took its toll and produced protest. The Alianza Hispano Americana, for example, wanted to eliminate the inferior educational facilities used by Mexican American children. School administrators in the affected areas pleaded that neither segregation nor discrimination was being practiced, but rather "separation on the basis of the lack of English proficiency on the part of Mexican-American children and the accompanying retardation of the English speaking children." In the early 1950s, Alianza lawyers Ralph Estrada and Greg Garcia, both of Phoenix, began to successfully challenge this premise in Tolleson, Glendale, and other valley farming community school districts.

Using landmark California cases as models, Estrada and Garcia brought civil rights for Mexican Americans in Arizona to the forefront. In *Gonzales v. Sheeley,* the Tolleson case, they argued in federal district court in Phoenix that placing Mexican American children in a separate school denied them their constitutional rights under the Fourteenth Amendment. Ample evidence showed that the school for Mexican American children was inferior to the Anglo school; it was separate but hardly equal. The evidence pertaining to unequal facilities went unchallenged, but lawyers for the Tolleson School District contended that the only reason for the segregation of Mexican American children was their English-language deficiency, which prevented them from competing with Anglo children. In turn, their lack of facility with the English language retarded the educational development of Anglo children. In this view, the segregation of Anglo and Mexican American students benefited both groups. The Alianza lawyers declared that no "literacy tests" were ever given to determine whether or not any students entering the Tolleson schools were deficient in language skills. Segregation based on literacy tests that did not exist, they asserted, was not justified. Moreover, Estrada and Garcia, again citing previous California cases, stated that language deficiencies did not "justify the segregation in separate schools of the children of Mexican ancestry from the rest of the elementary school population."

The California cases had established that language deficiencies did not justify the segregation of students in separate school buildings. They also had established that "inherent in the right of the student to equality is the right to 'commingle' with other students of other races, at the time of, and in the process of receiving an education, at the educational institution." As Paul J. McCormick, judge in the California case *Mendez v. Westminster,* stated:

> The evidence clearly shows that Spanish-speaking children are retarded in learning English by lack of exposure to its use because of segregation, and that commingling of the entire student body instills and develops a common cultural attitude among the school children which is imperative for the perpetuation of American institutions and ideals.

Judge McCormick deemed social equality to be a "paramount requisite in the American system of public education." His counterpart in Arizona, Judge David Ling, apparently agreed; in January 1952 he ruled that the Tolleson School District had deprived Mexican Americans of equal protection and was in violation of the Fourteenth Amendment. The Tolleson School District did not appeal the decision, which inspired the Glendale School District and others practicing similar forms of segregation to desegregate voluntarily when threatened with court action.[17]

Mexican American students in the barrios of south Phoenix continued to attend "racially isolated" schools. Lowell School and other "Mexican" schools produced some outstanding future leaders of the Mexican American community, but not everybody was pleased. There continued to be a lack of Mexican American involvement in the operation of the schools:

there were no Mexican American school board members or school principals and very few Mexican American teachers. Children were still punished for speaking Spanish in the schools or on the school playgrounds. The residential neighborhoods in which the schools were located reflected the low economic status of most of the schoolchildren. Many of those who went on to high school eventually dropped out and faced a bleak future. Inadequate schooling, housing, and employment opportunities made life difficult.[18]

During the 1950s laborers imported from Mexico, along with advances in mechanization in agriculture, further weakened the economic position of local farm workers, and the number of Mexican Americans on the welfare rolls rose. Mexican American leaders in Phoenix called for an end to the importation of *braceros,* or farm workers, from Mexico, but the practice continued. As many as five thousand Mexican nationals worked the valley fields each year. Manuel Pena, Jr., speaking for Phoenix Mexicans, declared that "as long as we have the imported worker, the local worker will never get a decent living wage." Anglo farmers preferred imported labor because it was cheaper and easier to control.[19]

Mexican American leaders were more successful in breaking down discriminating barriers in the valley for their people. Often it involved a struggle, but unofficial segregation in public accommodations such as theaters, restaurants, and swimming pools, as well as in the schools, lessened in the 1940s and 1950s. At the same time, one could continue to dine in Mexican American restaurants, read *El Sol* and other Spanish-language publications, listen to Spanish-language KIFN (La Voz Mexicana), dance to Spanish and Mexican music, hang out at the Ramona Drug Store (the "biggest Mexican drug store around here—where everyone converged and met and talked and so on"), see Spanish-language films at the Azteca and Rex theaters, and attend celebrations of Mexican Independence Day, Cinco de Mayo, and other holidays. Cultural identity remained important. As one patron of the popular Mexican American Calderon Ballroom later put it, "Tradition and heritage are important to Mexicanos. And at Calderon's the music, the familiar setting, the Mexicanos all together—it provided a sense of community."[20]

For those Mexican Americans who had the means, more housing opportunities opened up outside south Phoenix. Although critics often blamed members of the small but fast-growing middle class for deserting the barrios, successful Mexican Americans contributed to the community; the Vesta Club, for example, considered education to be the key to many Mexican American problems. Founded in 1954 by teacher Eugene

Marin, and composed of some of the outstanding Mexican American professional and business leaders in Phoenix, the Vesta Club adopted the motto "Progress Through Education." More active in Phoenix than LULAC and other largely middle-class organizations, it sponsored an extensive scholarship program for Mexican American youth throughout the decade. Only college graduates were allowed to join the Vesta Club. Mexican American professionals wanted an organization of their own; they held dances and other social events in order to raise funds. The annual Vesta Club Debutante Ball was a major social event in the city. Vesta Club leaders wanted to show Anglo Phoenix that Mexican American professionals existed, made valuable contributions to society, and deserved recognition.

As Marin put it, the Vesta Club's "immediate objective was to attempt to change the image, in the public eye, of the Spanish-speaking citizen."

> Up to that time, negative publicity absolutely overwhelmed anything positive that occurred in this valley, in the entire state for that matter. Where the news media publicized tavern brawls and roadside holdups, the club countered with benefit dances, scholarship award banquets, and testimonial dinners. When the news publicized destituteness or other depressing sights, the club worked to accentuate the positive by announcing stage productions at the Phoenix Little Theater, or cultural lecture series by its members.[21]

Another activity was political education. Marin, Val Cordova, Joe Acosta, Tony Vicente, Alex Cordova, Bennie Gonzalez, and other Vesta Club leaders over the years caught the attention of city power brokers, who recognized their success and influence and invited them to consider political and economic opportunities for Mexican Americans. The Vesta Club and its members, for example, often supported winning Phoenix City Council candidates such as Adam Diaz, Val Cordova, Ray Pisano, Frank Benites, Armando de Leon, and Rosendo Gutierrez.

Among Mexican Americans, Pena noted in 1962, "a fortunate few have succeeded." With a population of 61,460, or 14 percent of the total in 1960, they remained the largest and fastest-growing minority group in Phoenix. Up from 9,740 in 1940 and 16,000 in 1950, the Mexican American population needed all the help it could muster. In the barrios of south Phoenix, however, little was done; as Phoenix philanthropist Robert B. Choate, Jr., noted, "Social welfare in that part of town, from any possible direction, is insufficient for the demand." His organization, Careers for Youth, was especially concerned with the problem of improving the effectiveness of education in poor south-side neighborhoods.[22]

Many Mexican students dropped out of school to work and help support their families. The importance of duty and loyalty to family remained paramount. Although based on cultural values, the decision to leave school condemned many Mexican youth to low-income jobs in a society becoming increasingly technological and demanding in its need for educated workers.

A variety of voluntary associations served the community by trying to improve business, employment, housing, and educational opportunities. The Phoenix Mexican Chamber of Commerce continued to promote Mexican American business and businesses, while the Phoenix chapter of the Community Service Organization (CSO) did its best to eliminate blight in poor Mexican American neighborhoods. The Greater Phoenix Council for Civic Unity and the Phoenix All-American Council for Equality opposed discriminating practices in areas of public accommodation. Organizations such as Alianza Hispano Americana, LULAC, and the Committee for Americanism and Inter-American Solidarity worked on behalf of the Hispanic community in general, while local institutions such as the East Madison Settlement House and the Southside Improvement Organization brought a range of social services to the barrios.[23]

Friendly House remained a center of activity in the Hispanic community. Supported by the Phoenix Community Council and other financial sources, Friendly House continued its Americanization program and expanded its educational and charitable work. The beloved director of Friendly House, Placida Garcia Smith, served as the Mexican community's representative on important civic committees. At Friendly House she was ably assisted by Adam Diaz, who served as president of the private agency during the postwar years. A firm believer in education as the answer to Hispanic problems, Diaz proved to be a great fund raiser. He also was the first Mexican American to serve on the Phoenix City Council, being elected in 1952.

In 1956, with United Way as its biggest financial contributor, Friendly House increased its offerings. Citizenship and English classes, along with domestic training and employment programs, multiplied. Of utmost importance, Friendly House served as a meeting place for Hispanic groups and an informal community center where Hispanic problems could be discussed and resolutions considered. The gracious and talented Garcia Smith led Friendly House in fulfilling its motto of "Helping People Help Themselves." Also an advocate of the belief that education provided the key to progress, she was widely acclaimed for her leadership qualities. "Friendly House has given innumerable services to the community and especially to la colonia Mexicans," observed an admirer in 1961, and "Mrs. Placida Smith has been at the lead of this great work which has been conducted with intelligence and, above all, with a great deal of heart." In 1962, Placida Garcia Smith won Phoenix Woman of the Year honors.[24]

The career of Placida Garcia Smith illustrates the strong influence of outstanding minority women in Phoenix. She worked for community improvement and helped many Mexicans and Mexican Americans lead better lives in the city. Garcia Smith accepted her leadership role at Friendly House in the 1930s because she "wanted to do something for my own people." She led the organization in its quest to provide job opportunities and social services for men and women. Women especially benefited from Garcia Smith's work; most of the jobs she located were for them. She also inspired a day-care nursery for children and a well-baby clinic. The classes in English and citizenship she supervised were in demand in the 1930s because the government required United States citizenship to qualify for relief programs. As Garcia Smith put it, "The greatest need I found was the lack of being able to speak English." She also promoted an appreciation of Mexican culture in Phoenix. "I don't think you can live without culture, without music, without song, without dance, and we had a great deal of talent on the southside."

Garcia Smith also helped form the Southside Improvement Organization in the 1930s, a group dedicated to securing new parks and pools from the government. Grant Park and Harmon Park, both with pools, were built, and the result, according to Garcia Smith, who eventually was named to the Phoenix Parks and Recreation Board, "showed the people that you have to raise your voice and be heard." She encouraged people to speak for themselves and set an example by complaining to local businesses and government agencies about the lack of Spanish-speaking employees. The phone company and several banks, for example, heard from her and made gradual improvements. Also, as she later recalled: "I remember going through the offices in City Hall, in the Courthouse, and never seeing Spanish-speaking people working in any of the offices. There were a few, but not many." Some improvement eventually occurred in the public as well as the private sector, in part because of the leadership of Garcia Smith.

Young people concerned her. She often counseled them and their families. Troubled youths concerned her the most. Education was the key to progress, she declared time and again, but "there was a great deal of discrimination, and as result, the boys would say, 'Well, what's the use of going to school if you can't get jobs.' " Garcia Smith encouraged them to persevere and finish school. Later she stated: "It has always been my way to work with people individually. In my small way, I have tried to channel them into productivity." Moreover, she stressed that people of diverse cultures should learn from each other. "My main interest is that the people of the earth should understand each other—know each other's backgrounds and cultures," she once declared. "Society is responsible for what comes of its people. Peace and security will come only when people learn how the other half lives and take action." [25]

During the 1940s and 1950s, some Mexican Americans utilizing the G.I. Bill of Rights and taking advantage of other opportunities for advancement, broke new ground. As one veteran of World War II recalled: "The government educated us, and we consider ourselves more American than anything else. Fighting for your country doesn't give you the feeling of a second-class citizen. It really gives you the feeling that you did as much as the next guy did, so this is as much your country as it is anybody else's." Beneficiaries of the G.I. Bill were convinced education was the key to progress for Mexican Americans. Moreover, more female as well as male Mexican Americans were going to college following World War II. As one observer declared, "Before, Mexican-American women would get married or get a job as a clerk in clothing stores or five and ten cent stores, or in offices as typists, and that was it, but now after World War II, more are going to college." [26]

3 PROGRESS AND PROBLEMS, 1960-1992

Despite the success of some individuals and organizations, neighborhood surveys and civil rights hearings in the early 1960s described inadequate conditions in the Mexican American community. Residentially isolated in the barrios of Phoenix, most Hispanics continued to experience low economic status. Inadequate housing, schooling, and employment opportunities continued to make life difficult for them; in some areas such as education, surveys indicated a lower level of attainment for Mexican Americans than for African Americans.

In the 1960s the Mexican American Political Association (MAPA) and other activist organizations promoted increased voter registration and political involvement. Mexican Americans Leonard Calderon, Jr., David Valenzuela, Manuel Pena, Jr., and Tony Abril served in the state legislature. In 1965, Val Cordova became the first Maricopa County superior court judge of Mexican descent. Frank Benites became president of the Phoenix Building and Construction Trades Council. Although Mexican American membership in unions remained low, their total membership increased; moreover, the 1960s witnessed an increase in the number of Mexican Americans in civil service jobs.

At the same time, Phoenix and other Southwestern cities offered more opportunities than rural areas. In the 1950s and 1960s, Phoenix underwent a population explosion and economic boom that made economic upward mobility more possible than it had been in the past. Unskilled and semiskilled jobs in construction, for example, paid better than farm jobs. That opportunities to rise were improving was illustrated by the

Table 3.1. Social Indicators in Phoenix Mexican American
          Neighborhoods by Affluence, 1970

	% Women (35–44) Never Married with Children	% High School Graduates	% Men in Labor Force	% Women in Labor Force	% Foreign- Born
More affluent neighborhoods	3.174	53.1	86.5	46.5	3.1
Less affluent neighborhoods	4.020	18.9	77.5	34.1	4.3
All Mexican Americans	3.562	35.4	79.2	39.8	3.7
Citywide	3.115	58.9	78.6	44.8	3.4

SOURCE: John E. Crow, *Mexican Americans in Contemporary Arizona: A Social and Demographic View* (San Francisco: R and E Research, 1975), 79.

growing Mexican American middle class in Phoenix and other regional urban centers. Change, although limited, was taking place. Mexican American women, as well as Mexican American men, experienced higher expectations and hoped for a better future.[1]

Studies indicated that 83 percent of the Mexican Americans known to reside in Phoenix in 1970 lived in tracts with at least four hundred Mexican Americans. Higher education levels and smaller families existed in the more affluent areas (neighborhoods where family incomes were at least twice the level of poverty income), as did more working men and women. Working wives contributed to family incomes. Moreover, Mexican Americans outnumbered the foreign-born in the more affluent neighborhoods (see Table 3.1).[2]

By 1980, however, a segregated city clearly remained. In that year about 15 percent of Phoenix's neighborhoods contained more than half of the city's Mexican American population, and 32 percent of the city's neighborhoods had virtually no Mexican American residents (see Map 3.1).

As in the case of blacks, increasing numbers of Hispanic individuals made progress as more educational and employment opportunities

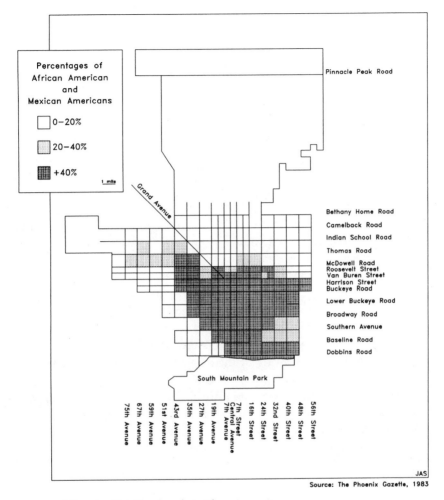

MAP 3.1 Minority Neighborhoods in Phoenix, 1983

opened up in the wake of the civil rights movement. Like blacks, Hispanics also continued to make political gains. In the early 1970s Calvin Goode, an African American, and Mexican American Rosendo Gutierrez assumed influential roles on the Phoenix City Council, while Art Hamilton, an African American, and Mexican American Alfredo Gutierrez (no relation to Rosendo) were elected to the Arizona Legislature. Alfredo Gutierrez did not expect to win the 1972 election, but he campaigned vigorously; black incumbent Cloves Campbell lost the close contest and later recalled that it "got down to who got out more votes—Hispanics or blacks. He got out more Hispanic votes." Many of the minority leaders, including Alfredo Gutierrez, were young, and they reflected the experiences of the civil rights movement.[3]

Alfredo Gutierrez, for example, was a student activist at Arizona State University in the late 1960s. A leader of the Mexican American Student Organization (MASO) at ASU, he and his supporters had successfully protested practices seen as unfair to Mexican Americans. Gutierrez not only engaged in Chicano causes on campus but also helped form Chicano organizations in the Phoenix barrios to fight discrimination in the city. The new Chicano organizations attempted to go beyond the services provided by Friendly House; the new leaders and their organizations, notably Chicanos por la Causa (CPLC), represented a new determination and direction in improving conditions in the Hispanic community. Integration appealed to them less than justice.[4]

In the fall of 1970, when conflict erupted at Phoenix Union High School, for instance, CPLC organized a Hispanic boycott of the school until changes occurred. Gutierrez, Joe Eddie Lopez, Earl Wilcox, Manuel Dominquez, and other CPLC leaders and members of the Parent-Student Boycott Committee publicized the dissatisfaction of the Chicanos and made the public more aware of their plight. For a long time PUHS had needed programs more responsive to the needs of the minority group students who made up the majority of the school's enrollment, but few materialized. Calls for more minority teachers and counselors also went unheeded. Noting in 1969 that PUHS and other schools in Phoenix were "full of discrimination and exploitation," Father Robert Donohoe, a Catholic priest, declared that they "have failed miserably to provide equality and equitable education and opportunity to the citizens of Mexican origin." Especially disturbing to minority parents was the inclination of advisers to channel minority students "toward manual rather than intellectual development, without consideration of the fact that such a choice produces and perpetuates economic-racial discrimination."

While the black and Chicano student population at PUHS increased during the 1950s and 1960s, the physical facilities deteriorated from age and neglect. White flight accelerated; from 1967 to 1970 alone, the number of Anglo students at the school declined from 35.1 to 19.3 percent. PUHS had become a "minorities" school, but minorities had little voice in determining and conducting education at the institution. Moreover, violence between blacks and Chicanos played a large role in the day-to-day life of the school, with each side blaming the other. Chicano parents and leaders from Chicano organizations protested. They "protested harassment of their children by black students and the school system's failure to cope with the high drop-out rate of Mexican American students." Marches and demonstrations were held, and Chicano leaders demanded official action. Finally, on October 9, 1970, they called for a boycott of PUHS.

The participating leaders of CPLC and the Parent-Student Boycott Committee insisted that law and order on the campus be restored. It was important that unlawful activity by black students be addressed by authorities; the situation only enhanced resentment between the two groups. According to the boycott leaders, the authorities were afraid to confront blacks because of their fear of possible conflict; the inaction of school administrators and law enforcement officials upset Chicanos, but there were other problems.

The lack of student security was an important issue, but it was one of many grievances. The protesters also wanted the general quality of education at PUHS to change to better reflect their aspirations for the Hispanic community. In response to demands made by the leaders of the Parent-Student Boycott Committee and CPLC, Valle del Sol Institute, Barrio Youth Project, and other Chicano organizations, school officials promised to hire personnel and to implement programs more responsive to the educational needs of Chicano students. During the month-long boycott Barrio Youth Project operated classrooms for boycotting students, and Valle del Sol Institute offered tutoring sessions during and after the boycott; much of this activity was organized by Father Frank Yoldi and held in local Mexican American churches and community centers. During the 1970s these groups, along with Chicanos por la Causa, joined Friendly House and other agencies in providing valuable educational, economic, and social services to Phoenix Hispanics.[5]

The Alianza Hispano Americana and other older organizations not attractive to younger Chicanos declined during the period, while new and more timely groups such as CPLC gained ground. In order to retain its importance, Friendly House adopted a more aggressive approach in the 1960s and 1970s. From its new quarters acquired in 1961, it expanded its operations during the War on Poverty, despite objections from some Anglo board members. Mildred Brown, an Anglo, took over as head of Friendly House in 1965, and under her direction changes occurred; the Americanization programs remained most important, but more emphasis was given to welfare services. Nevertheless, Friendly House's agenda failed to prevent young Chicano leaders from forming CPLC and other new Chicano-oriented organizations to represent the Phoenix Hispanic community.[6]

The Vietnam War and the civil rights movement, with their many Hispanic American participants, had helped encourage more active involvement at the local level. Hispanics complained that blacks were the major beneficiaries of most government assistance inspired by protest. Observers declared that "blacks are out for blacks; Mexicans are out for Mexicans." Others noted that "Mexicans are more white than blacks." Being "legally Caucasian," they preferred to protest within organizations distinct from black groups. Few Hispanic leaders marched with African American leaders during the early 1960s, but among those who did were Grace Olivarez, Joe Robles, and Larry Huerta, whose support was appreciated.

In the late 1960s a variety of Hispanic organizations emerged, many of them wanting a fairer share of Great Society programs and projects; among the more successful was Chicanos por la Causa. Formed in 1969 to secure aid to confront the "oppressing problems threatening to overwhelm the Phoenix Chicano community," CPLC initiated many community service programs in the 1970s, including housing, counseling and rehabilitation, small business projects, job training centers, and neighborhood health clinics. By 1977 it had an annual operating budget of $676,000; with heavy infusions of federal funds, the budget had grown to $6.3 million four years later. CPLC also served as a school of Hispanic leadership. Alfredo Gutierrez, Joe Eddy Lopez, and other Chicano activists, who founded CPLC to confront discrimination against the Hispanic community and improve barrio life in Phoenix, set the pace, while Ronnie Lopez (no relation to Joe Eddy), Tom Espinosa, and others later joined and contributed to the realization of many of the organization's goals. Espinosa, who became head of CPLC in 1974, proved to be especially effective in relating to and securing support from Anglo business and political leaders in and out of Phoenix.[7]

Despite gains made under the leadership of CPLC and other Chicano organizations, problems remained at the end of the 1970s. South Phoenix residents still needed more of everything most north Phoenix residents already had or expected to have in the near future. More well-built homes, more paved streets, more public parks, more health facilities, more libraries, more shopping centers, more police stations, more firehouses, and so on. Moreover, Phoenix Union High School and other educational institutions failed to do enough to spur confidence in their programs. Chicanos continued to head the drop-out list, which contributed

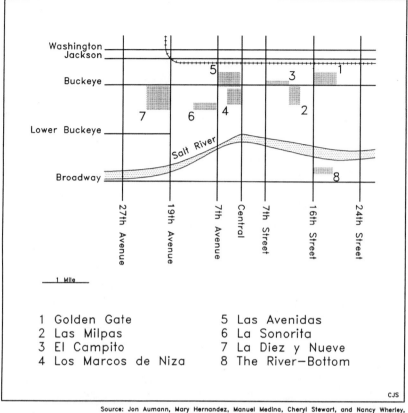

Source: Jon Aumann, Mary Hernandez, Manuel Medina, Cheryl Stewart, and Nancy Wherley,
"The Chicano Addict: An Analysis of Factors Influencing Rehabilitation in a Treatment and Prevention Program"
(MA Thesis: Arizona State University, 1972)

MAP 3.2 The Barrios of South Phoenix, circa 1970

to high crime rates in Phoenix. In 1979, Reuben Ortega, a Phoenix police community relations officer and future police chief, declared that "more than half our crime problem is directly related to youth." In that year it was estimated that more than forty organized street gangs operated in Phoenix, many of them in Hispanic neighborhoods on the south and west sides (see Map 3.2).[8]

Critics blamed the lack of educational, recreational, and social programs, along with the lack of employment opportunities, for the popularity of the groups. They insisted that "no real gangs existed in Phoenix, just hordes of drop-outs with nothing to do." At the same time, a young gang member asserted:

Kids never get out of their own neighborhood. Gangs evolve from groups of bored friends. And they end up fighting over stupid things—girlfriends, over their "turf." They fight over a piece of dirt, man. They get into drugs. It all starts because they are bored to death. South Phoenix is dead. There are no big discos, or good theatres and pinball places, or concerts and things they can afford. But there's a liquor store on every corner where a kid can go and buy booze.

Chicanos resented the negative publicity given to the barrios by reporters. In most neighborhoods the residents were hard-working, family-oriented people. Pete Garcia, a CPLC spokesman, regretted in 1979 that there was so much emphasis on "crime and drugs and violence" in the Hispanic neighborhoods:

It becomes guilt by association. If you live in these areas, you're stereotyped as having that kind of lifestyle. The news is out of proportion. Someone is killed in Scottsdale and you don't hear that much about it. One person gets shot in South Phoenix and it's made to sound like a massacre.

Garcia and others particularly lamented the image fostered by the "gang problem." Hank Molder, a Maricopa County juvenile probation officer, stated:

It's fair to say there is some violence and destruction going on. But maybe there is also a bit of injustice when kids in cowboy hats and pickups, drinking beer and cruising Central, aren't thought of as a gang. But when you have Chicano kids driving lowriders, wearing bandannas and smoking marijuana they are singled out as being gangs.[9]

Thousands of illegal aliens also posed a "problem" in the barrios. "Phoenix is like a hub," a federal investigator noted in 1979. Over one hundred "coyotes," or smugglers of illegal aliens, lived in Phoenix at that time, and they often contracted with local growers to provide farm workers. Exploitation of the illegals continued; many of them, observed a reporter, "sleep in the groves or fields, their only water coming from irrigation ditches; they are contaminated by pesticides; victimized by flies and mosquitos in summer, the cold and rain in the winter." Illegals also lived in the barrios, where they spent much of their low pay on high rents; on any morning truckloads of workers could be seen leaving for the groves or fields. Others eschewed agricultural labor and worked in a variety of other jobs ranging from building construction to domestic service. Illegals usually appreciated the opportunities presented to them, but they were vulnerable. "There are a lot of employers getting rich off their sweat," a Friendly House official noted in the late 1970s; "they're victims of anybody who wants to take advantage." They were often disliked by citizens critical of their siphoning off jobs and services; in many cases they were reported and returned to Mexico. A "feeling of separation" existed between many Mexican Americans and Mexican nationals.[10]

During the 1980s the Mexican percentage of the total population of Phoenix increased; by 1990 it had climbed to nearly 20 percent (176,139), up from 15 percent in 1980 (116,875) and 1970 (81,239). Mexican Americans remained the largest minority group in Phoenix; in 1990 the total population of Phoenix reached 983,403, up from 789,704 in 1980, sustaining the city's ranking as the ninth largest city in the United States. During the decade more Mexican Americans, many of them professional and business people, moved into the middle class. The positive effects of civil rights awareness and economic growth and prosperity made it easier for individuals to benefit from new economic and political opportunities, but progress for Mexican Americans as a group within the larger Phoenix population remained slow.

Educational and employment gains for individuals were noted during the decade, and structural changes in the city's political system allowed for more minority group representation. After the move to the district system in 1983, south and much of west Phoenix elected minority group members to the city council. Before the district system, minorities felt neglected; as Alfredo Gutierrez observed in regard to members of the Anglo power structure in Phoenix, "Hispanics have been totally out— when they do talk to us, it's like they're addressing ambassadors from a foreign country." Mexican American Mary Rose Garrido Wilcox represented District 7, which was populated mostly by Mexican Americans, and Calvin Goode represented District 8, where large numbers of both Mexican Americans and African Americans lived. Hispanic and black members of the Arizona Legislature from south and west Phoenix, including Alfredo Gutierrez and Art Hamilton, continued to make their presence felt in that body. Yet, in an article published in 1986 on "the 50 most influential people in Arizona," Alfredo Gutierrez and Art Hamilton were the only minority members mentioned. A similar article published in 1981 declared that "the twenty most powerful people in the state of Arizona were Anglos from Phoenix."[11]

The southern section of the city continued to contain a wide range of socioeconomic neighborhoods. South of the Salt River the population in 1986 was the most racially balanced in the city: approximately one-third Anglo American, one-third African American, and one-third Mexican American. The area contained a variety of housing ranging from shacks to mansions. As the 1980s evolved, developers as well as residents began thinking about its future. One resident called it "a gemstone in the rough." A builder called it the city's "last frontier," a section still retaining large tracts of developable land. Many residents fought hard during the decade to keep what they considered to be unwanted industrial, commercial, and residential development out of the area.

At the same time, many poorer residents looked to the jobs such development could provide for minority group members. The low-density area provided a pleasant, upscale, rural lifestyle for those who could afford it, but for those who resided in substandard housing in the poorer neighborhoods, general development meant economic opportunities and a more prosperous future for the area. One minority leader asserted it was time to "move south Phoenix forward" and "take advantage of the growth and opportunity that the rest of the city enjoys." For too long the section had been Phoenix's "dumping ground" for sewer plants, major landfills, and other "undesirable" projects. The conflict over the future of south Phoenix below the Salt promised to persist; observers hoped that the residents, developers, and politicians involved would eventually work out a plan beneficial to all concerned.[12]

In the meantime, although numerous middle-class minority neighborhoods existed in the area, the image of south Phoenix as primarily a low-income minority community discouraged more economic development. "There definitely is a stigma as far as getting people to want to invest in south Phoenix," a real-estate broker declared in early 1987; "without saying the term redlining, it's apparent it exists." A problem from the beginning, redlining referred to the "systematic refusal by banks to give loans on properties in neighborhoods regarded as deteriorating." The Association of Community Organizations for Reform Now (ACORN), a neighborhood action group, made some progress in securing loan commitments from local banks, but the problem remained. For example, a 1991 report noted that lenders turned down Mexican Americans and African Americans for home loans much more often than Anglo Americans and Chinese Americans. Moreover, continued the critics, when development took place, it did little to lessen the area's high unemployment rate; too often businesses brought employees with them. "During the past 10 years, we've had these developers come in and ask for zoning changes, making these grandiose promises about jobs, then they don't come through," neighborhood leader Carlos Avelar stated. "If they do, they are low-skill, low-paying types of jobs, like gardeners or janitors."[13]

South Phoenix, both south and north of the Salt River, and parts of central Phoenix contained some neighborhoods with conditions as bad as any elsewhere in the country. For example, the predominantly minority low-income neighborhoods in the area bounded by McDowell Road, Broadway Road, Thirty-fifth Avenue, and Forty-eighth Street were plagued with the problems of substandard housing, decaying schools, poverty, and unemployment. Observers referred to them as "low-density slums." They helped support the view of critics that Phoenix increasingly "resembled many other cities with a minority-populated, impoverished core surrounded by affluent white enclaves." Especially burdened were neighborhoods such as the barrio bordered by Roosevelt and Van Buren, Seventh and Sixteenth streets. In that area, noted reporter Andy Zipser in 1983,

> "For Rent" signs are everywhere, some posted on homes that are merely tired and untidy, others that verge on collapse. A few of the houses are only memories, marked by gravestone pilings or a rectangle of foundation, broken glass glittering like sequins on the broken ground. The dirt alleys that bisect each block turn to mud at just a kiss of rain. Graffiti is omnipresent, the distinctive, diamond-shaped letters sprayed on trash-containers, telephone poles, stop signs, buildings that have been abandoned and buildings that are still occupied.[14]

During the 1970s and 1980s the criminal activity of gangs increased considerably, especially drug deals and violent assaults, including drive-by shootings. Confrontations occurred almost daily, with more than 110 gangs operating in Phoenix by 1990, many of them in minority neighborhoods. "It's getting to be like what LA was like 10 or 12 years ago," said Phoenix police detective Johnny Vasquez, a member of Operation Safe Streets, a task force created in May 1990 to help lessen rising gang violence. "We're still in the infancy stages here," he asserted. "We don't have the numbers or the violence to rival California yet. But if we don't curb their activities now, chances are, Phoenix could become another LA."

The violence seemed senseless to many observers, but gang members, as one of them declared, "see it as a way of life." An innocent Mexican American resident of a troubled neighborhood was alarmed that "it's getting to be like a war zone here." In addressing gang-related problems, Phoenix Police Chief Reuben Ortega endorsed the need for more police and law enforcement, but he also recognized the need for education, community outreach, and family-support programs. One of the first Hispanic police chiefs in the country, Ortega had a history of community relations work and knew the Hispanic community. Other Hispanic role models stood out, but there were too few of them; world boxing champion Michael Carbajal, for example, lived in the south Phoenix neighborhood where he grew up. He could live anywhere he chose in the Valley of the Sun but chose to remain in an area where he might do some good. "Neighborhood kids no longer idolize gang members," a reporter observed, "they idolize Carbajal." Private and public programs involving many dedicated individuals and groups brought some relief to afflicted neighborhoods, but problems persisted.

One was the problem of motivating Hispanic young people to prepare for and attend college. Part of the problem, according to a report published in 1992, "is that there isn't a great value attached to a college education in the Hispanic community." The problem "is compounded by poverty and the perception that a college degree simply isn't attainable." As one Hispanic student at Arizona State University lamented, "There just are not enough Hispanic kids (academically qualified) to go to college. They're not being shown the road to success. Kids in south Phoenix see someone with a lot of money—a drug dealer—and that's how they define success." [15]

Also, during the 1970s and 1980s, some viable and vibrant Mexican American neighborhoods were destroyed by private and public pressure, including the Golden Gate barrio, a Mexican American neighborhood since the 1920s. Sky Harbor Airport expansion and the potential industrial and commercial development of Sky Harbor Center in southeast Phoenix forced the destruction of Golden Gate and other adjacent neighborhoods, resulting in the relocation of their inhabitants, mostly Mexican Americans. Done in the interest of "progress," the process contributed to strained relations between city officials, private developers, and Mexican American inhabitants. The neighborhoods were old but dear to many of the displaced residents. The experience proved to be highly emotional, and the destruction of the neighborhoods, like earlier freeway displacement on the south side, reinforced a long-held feeling that the neglected and often ignored minority groups in Phoenix had enjoyed little success against the Anglo establishment.

Most of those who were displaced relocated to growing Mexican American neighborhoods on the west side. Although many were relieved to get away from the noise, jet-exhaust pollution, and other unwelcome hazards present in the old neighborhoods, they encountered new social problems. Often they suffered from the forced break from family members, friends, churches, and schools. "Almost everyone has left, and their homes have been razed. Block after block appears literally Godforsaken," wrote a reporter of the area in March 1986. The city of Phoenix and other promoters kept justifying their actions as being in the "public interest," but many of the 5,000 displaced Hispanics had difficulty accepting the Anglo idea that the process benefited them as well as the larger community. As usual, the prevailing view left them little choice. The former Golden Gate barrio became a memory for many Mexican Americans. The "neighborhood was like a family. Where I'm at now is just a place to live," declared Esequel Chavez, who lived in the barrio for thirty years before being relocated to west Phoenix in 1978.[16]

Segregated neighborhoods and segregated housing contributed to segregated schools. Anglo flight to the suburbs, high minority drop-out rates, and federal and state cutbacks encouraged Phoenix Union High School to close in June 1982, but problems persisted in the school district. In 1987, for example, the Phoenix Union High School District remained under a federal court order to desegregate. The continued expansion of segregated housing patterns, however, compounded the problem of compliance. The high school district developed magnet schools and tightened enrollment policies to prevent "white and bright flight" to promote school desegregation. Such steps helped, but the problem persisted.

Moreover, minority group students rarely made it to Arizona State University, and those who did often dropped out. In 1984 the *Republic* noted that "only 2 to 3 percent of the more than 40,000 students at ASU are Hispanic and the percentage of faculty members is even smaller." Blacks also were poorly represented. Critics declared that "too few minority children receive the education they need to succeed in metropolitan Phoenix." Recruiters at ASU lamented "the lack of qualified ethnic students available." In 1987 statistics showed that the percentage of Hispanic students who attended ASU represented only about one-third the percentage of Hispanics in metropolitan Phoenix. The percentage of blacks was about half the rate of the black population in the area. "Attempts to increase the college enrollment and graduation rates need to begin in elementary school," ASU officials declared, and "they need to consist of a combined effort by many community organizations—including businesses, churches and public schools." Phoenix and Valley of the Sun civic and economic leaders, prognosticators emphasized, "must conclude it is in their best interest to improve efforts to educate minority children." By the end of the decade, critics complained that ASU still lagged behind in the recruitment of minority students, faculty, and administrators. As for the lack of high-level Hispanic administrators at

ASU, "it is unacceptable for ASU officials to claim that there are 'no qualified' candidates," declared Arizona Hispanic Community Forum leader Edward Valenzuela in 1990. "That ruse is old hat."[17]

During the 1980s more members of minority groups who could afford it dispersed throughout the city, but not without difficulty. Middle-class Mexican Americans found it easier than middle-class African Americans to relocate in predominantly middle-class Anglo American neighborhoods; as a result, more Hispanics were living in high-income neighborhoods. Not only did they reflect higher educational levels and smaller family sizes, but most of them represented recent generations. Moreover, more wives in the Hispanic middle class were in the work force. Historical gains encouraged the gradual integration and assimilation of the Hispanic middle class into the more general society. The less successful, however, remained in the poorer neighborhoods in Phoenix, and new immigrants kept joining them. According to one critic writing in 1983, "The Chicano middle class, like the black middle class before it, is more defined by economic considerations than ethnic ones—is more middle class than Chicano." That development, "although perfectly natural and understandable, doesn't solve any problems. It simply means that the disadvantaged have to turn to themselves—again—for the kind of leadership that was so effective in the 1970s."

Some progress was made, but it was never enough; setbacks occurred, yet Chicanos por la Causa (CPLC) and other important organizations continued to serve the Hispanic community during the 1980s. CPLC and its affiliates remained partly self-sustaining but depended upon federal grants and private grants and donations. "The Reagan administration's cutbacks have drastically affected us, which means we've had to turn more and more to foundations and corporations for help," declared Pete Garcia, new director of CPLC, in 1984. Cuts in staff and services had their effect, but some programs and projects went ahead. CPLC also continued to serve as a training school for Mexican American community leaders. "Some very outstanding people have come out of CPLC," noted Frank Hidalgo, a director of community relations at ASU, in 1984. As Phoenix developer Tom Espinosa, former executive director of CPLC, put it, "We need to develop a cadre of leadership that feeds into the community—a cadre composed of successful Chicano individuals who will donate their time and effort back into CPLC and the Hispanic culture." Espinosa served as a role model for many young Hispanics. His Espinosa Development Corporation demonstrated that success was possible for the ambitious and talented Chicano. As he related it, "Chicanos from south Phoenix can be successful."[18]

Hispanic women as well as men were making progress in the professional world, but it proved difficult. Discrimination hurt, but their ethnic background also slowed their progress. As much as they cherished their distinctive culture, they also objected to the limits it placed on women. "We feel a great deal of responsibility and pressure," noted Carmen Arroyo-Duran, a member of MUJER, a professional women's organization in Phoenix, in 1983. "Even today when so many of us are working outside the home, many of us feel a great deal of pressure. They say, 'Hey, why don't you stay home and take care of your family and your husband.'" Economic necessity is a major reason roles are changing, declared another member, "but with that comes a lot of social values, a lot of personal traditions that now have to be restructured and some discarded because they've become obsolete." For example, she continued, "It used to be that it was an embarrassment among Hispanic males if the wife had to work." MUJER members attempted to serve as role models for younger Hispanic women still in school. "Women in general need role models," stated one member. "For the Hispanic woman, particularly, there has been a dearth of role models."[19]

Statistics clearly indicated that Hispanic males and females in the middle class increased in Phoenix during the 1980s, but as a group Hispanics did not share proportionately in the growing prosperity of the decade. Immigration helped explain the failure, but Hispanics still suffered from fewer educational opportunities, more low-paying jobs, and poorer housing than Anglo residents. According to 1991 polls, nearly 85 percent of Arizona's Hispanics said they "feel there is discrimination."

Moreover, Hispanics and blacks continued to have a hard time supporting each other. Cohesion proved difficult in the face of competition and cultural differences, and the lack of cooperation proved at times to be counterproductive. As Hispanic leaders declared in January 1991, "We've fought over limited resources, and we're tired of doing that. We want to unite for a greater share of the resources." Some applauded the idea, but its realization proved difficult. Each group wanted to succeed, and racial rivalry often prevailed. In September 1990, for example, black parents wanted Roosevelt School District superintendent Alexander Perez ousted for being "insensitive" to the needs of black students and black personnel. The Hispanic superintendent of the largely minority south Phoenix school district was also accused of favoritism; several leaders of the African American Parents for Quality Education accused him of hiring more Mexican Americans than African Americans to work in the school district. For several months turmoil prevailed in the district as Mexican Americans and African Americans engaged in "educational politics." While some observers denied a rift between blacks and Hispanics in south Phoenix, the situation deteriorated. The competition between the two groups for jobs in the school district, the largest employer in south Phoenix, proved to be fierce. In an area where economic distress and high unemployment rates existed, jobs at all levels were important, and each group wanted its share. Finally, the Roosevelt School District Board bought out the contract of Perez; the vote was three to two, the three blacks on the board voting yes and the two Mexican Americans on the board voting no.

There existed some excellent schools in minority neighborhoods in Phoenix, but the question of who should run them caused problems. Anglo Americans were still the main challenge. In 1990, for example, Hispanic leaders were disappointed when the Phoenix Union High School District did not hire a Hispanic superintendent. They also complained to Victor Herbert, the new Anglo superintendent from New York, about "racism and high dropout rates in the school system." Sixty percent of the 19,600 students in the Phoenix Union High School District were minorities, and 40 percent were Hispanic, yet no minority person served on the school district governing board. Poor minority youth accounted for most of the district's 30 percent dropout rate, and Hispanic leaders wanted changes. They suggested hiring more Hispanic teachers and administrators, developing a more culturally sensitive curriculum, and bringing more minority organizations and parents into the educational process.

From without and within, the minority community experienced challenges. In 1987, for example, to the relief of Hispanic leaders, an effort in the state legislature to make English the "official language" in Arizona failed; a popular vote had approved of the measure, but a federal court ruled against it. Proponents appealed and all concerned waited for a final decision. According to Hispanic leaders, the issue caused "a renewal and resurgence of discrimination." Ray Gano, Arizona director of LULAC, noted that "a lot of people resented the Hispanic opposition to the measure."

In Phoenix, banker and Spanish-language radio station KPHX executive Jose Ronstadt, State Representative Armando Ruiz, developer Tom Espinoza, lawyer Daniel Ortega, Maricopa County official Adolpho Echeveste, and other Mexican American leaders served in the forefront of protest. While supporting efforts to encourage English-language competency in Arizona, critics argued that those who wanted to make English the "official language" of the state were going too far. "Yes to English Excellence, No to English Only" read the signs, as thousands of Spanish-speaking Arizonans marched in protest. "This type of legislation is really very divisive," asserted Ronstadt, a protest leader and organizer of the 1987 march. "You cannot separate language from culture, and our culture is something we want to keep." Another protester believed that "the people backing this English-language campaign view the growing Hispanic population as a threat. They want to make it so every other language would be inferior, and that's not fair." Still another opponent said that he "would like to see more understanding and respect for different cultures, and 'English only' undermines that effort."

Splits within the Hispanic community also persisted and hurt it. Cooperation often fell by the wayside as competition created hard feelings and counterproductive behavior. "In the 1980s," asserted an observer, "personal goals for higher political office and greater material wealth eroded that one-for-all sense of solidarity" that had existed in the past. Hispanic leaders "no longer see themselves exclusively as part of a struggling community, but, like so many of their Anglo, me-generation contemporaries, have begun to look out for *numero uno*. Competing ambitions have, at last, emerged."

In the 1980s many of the leaders of the 1960s and 1970s became part of the establishment. Their contributions remained significant, but they became less involved in CLPC and other organizations. As one observer put it in 1985, the "current Chicano leadership, a product of the activist Sixties and Seventies, may be the victim of its own earlier successes." The prevailing mood among the leaders appeared to be one of "middle-class malaise," with too few "flashes of 'minority' concern." The "good life" seemed to have carried them away from "the struggle." Hispanic leaders, it was said, were losing touch with the people they were supposed to be leading. Splits fragmented the Hispanic community and made it tougher to solve common problems.

On those occasions when Hispanic unity prevailed, positive results continued to occur. For example, one of the "old guard," Ed Pastor, reached a new plateau in the fall of 1991 when he became Arizona's first minority congressman. A Mexican American Democrat from Phoenix and former Maricopa County supervisor, he won election to the U.S. House of Representatives in a special election to replace the ailing

Morris K. Udall. Pastor's ascension to the Second Congressional District seat held by Udall for thirty years was applauded, especially by the large numbers of Mexican Americans in and out of the district who supported him. It was truly a historic event for the Hispanic community. "This victory is for all the Hispanic people, for all his supporters who worked so hard for him," declared the new congressman's father, Enrique Pastor. "This is a big victory for the Hispanic community." He added, "I hope my son's victory will be repeated with other Hispanics."

Also during the 1980s, neighborhood churches and community organizations, such as Alma de la Gente (Spirit of the People), helped Hispanics retain their cultural identity and heritage. Fiestas Patrias and Cinco de Mayo took place annually, as did a host of events ranging from informal family gatherings to formal balls (notably Quinceañeras, sponsored by the Vesta Club) to Chicano art shows supported by Movimiento Artistico Del Rio Salado. Spanish-language radio and television offerings, magazines, and newspapers, along with theater, music, and dance groups, drew appreciative attention. For Mexican Americans who were unaware of their past or at risk of forgetting it, a variety of organizations continued to promote cultural pride and awareness.

The constant flow of immigrants from nearby Mexico worked to reinforce the Spanish language and heritage in Phoenix, but not all Mexican Americans welcomed the flow. Mexican American barrio gangs, for example, spent considerable time discouraging the influx of illegal aliens into Phoenix from south of the border. In turn, Mexican gangs, at times referring to themselves as "wetbacks," retaliated. Job competition and different social styles also caused friction and occasional violence. New immigration laws penalized employers who hired illegal aliens, causing them to discriminate against Hispanics in general. Job bias against Hispanic Americans encouraged them to object vigorously and submit discrimination complaints. What Hispanic unity existed was further shattered by the growing cultural clash between local Hispanic Americans and the poor newcomers from south of the border, most of whom were Mexicans.

Some established Mexican American neighborhoods in Phoenix were heavily infiltrated by illegal aliens, so much so that they reminded observers of Mexico. Some Mexican Americans who had lived in the neighborhoods for decades—sometimes generations—found it difficult to accept the increasing numbers of illegal aliens in their midst. If it continued, critics noted, the clash would split a growing minority that needed unity to wield meaningful political power. This problem, according to accounts, was most obvious in the lower-income Mexican American barrios where longtime residents often competed with the newcomers for low-income jobs, low-income housing, and low-income social services.

Friendly House offered a more hospitable reception to the immigrants, and it was busier than ever in early 1987 when it began to meet the needs of countless local illegal aliens who had lived in the United States more than five years; under the controversial Simpson-Rodino Immigration and Reform Control Act of 1986, they became eligible to apply for amnesty and United States citizenship, and thousands of them did. Friendly House, the metropolitan area's only social agency specializing in Americanization services for immigrants, felt the strain. As Friendly House immigration specialist Jose Figuero put it, "There's just not enough of us. We're all so frustrated, and physically drained. It's sad, because these people really need help." Friendly House officials asked for volunteers and donations to help, but they received little response from the Mexican American community. Many Mexican Americans were in no hurry to see more illegal aliens become citizens under the new immigration laws. For reacting in such a manner, critics accused them of forgetting their own origins.[20]

The conflicts between individuals and groups within the Hispanic community in Phoenix illustrated the difficulty of portraying it as monolithic in its composition. Diversity existed, and although a large portion of the community gathered in unity on occasion, much of the time disparate elements went their own way, as did disparate elements in other communities making up the Phoenix mosaic. Generally, over the years considerable progress took place, with some individuals and groups within the larger community gaining more than others. More progress for all, however, was needed, and those concerned called for it. For many the struggle continued.

PART 2   THE CHINESE AMERICANS

4 COMMUNITY DEVELOPMENT TO 1930

Fewer than fifty Chinese lived in America prior to 1848. The discovery of gold and the construction of railroads in the American West brought unprecedented numbers of young Chinese men to work in the mines and on the railroads. By 1880 just over 100,000 Chinese, mostly male, were listed by the census as residing in Western states and territories. Most Chinese immigrants to America came from the province of Guangdong in southeastern China. Turmoil in that province had imposed hardships upon the workers, and many of them left their homeland to find employment in the United States. Some managed to pay their own way, while others, utilizing the credit ticket system, exchanged their labor for passage to the new country. They hoped to amass enough money to return home to China to their families and live a comfortable life.[1]

Most Chinese were sojourners who felt unwelcome in America. They worked hard but were discriminated against and subjected to verbal and physical abuse. When the mines became exhausted and the railroads were completed, the majority of Chinese in the United States returned to their homeland. Chinese exclusion acts passed by Congress in 1882 and 1892 limited Chinese immigration into America in the late nineteenth century, and their total population rapidly declined. Most of those who remained settled in the Western United States, especially in California and notably in San Francisco. Established in the 1850s, San Francisco's Chinatown evolved into the vital center of Chinese life, setting the tone for other Western Chinatowns.[2]

The first Chinese arrived in Arizona in the late 1860s. As mines played out and railroad construction in the American West reached completion, some Chinese who chose not to return to China or go elsewhere settled in the towns of Arizona Territory, where they assumed a variety of occupations available to them and worked to form Chinese communities. Although faced with increasing prejudice, they survived discriminatory attitudes and actions with determined tenacity in Prescott, Tucson, Phoenix, and other Arizona urban centers. Anti-Chinese feeling in Arizona never reached California levels, but it was present, especially among white workers who felt threatened economically and culturally. When three Chinese newcomers appeared in Prescott after the completion of the Central Pacific Railroad in 1869, a local paper decried the addition of "MORE CHINAMEN—Three more Chinamen arrived here during the week, and have gone to work. There are now four of them which is quite enough." Despite the opposition, a growing Chinatown was established in Prescott in the 1870s. In 1879 the same paper declared that "Prescott has about 75 or 80 Chinamen, which is 75 or 80 too many. Now is a good time to get rid of them." [3]

The construction of the Southern Pacific Railroad across southern Arizona in the 1870s brought a number of Chinese to Tucson. The 1880 United States Census listed 1,630 Chinese in Arizona Territory, 160 of them in Tucson. Tucson's Chinatown became a vibrant center of economic and cultural activity; not far from town Chinese farmers tended vegetable gardens. Limits existed, however; anti-Chinese sentiment encouraged Chinese settlers to avoid competing with others by engaging in occupations and businesses few others could or cared to engage in. To do this, Chinese often worked together to promote mutual business and social pursuits. Organizational structure allowed them to hold together, support each other, and build a community in the midst of an alien world. Clans, or family associations; benevolent societies, comprising people who had originated in the same village or region in southeastern China and spoke the same dialect; and tongs, or cliques, allowed the Chinese to retain their ethnic identity and perpetuate their traditions and rituals. Institutions for interaction included joss houses or temples, Chinese stores, and opium dens. Restaurants, groceries, laundries, and other business buildings often doubled as residences in Chinatown; other Chinese lived in centralized tenement quarters and boarding houses. At home, in the community, the Chinese language, food, music, and games could be appreciated, and topics of conversation ranged from the good old days in China to the difficulties of adjusting to life in the American West. [4]

Living in Chinatown, Chinese could resist the dominant culture and retain their own. Being sojourners, they had no desire to become part of the larger community, and the negative attitudes and actions of that community only made them less eager to adopt American ways. Cultural distance was kept, as socially isolated Chinatown became for its residents a self-sufficient refuge from the outside world.

Chinese rituals perplexed the residents of Arizona and other places in the American West. Chinese views of the passage to the next world, for example, inspired a Prescott reporter in 1879 to write an article entitled "Feeding the Dead."

> R. J. Rutherford, the pioneer expressman, this morning performed the pious duty of taking two of the followers of Confucius, with a lot of roast pig, peaches, grapes and a bottle of brandy to Lynx Creek to feed a dead countryman, who was lain beneath the cold gravel of the lonely canyon, where he was murdered, a whole year, without a morsel of food or a drop of anything to cheer him on his journey to that flowery kingdom where all good Chinamen at last bring up. Rutherford says that they left plenty of food and that which was good, on the grave, and as the two live celestials returned to town with him, there is no probability of their returning to bring away what their defunct friend may leave after satisfying his appetite.[5]

Although Chinese sojourners were willing to adapt to some American ways when it suited them—learning a few words of English, for example—they insisted on maintaining their own cultural traditions, but several Chinese customs and observances bemused the general population. Their dress, food, music, spiritual beliefs, and celebrations of Chinese holidays differentiated them from others. Family relationships also differed from the mainstream, for few Chinese women located in the United States or in Arizona Territory. The first Chinese woman arrived in Prescott in 1871; most of the women who arrived in Arizona reunited with husbands who had immigrated earlier. Most of the bachelor Chinese remained single, but some married women of other minority groups. A 1901 Arizona law prohibited Chinese from marrying Anglos, declaring "the marriage of a person of Caucasian blood with a Negro or Mongolian is null and void."[6]

The 1870 United States Census listed 21 Chinese males and no females in Arizona Territory. The Chinese males were poor, uneducated, unskilled, and most of them came from Guangdong Province in southeastern China, especially the city of Canton. The great majority of them worked as cooks or laundrymen. The greatest entry of Chinese into Arizona occurred during the late 1870s, when the Southern Pacific Railroad was under construction across the territory. During the course of construction, many Chinese left the employ of the Southern Pacific but remained in Arizona.[7]

The anti-Chinese movement in California at this time also motivated Chinese sojourners to seek refuge in Arizona. White workers in California feared Chinese competition for jobs and the presence of "unassimilable and unscrupulous foreigners." The "yellow peril" and "Chinese must go" cries heard in California would affect Arizona, but not to such an extent. Nevertheless, Arizona officials worried about Chinese taking jobs from white workers and warned against "Chinamen" competing with American businessmen. The *Arizona Gazette* in 1886, for example, called for an end to the influx of Chinese. It declared "there is no town on the coast where the Chinese have as strong a foothold as in Phoenix. They have a virtual monopoly of the gardening trade, control every restaurant, perform most of the household work, and all of the laundry business."[8]

In 1880, of the 1,630 Chinese in Arizona, 164 resided in Maricopa County, 110 of them in Phoenix. Some of them opened laundries, groceries, restaurants, and bakeries, while others worked as household servants, cooks, gardeners, small farmers, or vegetable peddlers. They often filled voids in the local economic structure, doing work undone or unwanted by others. Also, considering the mood created by the anti-Chinese movement, they did not wish to compete with those who criticized them. In 1880 the Chinese made up 4.6 percent of the Phoenix population of 1,708, a peak year for them in this regard.[9]

Arriving in Phoenix in 1872, the first Chinese opened a laundry. Additional Chinese trickled into town, increasing in number in the late 1870s. In 1880 the *Herald* declared that it would like to see "fewer Chinamen in Phoenix." During the 1870s and 1880s, the Chinese in town settled in an area bounded by Jefferson, Monroe, Cortez (First Avenue), and Pima (Third Street). Chinese living quarters and stores clustered on Montezuma (First Street), one-half block north and south of Adams, but several Chinese laundries, restaurants, and shops were scattered throughout the area. Lines of credit and trade with established San Francisco and Los Angeles Chinese firms existed, so that local Chinese businesses stocked a wide range of Chinese goods. Chinese businesses provided goods for the Chinese community and other elements of the population. They also enhanced the economy by buying from local wholesale merchants. Phoenix wholesale houses, it was said, profited from supplying small Chinese businesses. In an area south of town known as the Chinese

Gardens, Chinese vegetable farmers provided produce for the markets and residents of Phoenix. Their vegetable wagons could be seen in all parts of the community. By the 1890s most of the truck farms in the Phoenix area were Chinese. The heart of Chinese life, however, was Chinatown. The concentrated Chinese community in Phoenix, much like Chinatowns in other frontier towns, served as a place of refuge in an alien world where members could be among their own kind, speak a familiar language, and live a Chinese life as much as possible.[10]

Phoenix's Chinatown over the years was small but vital. Never very large, it remained the center of Chinese activity in the Arizona urban center for many decades. From the beginning, however, Chinese increasingly established businesses throughout Phoenix, often in other minority group neighborhoods. They also lived in their business establishments rather than in housing available in Chinatown. Although Chinatown catered largely to a "bachelor society," Chinese community offerings attracted Chinese men, women, and children from all over Phoenix. A visit to Chinatown was essential and anticipated by those who lived and worked elsewhere.

The customs of Chinese life could be as bemusing to the general population in Phoenix as elsewhere, due to their lack of awareness of Chinese culture. Local newspapers occasionally printed articles describing Chinese rituals. In August 1880, for example, a Phoenix reporter noted:

> Our streets were enlivened for a short time yesterday by a Chinese funeral procession. We fell in with the heathen and followed the corpse to the place where it will remain until the bones are sufficiently dried for shipment to China. One of the brethren was perched upon the top of the hearse and hired the devil, by scattering money (which was counterfeit) along the road to not follow them. After arriving at the grave, the members of the procession formed in a circle around the grave, a lot of sticks were set on fire, several bunches of firecrackers were set off. After filling up the grave, a nicely cooked side of bacon, a couple of roasted chickens, and lots of other "goodies" were placed upon the top as food for the departed spirit, but from the number of Maricopa (Indian) vultures which we saw hovering around, we rather opine that those delicacies were devoured by material beings ere the spirits had time to make their appearance.[11]

Despite problems, Chinese continued to observe their traditional culture. When necessary, however, they modified their rituals. On April 5, 1886, for example, the *Arizona Gazette* reported the following:

> Yesterday a number of Chinese observed the ceremony of feeding their dead. Two roast hogs, rice, oranges, brandy and other delicacies in abundance were

taken to the old cemetery where paper was burned and other ceremonies indulged in. Heretofore the festive Indian, hungry as well as sacrilegious, has been the beneficiary of these feasts, stealing and eating the provisions left on the graves. But the heathen outwitted the savage . . . little rice and tea scattered about the graves, roast hogs, oranges, etc., after remaining in proximity for a sufficient length of time, reloaded in wagons and brought up to town.[12]

It was, of course, extremely important to the sojourners that they be able to experience their culture, but it often threatened other residents. The strange dress and manner of the Chinese alienated other members of the population. To them, Chinese appeared aloof, arrogant, too clannish. That aloofness and the threat of economic competition inspired the *Herald* in March 1880 to urge the "yellow heathen Chinese of Phoenix to go to New York." If enough of them from Phoenix and other Western centers went to New York, declared the paper, New Yorkers would soon be chanting "the Chinese must go." Phoenix Chinese quietly declined the invitation to leave.[13]

Internal quarrels as well as outside threats hurt the Chinese community. Opium and gambling den rows occurred frequently. Quarrels and murders among themselves did little good for Chinatown's image. Factions, or tongs, caused serious trouble on occasion. In September 1885, for example, Wong Tie shot to death Tung Wong in a Chinese house at the corner of Montezuma (First) and Adams streets. A quarrel had been going on between Tung Wong and his backers and Wong Tie and his friends for possession of a racially mixed girl, said to have had a Scottish father and a Chinese mother. Tung Wong was buried by his friends with "great honors." A Chinese brass band played and "considerable display occurred." The two factions or tongs involved, according to the *Herald*, "now glower at each other in a way that means more fight, on the slightest provocation." Wong Tie fled town.[14]

While the murder of Tung Wong boosted negative feelings toward the Chinese, the Anti-Chinese Labor Association of Maricopa County adopted resolutions. Meeting in Phoenix in September 1885, it asserted that the prosperity of the country was "based upon the industry and intelligence of the white laboring masses of our citizens." It "extended to downtrodden Caucasian residents of every continent who seek our land for honest labor, the hand of welcome," while it "looked with foreboding and horror upon all public manifestations in favor of Chinese immigration, for their touch is social and moral pollution; their presence a perpetual menace of the public peace." The local organization expressed "to the great mass of white laboring people of California and the other states and territories of the West our earnest sympathy and cooperation in their efforts to rid themselves of the curse of Chinese labor," and "we do hereby pledge ourselves to do all in our power to secure the passage of such laws by Congress, as will totally prohibit Chinese immigration to our country." It also wanted the enactment of "such laws as will absolutely prohibit the return to our country all Chinamen who leave our country for any purpose whatever." The *Gazette* agreed, and offered additional advice. "By boycotting Chinese labor and Chinese goods," it declared, "we may peaceably drive the coolies from our midst." [15]

Fewer in number in Arizona Territory, Chinese did not experience the violent treatment they suffered elsewhere in the American West, especially in California. In Arizona and Phoenix there was comparatively little discriminatory legislation and no riots or lynchings, but plenty of unofficial segregation and verbal abuse. The Chinese, like other minority group members in Phoenix, faced barriers infused with racial and cultural overtones. The influence of race made equity impossible for them; allegations of inferiority and incidents of unfairness supported systematic injustice. Chinese responded to prejudice and persecution by creating Chinatown, a community that needed little from the dominant culture; moreover, as one historian has put it, Chinese often "swallowed their anger" and displayed "a stoic willingness to persevere, and to take without complaint or resistance whatever America dished out." Their self-sufficiency, according to a Chinese observer, was "a specific response to persecution."

National legislation made it clear that Chinese were not welcome in America. The Chinese Exclusion Act of 1882 was the first immigration law in American history to bar a specific nationality. The act prohibited the immigration of laborers but allowed the entry of merchants, their wives and children, and other "select" groups such as teachers, missionaries, students, travelers, and Chinese born in this country and their children. Legal and illegal candidates sought entry, and many managed to get in, especially after the San Francisco earthquake in 1906. It destroyed the records of most Chinese already in this country, and many of them now claimed to be American-born citizens. They also claimed that on visits home to China they had fathered sons eligible for immigration. Many "fathers" sold immigration documents to young men in China, and many "paper sons" (sons on paper only) gained entry. Immigrants whose status was questionable, however, were held up, sometimes for months, at the feared immigration detention center on Angel Island in San Francisco Bay, where determined immigration inspectors checked the authenticity of their status. Angel Island acquired a terrible reputation among the Chinese as a nightmarish experience; fortunately, only about 10 percent of the Chinese who spent time there were deported.

The Chinese exclusion legislation of 1882, 1888, 1892, 1902, and 1904 and related laws kept the Chinese population in the nation and in Arizona low. Although the federal courts in territorial Arizona did not enforce, to any effective degree, the various exclusion acts legislated by Congress, the fear of arrest and deportation took its toll on the minds of Chinese. When arrested, accused Chinese used a variety of defenses, and few of them were ever deported. Chinese merchants and other "select" groups were exempt from the laws, providing they could "prove" their status, and fraudulent ways emerged to gain admission, including the smuggling of Chinese in via Mexico.

The Chinese population in the nation grew increasingly smaller until World War II arrived and encouraged more liberal immigration laws allowing for the entry of more Chinese. By 1940 the Chinese community in the United States had shrunk to 77,000, less than three-quarters of its 1880 peak of 107,000. Not surprisingly, the Chinese population in 1940 remained largely male. Arizona's Chinese population peaked in 1880 at 1,630; in 1940 Chinese in the state numbered 1,419. Phoenix's Chinese population rose from 110 in 1880 to 431 in 1940, indicating that Chinese Americans preferred to live in urban America and urban Arizona.[16]

Considering the turmoil faced by Chinese inside and outside their community, it is not hard to understand why they kept to themselves. The mystery surrounding their existence often intrigued outsiders. Determined to lay before the public a "true picture of the vice and misery presented in the Chinese opium dens," a reporter in 1879 visited the "principal resorts of opium smokers in Phoenix." The first reached was located in the rear of the laundry on the corner of Montezuma (First) and Adams streets.

> Passing through the front room which is used as a wash house, and by a Chinese door helper, the visitor finds himself in a room about 15 feet square, along the walls of which are ranged about a dozen bunks. . . . The smokers, with the exception of three, were Chinese—of these three, two were men—Americans—the other, a young woman. All seemed to be so totally under the influence of the drug, as to be unconscious of what was taking place around them. The expressions on the faces were very much alike, eyes glossy and though open, unseeing, some smiled, others chattered, while others remained

perfectly immobile in feature and limb. . . . In stating his experience, a smoker said the first pipe had no apparent effect on him, the second caused a slight feeling of lassitude together with a bell-like tinkling in the ears; the third seemed to have a tendency to make him feel very indolent and dreamy, and entirely indifferent to what was transpiring around him; this feeling grew irresistible after the fourth pipe had been consumed. To concentrate the reasoning faculties on any subject for any length of time was impossible, all control over the mind seemed lost. Dreams of the most enchanting kind only filled the brain. All were vagaries of the wildest degree. In these dreams the desires of a lifetime were realized.[17]

Several opium dens operated in Phoenix, and observers noted that "many Americans—men and women—were in the habit of smoking opium in these holes." The Arizona Legislature in 1883 passed laws preventing the sale of opium and the keeping of "opium joints," but they proved largely ineffective. Local reporters continued to point to the locations where police could make "a number of arrests that would surprise our own people." The "vice is rapidly spreading in our fair city," declared the *Gazette* in March 1883, and "the means to check it cannot be too prompt or rigid." Periodic raids brought in welcome fine money, but few opium dealers or "joints" ceased their operations. Much of the activity took place underground. "The Chinese are making extensive excavations under their building on the corner of Montezuma and Adams Streets," an observer noted in April 1886, and "the intention of the same is doubtless to establish a quiet and retired opium joint." Nearly two years later, the earth in the vicinity of Montezuma and Adams streets was said to be "honeycombed with secret chambers."[18]

Fines helped to finance city government, and local authorities sought to gain as much money as possible from Chinese. Chinese gambling establishment owners, arrested for operating without a license, often paid fines. License taxes, like fines, provided another means for the city to extract funds from Chinese. The laundry license tax levied in early 1886 serves as an example. All of the laundries, or "wash houses," in Phoenix were run by Chinese and were constantly criticized as "public nuisances." The "filthy practices of the Chinese in allowing pools of dirty and stinking water to accumulate around their laundries produce breeding places of disease," the *Gazette* warned, "which it is most wise to guard against." In April 1886, when Chinese refused to pay the license on laundries levied by the city, court authorities ordered them to pay it, along with a fine. The racist *Gazette*, pleased with the result, continued to explore ways to rid Phoenix of the Chinese; indeed, much of the anti-Chinese sentiment in Phoenix was stirred up by the "success" of Chinese businesses. The *Gazette* urged more laundries and restaurants run by white people, as the following statement from September 1887 illustrates:

A steam laundry would be one of the most profitable investments that could be made in Phoenix. The different Chinese laundrymen of this city collect about $8,000 per month for washing, nearly all of which could be secured by a steam laundry, conducted by white help. The practice of permitting this race to control both the laundry and restaurant business of Phoenix is not in keeping with her advanced ideals on other business matters. Every restaurant in this city is under control of this filthy class, and why it should be thus, is beyond our ken. The *Gazette* would rejoice to see some enterprising citizen make an effort to open up and maintain an eating house which would be in keeping with a city, with the pretensions of Phoenix. These people are of no material benefit to the community; on the contrary, they are a curse, they neither contribute towards its support, nor aid in its advancement or prosperity. As our city increases in size, population and wealth, this class of undesirable people will flock here by the hundreds if something is not done whereby their presence is not in demand. If our people are dependent entirely upon them for caterers and laundrymen, they will as a matter of course be here to supply the demand, but should responsible white men compete with them for this necessary trade, we feel confident that they would be liberally patronized. The Chinese men of this city collect from its white population fully $150,000 annually, nearly all of which finds its way across the ocean to the flowery kingdom of China.[19]

Several attempts by white people to operate a steam laundry during the 1880s failed for lack of skilled workers. Chinese restaurants remained popular in the face of criticism because they met the demand for hearty, inexpensive food. Many in the general population also enjoyed Chinese holidays, especially the popular Chinese New Year celebration, which lasted for several days. "Noisy Chinamen" may have made the "night hideous by their attempts to frighten off the devil," as one reporter in January 1881 declared, but numerous enthusiastic whites also enjoyed themselves.

Eight years later critics still complained about the noise, but participants insisted that "loud celebrations—the louder the better" were needed to "scare off the devil." Firecrackers provided most of the noise, and Chinese turned out looking their finest for the festivities. Bright banners and "dragons" added to the excitement. In February 1893 the *Herald* noticed that "the Chinese around town are dressed in their Oriental best, smoking cigars and indulging in dissipation on account of their holiday." The same paper in January 1895 remarked how the Chinese population was "making life miserable for those who are domiciled close to them by their methods of celebrating the opening of the New Year."

> Each Chinese joint in the city is an open house today and the celestials are putting in their time by making, exchanging compliments of the season, smoking, eating and drinking a fiery decoction that would stagger a well-seasoned toper. Each joint has its Joss in place, before which a table stands and on which edibles, fruits and choice heathen delicacies are spread, to say nothing of the rats done a la mode. They have music also; and such music! The musical instruments are a keg with a raw hide top for a drum, three gongs, a tenor, a soprano and bass and a pair of old-fashioned cymbals that are so large that it makes the son of the heavenly kingdom exude large and full-drawn drops of sweat as would put to blush the once-famed "nigger at an election."[20]

The Chinese New Year, the most celebrated of Chinese holidays, was only one of many festive occasions observed by Chinese in early Phoenix. Another reason for celebration occurred when a sojourner returned to his homeland. Some of them returned to their wives and families in China to live out their lives. Others visited in China for a time and then returned to Phoenix, although re-entry was often difficult following the passage of the exclusion acts. Of course, local critics expressed their feelings about the departure of Phoenix Chinese in their usual sarcastic manner. As the *Herald* put it in April 1891, "Eight Chinese left this afternoon for the Flowery Kingdom, having been lucky enough at tan, faro, chopsticks and other games of chance to secure a fiscal wad that will enable them to spin opium smoke rings and burn frankincense in the pagodas of Hong Kong for this life and several centuries in the next."

Critics especially hated to see Chinese taking or sending money back to China. "A white man or woman spends their money in the community where they reside, and assists its progress and development," noted the *Herald,* while "a Chinaman lives in a hut and hoards and forwards his earnings to China"; thus "it does not require a philosopher to discern where the injury to our country's progress comes in as between the two nations." Mexicans and blacks also resented Chinese, who competed with them for some jobs and often accepted less money for the same work. Cultural differences between the three groups also hindered mutual fellowship and cooperation. Ethnocentrism, an inherent tendency of all cultures, generated considerable divisiveness. At times, members of each group exhibited their own prejudices toward others.

Generally, each group resented the presence of the others. Not only economic competition was involved, but also cultural status. Each group adopted Anglo attitudes toward the others; both blacks and Anglos, for example, were suspicious of sojourners. They did not appreciate transient people unwilling to "Americanize" themselves. Blacks saw themselves as more "American" than Mexicans and Chinese. Many black Protestants felt uncomfortable with Catholic Mexicans and "heathen" Chinese. For blacks as well as Anglos, Chinese business success caused jealousy and bitterness, resulting in black support for anti-Chinese legislation, including exclusion laws. Blacks also disliked Chinese because they believed Chinese were prejudiced against them, and antiblack sentiment did exist in the Chinese community. Blacks accepted the Anglos' negative image of both Mexico and China as backward countries populated by inferior people with inferior cultures, and they resented and disliked Mexicans for many of the same reasons they resented and disliked Chinese. In turn, Mexicans, feeling resented and disliked by blacks and Chinese, had no love for either group. All three groups suffered from many of the same problems, but rather than join together and become partners in the struggle to overcome dominant Anglo prejudice and discrimination, they viewed each other as rivals.[21]

Many critics wanted Chinese to return to China, but if that desire went unfulfilled, they at least wanted Chinatown removed to a less conspicuous location. In the middle 1890s they rejoiced in seeing the concentration of Chinese in the vicinity of First Street (Montezuma until 1893) and Adams Street shift south to a new location bounded by Madison, Jackson, First, and Third streets. The joss house (221 South First Street), Chinese businesses, and residences concentrated in the half-block area bounded by First and Second streets, Madison Street, and China Alley, a block dividing line to the south halfway between Madison and Jackson streets (see Map 4.1). From the beginning of the decade, a movement to relocate Chinatown gathered momentum. As the *Arizona Republican* declared in June 1890:

> Limit Chinatown. The wily Mongolians have a faculty of locating in the most favored section of every city which they determine to occupy. They are now doing this in Phoenix and their "town" is fast becoming a nuisance that will soon require abating. Just now it is tolerable, but the date is not far distant when we will have the same troubles that San Francisco, Los Angeles, Fresno and other cities now have to contend with. It will simplify matters to designate limits as possible, for an evil it is, sure and simple, and so it will be recognized by and by.[22]

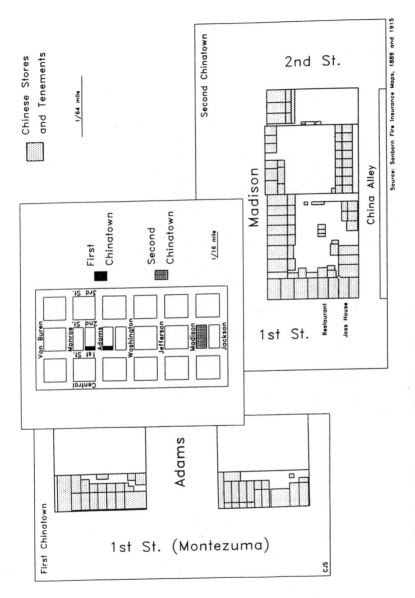

MAP 4.1 The Two Chinatowns of Phoenix, 1889 and 1915

Reluctant to leave Chinatown, residents resisted, but the movement to relocate them persisted. Especially alarming to Phoenix promoters was their vision of conditions on First Street, between Washington and Adams. In August 1895 the *Phoenix Herald* insisted that "the Chinese and the unsightly, unhealthy buildings they occupy be removed." It wished to see the area redeveloped by others. "There is no finer business property in Phoenix than this," it noted, "and now that the First Street railroad line begins here just in front of this property, retail business houses in this locality would get a larger portion of the trade of the northeastern quarter of the city." The "fearful sanitary condition of this locality has attracted general attention and the class of establishments allowed to exist on the property now will no doubt soon be declared a public nuisance, as they are." Signed petitions to remove the "Chinese colony" were submitted to authorities. The "question of ridding First Street of the Chinese hovels is agitating a great many of our people and in fact all who have an interest in the development of the city are interested in seeing those hovels torn down and the filthy neighborhood cleaned up."[23]

In October 1895 a syndicate of local businessmen purchased the part of Chinatown running from the alley on First Street to the corner of Adams Street, with a frontage of 100 feet on Adams. The property on First Street, just off Washington, housed Chinese opium joints and gambling houses, and the new developers, calling Phoenix a progressive place, announced that they would soon change the nature of the area. On October 22 they notified the occupants of the buildings that at the expiration of one month they "must be conspicuous by their absence or suffer the general destruction which will overtake every building now on that property." The developers who bought the property planned to "rid the heart of the city of a most miserable class of residents." They hoped to "entirely clear the business district of Chinese joints and hovels" and erect "a handsome four-story business block, which will be second to no structure of the kind in the Territory."[24]

By December 1895 the *Herald* happily declared that "the residents of the Chinese quarters on First Street are on the move and soon that delectable quarter will be occupied by white people." It was hoped that in their new location Chinese would be less visible and bothersome. Chinatown "has gone glimmering," the *Herald* reported, "and the light of the balance is rapidly waning." While the "Celestials will still revel in hop and stake their earnings on the fortunes of tan they will present a more decent appearance to the outside world." The idea was to remove Chinese as much as possible from public view. City boosters did not promote Chinatown as a Phoenix attraction. A Phoenix directory in 1895 made no mention of the Chinese community other than the following statement:

> The growth of the city is clearly evidenced by the increase of names in the Directory. The present volume contains 2116 names (not including Chinese and many other objectionable classes) being a gain over the last publication of 361, indicative of an increase in population of 1444 inhabitants.[25]

A new Chinatown emerged in Phoenix in the late 1890s. By 1900 it was well settled in the vicinity of First and Madison streets. Because of its cultural attachments, as well as its unwelcome reception in the larger city, the Chinese community remained tightly composed and presented an enigma to much of the Phoenix population. Few of the mostly male sojourners made much money in Phoenix, and they lived a harsh existence. Most of them came from the same village in the district of Hoiping in the province of Guangdong in southeastern China, and they yearned to return. Denied participation in an egalitarian society in Phoenix, Chinese found refuge in Chinatown and its offerings. Chinatown made it easier for them to retain and cherish their cultural heritage. The transient nature of the Chinese community and the scarcity of females within it made for social instability. A familiar neighborhood helped Chinese immigrants to survive an unfriendly larger city, just as it did other proscribed groups.

The occupational structure of the Chinese community may be seen in Table 4.1. As in the case of Chinese population elsewhere, manuscript census returns from 1870 to 1900 underrepresented the number of Chinese in Phoenix. The census figures, however, are included to bolster the impressions of observers regarding Chinese participation in the economy. Operating groceries, laundries, restaurants, and a variety of shops, and working as unskilled and semiskilled laborers, Chinese filled occupational voids and provided for themselves and others as best they could.

In Phoenix's new Chinatown, the Chinese built an impressive joss house and established boarding and tenement houses, stores, shops, and other businesses, including restaurants and laundries, nearby. Opium joints and gambling dens also opened, many of them underground. Chinese often lived as well as worked in these places of business. They rented, leased, and occasionally bought property. National legislation prohibited alien Chinese from owning property, but as early as 1878 land

Table 4.1. Occupational Structure for Chinese Population,
        1870–1900[a]

Occupations	1870	1880	1900
Unskilled	—	31	32
Semiskilled	—	31	16
Skilled	—	1	2
Farming/Ranching	—	—	1
Mercantile	—	14	31
Professional	—	—	—
Totals	—	77	82

SOURCE: Federal manuscript census schedules, 1870, 1880, 1900.
[a]Chinese populations derived from place of birth for individuals or parents, and enumerator classification of "C" or "CH" for Chinese.

deeds involving Chinese were filed with the Maricopa County recorder; on occasion, laws were ignored or overlooked, and increasingly real estate transactions occurred in the names of American-born children, who were citizens.

Not only did the typical Chinese sojourner find security and solace in the economic and social life of Chinatown; he gained cultural and psychological satisfaction from clan/regional associations. Based on familial lineage and/or territorial ties (including village dialects) in China, these associations offered aid and protection and generally took care of their own as much as possible in the Chinatowns of America. In San Francisco the Chinese Consolidated Benevolent Association, known widely as the Chinese Six Companies, set the pace for organized Chinese America. It settled disputes within the Chinese community, and it spoke for the general interests of Chinese America and Chinese Americans. In Phoenix clan/regional associations, although theoretically tied to the Chinese Consolidated Benevolent Association, actually enjoyed considerable local autonomy.[26]

They also provided ambitious Chinese with economic opportunities not available in sufficient quantity to other minority group members. Local banks preferred not to lend money to minority individuals and groups, but Chinese tradition and custom encouraged small business proprietorship. To fill the need, Chinese organizations served as credit institutions; the capital formation necessary to start a small business was available to applicants through clan/regional associations. Discrimination against Chinese by banks plus distrust of banks by Chinese made the associations a major means of acquiring capital for business enterprises; without them very few businesses could have been started. Henry Ong, Jr., later recalled that "the Chinese didn't want to go to the bank. They would have to disclose all their information and it might get them in trouble with immigration." Violet Toy later added, "Chinese didn't need a bank; they just sort of stayed together and helped each other out." Moreover, the mutual trust of those involved, along with clan/regional loyalty and honor, usually made such financial transactions mutually satisfying.

In the beginning, representatives of several clans showed up in Phoenix, but many of them soon left. The Ongs predominated in early Phoenix, and over the years they encouraged many of their kinfolk from the province of Guangdong and from San Francisco to join them in Phoenix. Ong Louie, or "China Dick" (as he was popularly known), early pioneer, successful merchant, and leader of the Ong clan, served as the unofficial mayor of Chinatown. Secret societies, or tongs, also existed in the Phoenix community, engaging at times in illegal activity according to American law; tong membership was not necessarily based on clan affinity or place of origin. A local lodge of the Chinese Free Masons of America, a secret society headquartered in San Francisco, played an active role in the legitimate (and illegitimate) life of Phoenix's Chinatown beginning in the 1870s. Lodge members included Ong Louie and other prominent residents. All of these associations helped Chinese to survive economically and culturally, but they also slowed their acculturation in Phoenix.[27]

The associations in Chinatown offered generous rewards to those helpful in the apprehension and conviction of criminals guilty of violent crimes against members of the Chinese community, and they hired successful, expensive Anglo lawyers to represent Chinese accused by city authorities of unlawful activity. Also, if convicted, a Chinese offender could usually count on his "countrymen" to come to his rescue and promptly pay the fine assessed against him, no matter what the amount. For the most part, however, Chinese policed their own community, and Chinese "justice" proved to be effective the majority of the time. In November 1911, Phoenix Judge C. W. Johnstone made the "unrestricted statement" that "the Chinese are the most orderly of all the people in Phoenix." He claimed he had the police and court records to back up his statement, which "did not except even white people." "The Mexicans, the books show, comprising about 15 percent of the population in Phoenix are in court more than all the other residents put together," while "the Negroes come next, though there are not a great many Negroes in Phoenix, then the Japanese, and following them the whites."[28]

That the Chinese to a large extent policed their own community may be seen from the role played by Ong Louie. In September 1911, while visiting the city, the famous black leader Booker T. Washington interviewed "Mayor Dick, the supreme authority in Chinatown." Washington asked the Chinese leader how he came to be called mayor, and Ong responded: "Well, you see, I am here 30 years. I know American custom. When Chinaboy get in trouble he come to see me. When policeman get in trouble with Chinaboy, both come to see me. I know how to make it right. So the newspapers say I am Mayor of Chinatown. Yes." As Washington put it:

> Whenever a Chinaman is arrested for a small crime of any kind—anything less than a felony, in fact,—it has become customary for the police and authorities to turn the man over to "Mayor Dick."
>
> They have found that they could get substantial justice more surely and more conveniently in that way than they could by dragging the culprit into the ordinary police courts and going through the ordinary processes.
>
> The reason for this seems to be that the Chinaman has very little understanding of and apparently little confidence in the American methods of administering justice. And so the Chinaman in Phoenix, even though he is not a citizen, gets in this indirect way, a certain amount of self-government.

Washington described Ong as "a little dried up, yellow man, who spoke very broken English," but he "seemed to have a pretty clear understanding of American customs and manners." Ong also explained to Washington that the Chinese population of Phoenix was gradually decreasing because "every Chinaman must sometime go back to China. He is never more than a sojourner in America. If he does not go back alive, he goes back in his coffin." And the Chinaman, Ong noted, reflecting on the Chinese immigration restriction laws, "once out of the country, unless he has a certificate showing that he is a merchant, is not permitted to return." Recalling his conversation with Ong, Washington was especially impressed with the extent to which "the Chinaman is also an alien in this country. I doubt whether any other portion of the population remains so thoroughly foreign as is true of the Chinaman."[29]

Ong Louie had first-hand experience dealing with the immigration laws. In June 1902, for example, he received a letter from Ah Yip, a friend and local merchant who had been in China for some time, visiting members of his family. Ah Yip wrote that he was being held on board a steamer in the San Francisco harbor by immigration authorities who refused to allow him to land because they believed he was a laborer and not a merchant. Merchants, not laborers, were allowed re-entry, and Yip needed confirmation of his status. Ong quickly sent letters of confirmation from "reputable citizens" of Phoenix to authorities in San Francisco, and Yip was allowed to re-enter the country.

Chinese resented the immigration laws and struggled with them. Another example of national legislation that offended them was the Geary Act, passed in 1892, which extended the Chinese Exclusion Act of 1882 for another ten years. Among other anti-Chinese regulations, it required them to possess residence certificates. Those who failed to register and acquire certificates were in danger of being deported. Chinese in Phoenix and elsewhere refused to cooperate; no mass arrests or expulsions followed because there were no funds for enforcement. The *Phoenix Daily Herald* noted that "unregistered Chinese" in Phoenix did not worry about the deportation act. "Take um long time catchee Chinaboys in California; no time monkey with Arizona," the biased paper quoted a Chinese spokesman. Representatives of the Chinese Six Companies in San Francisco and local leaders urged members of the Chinese community not to register; they hoped the issue would be settled in court in their favor. "The Chinamen who have registered are very shy about it and ask that their names be withheld," declared a reporter. "They dread the torment to which their registration will subject them. Their neighbors who will not register hold those who do in contempt and intimate that they are not good Chinamen," the reporter added. "It looks now as though there would not be a dozen of them registered all told in Phoenix." The Chinese hoped to win in the courts, but after the Supreme Court declared the Geary Act valid, they ended their boycott of registration and increased their participation in the process. Another protest lost.

Ong Louie and other members of the Chinese community also looked upon gambling and opium smoking differently than did law enforcement authorities. Both gambling and opium smoking were against the law in Arizona, but for isolated, lonely Chinese males far from "home," they were games and custom. As one observer asserted, "Corporeally, the Chinese are in Phoenix, but in spirit they are 10,000 miles away, in a land where one can play fan-tan or mark a lottery ticket or inhale the fumes of a little yenshee without having an American cop throw him in the calaboose." For the Chinese, opium dens provided useful services other than recreational; for example, as "medical clinics" they offered to those who did not want to go to an Anglo American doctor a form of relief for physical or psychological pain.[30]

On occasion, Ong accompanied white acquaintances to gambling and opium establishments. Mrs. William Henderson recalled a visit she and her husband made to an opium den with Ong. He had invited the Phoenix couple to attend the Chinese New Year celebration in Chinatown. After enjoying the elaborate firecracker display, Ong took them "down into an opium den, which thrived freely." On entering the den, he warned Mrs. Henderson to hold her nose, because "we don't want you to go to sleep down here." She "curiously observed men playing mah jong, making little pellets over burners, and smoking long-stemmed pipes. The air was tinted with a blue smoke that hung like a cloud over the room." She noticed "a little Chinese woman come out of a door in the side of the room" who appeared frightened. Mrs. Henderson felt compassion for her and the other women "brought here for the convenience of the men." The Hendersons and other members of the Central Baptist Church did much religious work with the Phoenix Chinese and helped stir interest in the future formation of a Chinese Baptist church in the city.[31]

Ong Louie arrived in Phoenix in the 1870s and lived in the city until he died in January 1929. A successful entrepreneur and "beloved by all," the *Republican* declared, "Mayor Dick is said to have ruled his countrymen with an iron hand. Relentless in his persecution of an offender, he was said to be always fair and just—a court and jury for the transgressor, meting out punishment in accordance with the gravity of the offense; a kindly kindred advisor for the righteous." Because of his "knowledge of American ways and manners, he practically guided all his countrymen in their business affairs and negotiations." Ong through the years "was a power for law and order, though it was seldom that American courts ever were called upon to intervene in settlement of a dispute or business transaction. The 'city of expressionless faces' had its own methods of weighing judgement and invariably it was China Dick who had the final say." He "has, for more than a quarter of a century," the paper continued, "been the 'go-between' in dealings between the city and members of his own race." Ong died from injuries received in an automobile accident at First and Madison streets; he was seventy-six years old, and "all Chinatown was plunged into mourning as news of his death spread through the secret channels of the district."[32]

On occasion Chinese shared Chinatown with the general population, especially during the Chinese New Year celebration. The holiday seemed more exciting every year. In February 1902, the *Republican* declared, "The show was well patronized," and "if the Chinese theory that the devil may be scared by noise is correct, he flew so far last night that it will take him a year at least to get back to Phoenix." The Chinese New Year celebration had been going on for three weeks, the paper continued, and it ended last night "in a blaze of glory and pandemonium." The elaborate firecracker display in front of the joss house highlighted the show.

> It seemed as if half the town were there. Not only the sidewalks, but even the street in the block of the Chinese quarter was impassable. In the course of the evening thousands entered the joss house and had to fight their way out. A religious ceremony was going on, requiring the burning of a great deal of incense of a kind that suggested that if it was pleasing to the Chinese god, his sense of smell had become vitiated. There was an entertainment of some kind going on in all the stores and all were crowded. As late as nine o'clock the crowd moving in the direction of Chinatown was much larger than that going in the opposite direction.[33]

Chinatown opium joints and gambling dens also continued to attract customers and be raided occasionally by law enforcement officers. In March 1910 the Phoenix police raided Chinatown looking for narcotics. "Four opium dens were discovered, all in full blast, and packed to the doors with hop-smoking Chinks," declared the *Republican*. In a December 1919 raid, although "all of the inmates of the gambling dens escaped by secret passages and trap doors," evidence indicated that gambling and opium smoking had been going on "in a wholesale fashion." Dozens of tables with the "full complement of cards, dice, lottery tickets, poker chips and other paraphernalia were unearthed." Many of the gambling rooms raided "were of apparent new construction, with the lumber new and fresh from the mill." On March 16, 1923, in order to prevent any escape from the area under surveillance, federal narcotics agents assisted by local police surrounded "the heart of Chinatown, comprising the west half of the block bounded by Madison Street, China Alley, First and Second Streets," and arrested five Chinese opium dealers, confiscating in the process thousands of dollars' worth of drugs, mostly opium. The officers involved in the raid "made human rats of themselves in exploring the underground tunnels . . . which played an important part in the narcotics activities of the men taken into custody. A majority of the dope taken in the raid was discovered in these subterranean passages."

In August of the same year, large quantities of cocaine and opium were seized at Ong Foo's Chinatown Restaurant at 211 South First Street. "So carefully were the proscribed narcotics hidden," a reporter declared, "that it was fully an hour after the officers entered before anything was found. The raiders were thorough and systematic in their work and went through the establishment from cellar to garret." [34]

Other members of the general population, including whites, visited the illegal drug and gaming establishments in Chinatown. "That white residents of Phoenix are frequent habitués of this city's Chinatown for the purpose of smoking opium," declared the *Gazette* on March 26, 1926, "was freely admitted by the police department today following a sensational raid on opium joints last night." According to the paper, the police asserted that "the yellow fangs of the insidious poppy had ensnared not only the outcasts of society, but men and women prominent in Phoenix business and social life who are listed at the police station as drug addicts."

At first, police officials denied making the remarks. "The police department knows nothing of these alleged conditions," commented Captain James H. Allen, the officer in charge of the raid, and "it is certain that no prominent men or women of Phoenix have ever been found smoking opium or using drugs of any kind in Chinatown." A few days later, in an interview with a *Gazette* reporter, Chief of Police George O. Brisbois stated that he had no knowledge of "white people frequenting Phoenix opium resorts," and he insisted that "vice conditions" in the city "were vastly improved over those of former years."

> Candidly and honestly, I believe that vice conditions in Phoenix are 100 percent better than when I first went on the job. It was a common sight in those days to find white men and women, Negroes and Chinamen all in the same room happy in the dreams of poppyland. A consistent and determined campaign of enforcement, through frequent raids of resorts under question has had the effect of holding vice in check to a large extent, although it would be foolish to state that it had been driven out entirely or that it could be. [35]

The Chinese in Phoenix, as elsewhere in America, closely followed events in China. Most of them supported Sun Yat-sen's nationalist revolutionary cause in the 1900s. Sun, who was from Canton, the capital of Guangdong Province, sought to end the Manchu regime in Peking, and he received considerable political and financial backing from Chinese in the United States. On October 10, 1911, the Manchu government was overthrown and the Chinese Republic was established. The successful revolution in 1911 ended more than 2,000 years of dynastic rule in

China. Sun, according to Phoenix Chinese leaders, had visited the city early in 1911 and received a warm welcome, along with financial contributions. Most Chinese in America and Phoenix called the province of Guangdong home and believed that "real Chinese are Cantonese."

In front of Ong Louie's store, located at the corner of First Street and Madison, a new flag flew in October 1911. He noted that the flag of the new Chinese Republic had been sent to him by the Chinese in San Francisco. China continued to experience turmoil, but Ong insisted that "the China boys of Phoenix want the republic of China to stand." They "know that form of government to be the best, not only for China, but for all other countries of the world." In December 1922, Kerman L. Wong, general secretary of the Chinese Nationalist Party in the United States, with headquarters in San Francisco, came to Phoenix to form a branch of the organization to help "make China safe for democracy." Several prominent Phoenix Chinese merchants spoke, and a dinner was served in the banquet hall at 237 East Madison. A month later the new branch numbered more than one hundred members from the Phoenix vicinity, and a new office for the organization opened at 221 East Madison. At a meeting Wong discussed current events in China and appealed for funds to aid Sun Yat-sen. A Chinese play rounded out the evening.[36]

The changes in China influenced Chinese life in America and in Phoenix. Signs of Americanization became more visible; Chinese men, for example, began dressing more in American style, and some of them cut off their queues. Double Ten (October 10) celebrations, honoring the founding of the Chinese Republic, became an established event in the Chinese community in Phoenix and elsewhere in the years to come. Chinese tradition, however, remained paramount, and the lack of women retarded Chinese adaptation to American culture on national and local levels. Ninety-three percent of the Chinese in the United States in 1910 were male. Of the 110 Chinese in Phoenix in that year, 10 were women, all married and all mothers. Although the female population increased and the male population stayed stable after 1910, for many years Chinatown remained largely a bachelor society. The 1901 Arizona law prohibiting Chinese from marrying Anglos continued; although marriage between Chinese and other minority groups was accepted, it rarely occurred.

For the Chinese single men, the brotherhood organizations meant a great deal, fulfilling social functions normally assumed by wives and children, in addition to arbitrating disagreements and offering financial aid to the destitute and loans to those who wished to establish small businesses. Those who succeeded sent for wives and families in China or returned to China to marry. For example, Yee Sing, proprietor of the popular American Kitchen restaurant, returned to Phoenix in February 1923 from a long visit in his "home city" of Canton, "bringing his little wife with him, and the smile on his face was as glad and broader than ever when he walked into his place of business yesterday morning immediately after his arrival from San Francisco."

> And trotting demurely at his side was his young wife, whom he took as a bride on his last visit to China two years ago. Clad in the dainty garb of her race, and with a shy smile and a hand-shake for everyone to whom her husband introduced her, she made quite a sensation in the restaurant. Mrs. Sing could speak no word of English, but her smile and bow seemed to say that she was delighted to meet the friends of her husband and that she hoped soon to be able to converse with them in their own tongue.

Yee Sing owned the American Kitchen for forty years. According to his son, Sing Yee, Jr., he was extremely personable and outgoing; dedicated to pleasing his customers, he built his restaurant into one of the best in Phoenix and gave many Chinese "a start working in the American Kitchen."[37]

Yee Sing is a good example of one way the Phoenix Chinese community maintained ties with China. Typically, after years of working in the business of a relative and accumulating sufficient funds, a Chinese male would open his own grocery, laundry, or restaurant. Upon achieving some success, he would return to China to get married. In time, he would return to Phoenix with or without his wife and children. Yee Sing and other operators of Chinese businesses provided employment to family members newly arrived in Phoenix from China by filling vacancies left by relations who had acquired enough funding to start their own businesses. In addition, ties with China were kept by sending American-born children to China for a Chinese education. Phoenix Chinese also gave money generously to districts in Guangdong Province from which they or their forbears had emigrated.

Although most of the Chinese cared little about the world outside China and Chinatown, schools and missionaries in Phoenix introduced some of them and their children to English and the Christian religion. On occasion, members of the Chinese community participated in city-wide celebrations and contributed generously to city-wide funding drives. For example, a Chinese float, "one of the most beautiful ever exhibited in Phoenix," accompanied Ong Louie and other Chinatown residents in the 1918 July 4th parade, and in July 1922 the Chinese community pledged one thousand dollars to the Deaconess Hospital building fund. The Chinese of Phoenix also purchased their share of Liberty Bonds and sent their share of soldiers into World War I. Thirteen "China boys from Phoenix" served overseas, the *Republican* noted in May 1919, and "although some of them could scarcely speak English," they "were willing workers and fighters and labored for Uncle Sam with the same spirit as the boys who were born under the flag."

Chinese leaders accepted the respect paid to members of their community by the press and the larger community, but they objected to unfair accounts of their world in America. For instance, in April 1920, at a City Commission meeting, Phoenix lawyer F. C. Struckmeyer, representing the Chinese Merchants' Association, protested the showing of a motion picture entitled *The Tong Man* at a local theater "on the ground that it contained objectionable matter tending to create race prejudice." The City Commission notified the theater manager not to show the film until the city board of censors reached a decision.[38]

While opium joints and gambling dens were part of Chinatown, several other businesses flourished during the 1920s. Throughout the decade the neighborhood was known for its Chinese restaurants, hand laundries, grocery stores, and small shops that sold medicinal herbs and other imported goods. Some Chinese leaders encouraged members of the community to disperse to avoid too much attention and conflict. Wary of high-profile Chinatowns in San Francisco and New York and their problems, they wanted the Chinese in Phoenix to settle and do business throughout the city. As a result, grocery stores, hand laundries, and good restaurants continued to serve the Chinese and much of the general population in and out of Chinatown.

Indeed, Chinese businesses had always been located throughout Phoenix. Much of Chinese life centered in Chinatown, but Chinese families increasingly lived and did business beyond its borders. Beginning in the twentieth century, there appeared to be fewer Chinese sojourners and more Chinese settlers in Phoenix. For these early Chinese Americans, proprietorship brought dignity and profits. "Every Chinaman," it was said, had "the ambition to be a merchant." In 1929 there were fifty-three Chinese business establishments outside Chinatown, up from thirty-four in 1921 and eighteen in 1900. Some Chinese proprietors turned their businesses into large, successful enterprises.

Tang Shing, for example, came to Phoenix from Canton, China, via San Francisco in 1910 to visit his brother. Industrious and ambitious, he decided to go into business. With limited finances he opened a small grocery store at 622 South Seventh Avenue. Married to American-born Lucy Sing in 1914, Tang Shing worked hard and expanded his growing business into the Sun Mercantile Company, the largest wholesale grocery house in the city. In April 1929, when the company moved into its new $80,000 facilities at Jackson and Third streets, the *Republican* noted that it had "the most diversified line of any general jobbing merchandise house in the state." The history of its "remarkable growth is an outstanding chapter in the business and development of Phoenix and the Salt River Valley."

Tang Shing's wife, Lucy, shared the struggle for success experienced by her husband. She had worked hard and long in her father's store, with little time for rest or relaxation; life was "simply work and obedience to her father," according to one account. There was, however, one major decision Lucy helped make. Her father "allowed her to give approval in the choice of husband, even though traditional Chinese rule placed that power in the hands of the father, because of his age and wisdom." Lucy resisted many suitors who asked her father for her hand in marriage, but in 1914 she married Tang Shing, the aspiring entrepreneur, who had won the approval of both father and daughter. Throughout her life Lucy served as a strong role model for women in the Chinese American community.[39]

In 1940 the Phoenix Chinese population numbered 431, up from 227 in 1930, 130 in 1920, and 110 in 1910, but still less than 1 percent of the total Phoenix population. In the 1920s success stories such as that of Tang Shing occurred more frequently in Phoenix, as they did in the nation. Also, older Chinese declined in number while younger Chinese and American-born Chinese became more numerous. American ways were increasingly adopted as the Chinese lessened their orientation toward China. In the 1920s greater acculturation took place in the Phoenix Chinese community because success stories encouraged different expectations. More participation in the commercial and educational networks brought higher economic and social mobility for ambitious Chinese. Fewer Chinese exhibited the attitudes and actions of the sojourners. The children of Chinese settlers growing up outside Chinatown in the 1920s and 1930s later remembered it only as a place they visited.

More Chinese families adopted American customs while retaining important aspects of their cultural heritage. For example, while Chinese children studied English and received an American education in the Phoenix public schools during the day, in the evening in the Chinese homes and schools they learned to read, write, and speak Chinese. They also worked long hours helping out at home and in small family businesses. Education and hard work were viewed as the keys to success in America and in Phoenix. At the same time, discrimination and segregation persisted. As one participant later recalled, "When I was a child, even in third class theaters like the old Rialto [in downtown Phoenix], the Chinese had to sit in the balcony."

Although restricted in their use of movie theaters, swimming pools, and other places of recreation, Chinese youth adopted American styles and took advantage of opportunities open to them during the 1920s to participate in the mainstream of society. Young people retained Chinese ways but also became more Chinese American. "Oriental culture has faded from the Southwest though the Orientals haven't," declared a Phoenix observer. "Sons and daughters of the silk robed elders entered into the spirit of the 'Oh-you-kid' era with gusto, knocking off prizes in local Charleston contests and beating the tar out of us natives scholastically."

Still, in the 1920s and 1930s, very few Phoenix Chinese went to college; most of the small Chinese population continued to work in the grocery, laundry, and restaurant business or as truck farmers. And to ensure that the American-born children of immigrants received the benefits of a Chinese education, in addition to their regular schooling, Chinese schools continued to be established, including one that opened on Second Street between Jefferson and Madison in 1938. Frank Yue, a Chinese scholar, was principal, and Chinese language, history, calligraphy, and ethics made up the curriculum. If an American-born Chinese did go to college, it was usually located in China. The student might spend years in China before returning to the United States to commence a career.[40]

5 DEPRESSION, WAR, AND PEACE, 1930–1960

The 1930s brought the problems of the Great Depression to Chinese communities throughout the United States. The Chinese took care of their own to a large extent, their associations providing assistance to those who suffered from hard times. Their own institutional network proved successful enough to keep many depressed Chinese off the welfare rolls of the government. Following the death of Ong Louie, "mayor of Chinatown," in 1929, the Chinese Merchants' Association and other Chinese organizations assumed greater leadership obligations.

Competition in the marketplace, however, was fierce. In the 1930s, as in the 1920s, numerous small Chinese grocery stores were scattered throughout Phoenix; the 1929 Phoenix City Directory listed forty-two grocery stores with Chinese proprietors. They served the various neighborhoods in which they were located and their dispersal enabled them to exist relatively free from competition, but the Great Depression brought unprecedented problems. During the decade several stores closed due to the competition from Safeway, Bayless, and other large food store chains. Chinese grocers worked day and night, seven days a week, including holidays, but the growth and expansion of the supermarkets drove some out of business.

White competitors became "nasty towards Chinese." One placed full-page ads in Phoenix area newspapers that said, "Don't patronize the Chinese because they sleep behind the store; they make their money and send it back to China; and they live like pigs." In the late 1930s one chain store firm publicly accused the Chinese stores of being unpatriotic because they conducted business on Independence Day. Responding to these comments, Chinese grocery store owners, wishing to project a better image of their community, began celebrating Independence Day by closing their stores and flying the American flag; they also began sponsoring community picnics in honor of the holiday, complete with ball games and beauty contests. The Chinese Boy Scouts directed traffic for the large crowds. Late in the decade Henry Ong, Tang Shing, Yee Sing, and other Chinese leaders created the Chinese Chamber of Commerce to help protect and support the Chinese business community. The organization encouraged Chinese participation in annual Independence Day celebrations and worked to accelerate the Americanization process while preserving cherished parts of traditional Chinese culture.[1]

While the Chinese confronted their critics, the Japanese, who made up the smallest minority in Phoenix, bore the brunt of local resentment of Asians during the Great Depression. Only about fifty of them resided within the city limits in 1940, some of them in Chinatown, but several hundred lived outside the city in the valley, most of them engaged in agricultural work. Confronted with incidents of discrimination and segregation and possessing a sense of ethnic identity and cultural awareness, the Japanese in the Salt River valley, like the Chinese, created their own communal structure.

Beginning in the 1920s, the Japanese Association of Arizona, organized to protect the general interests of members, maintained an office on South Third Street in Phoenix. The Japanese Community Hall and the Japanese Language School building opened in 1928, and in 1932 the Arizona Buddhist Temple was formed in the Glendale home of Hiboshi Yamamoto. It listed more than one hundred members from Phoenix, Mesa, Tempe, Glendale, and Tolleson. Affiliate organizations were the Buddhist Women's Association and the Young Buddhist Association. As in the case of other groups making up the demographic mosaic, Japanese secular and spiritual organizations and institutions helped alleviate problems members faced individually and collectively during the Great Depression. The construction of a building to house the Arizona Buddhist Temple was completed in May 1935 near the corner of Indian School and Forty-Third Avenue. Through the last half of the decade, it served as a center of life in the Japanese community.[2]

The Japanese proved particularly successful as lettuce and cantaloupe growers, but competition with white farmers in the 1930s caused conflict. In the past, the Japanese in the Arizona capital, like the Chinese, had been subject to segregation in public places such as theaters and swimming pools, and state law prohibited them from marrying whites. Restrictive laws in the early 1920s limited the entry of Japanese immigrants into the United States, and state legislation such as the Arizona Alien Land Law of 1921 denied Japanese aliens, who by law were ineligible for citizenship, the right to "acquire, possess, enjoy, transmit, and inherit real property or interest therein." Aimed directly at the Japanese farmers, the legislation proved to be less than effective. Although designed to prohibit Japanese aliens from living in or owning land in Arizona, many of them gained access to agricultural lands through lease contracts and accommodating whites or through their American-born children.

Moreover, white farmers in Arizona did not test the land law until the Great Depression. In August 1934, frustrated at the continued success of the Japanese vegetable and fruit farmers in the Salt River valley, several militant white farmers organized the Anti-Alien Association and began calling for the strict enforcement of the law. Japanese farms were damaged and destroyed, while Japanese farmers were harassed and attacked. The Anti-Alien Association, which soon had hundreds of members, organized "anti-Jap" motorcades to drive throughout the valley to protest the "Yellow Peril" and to demand the removal of "the Japs" from Arizona. As acts of violence escalated, the Japanese community complained, and representatives of Japan and the United States, reflecting on the "bombings, shooting, floodings, and burnings," asked Arizona Governor B. B. Moeur to settle the dispute. As Tomokazu Hori, Japan's consul general in Los Angeles, put it to Moeur:

> Such wanton and barbaric assaults upon the law-abiding Japanese are damaging to the name of your state as well as to the friendship between the United States and Japan. Both for the sake of your state and American-Japanese friendship, I beg you to redouble your efforts in suppressing the agitators and vandals, and thus safeguarding the lives and properties of the Japanese.

Only after agents from the United States Department of Justice arrived did the violence stop. Especially effective was the warning by New Deal authorities in Washington that if the situation did not change, there might be a problem in granting Arizona federal funds and projects. With millions of dollars needed for relief and recovery, Arizona officials received the message and ultimately proved reluctant to commit the state to any policy strenuously disapproved by the federal government. By March 1935 the crisis was over. The Arizona Supreme Court ruled against the Alien Land Law of 1921, and the Arizona State Legislature, subject to a great amount of international, national, and local pressure, failed to pass similar measures. The crisis, however, established the Phoenix area as a focal point for racial prejudice and discrimination against the Japanese, an example of what contributed to the breakdown of Japanese–American relations that led eventually to World War II.[3]

Although the Chinese created more community welfare and protective organizations in the 1930s, such as the Chinese Salvation Society and the Chinese Chamber of Commerce, some of them, along with members of the general population, continued to frequent gambling dens and opium joints in a declining Chinatown. During the decade gambling and drug use posed persistent problems for local and federal officials, and Chinatown became less appealing to those who could relocate. As a result, Chinatown began to break up in the late 1930s and early 1940s. Successful Chinese business and professional leaders led the way in leaving the neighborhood. They believed that the area encompassing Chinatown would inevitably deteriorate, and rather than become part of a "skid row" in downtown Phoenix, they began moving and scattering to neighborhoods throughout the city. Gambling and narcotics trafficking had given Chinatown a bad image, and upwardly mobile Chinese wanted to avoid being part of that image. Chinese business interests also realized that "Phoenix would grow and that commercial enterprises would have a better chance of success if they were in areas of expansion." D. H. Toy, for example, had successfully operated his restaurant and food service business at Sixteenth Street and Camelback Road for several years, and others hoped to follow his lead.[4]

In fact, Chinatown represented only part of the story of the Chinese in Phoenix. From the beginning, Chinese entrepreneurs had established small businesses outside Chinatown as well as within it. Although few in number, some Chinese families lived in the neighborhoods they served and only visited Chinatown. Over time, more Chinese families and businesses located outside the downtown community, especially in black and Mexican neighborhoods. The decline of Chinatown signified the end of the old Chinese bachelor society and the strong sojourner mentality of the past as the population shifted from sojourners to settlers. D. H. Toy and other Chinese grocers and restaurateurs were determined to succeed in the larger city while retaining the best of their cultural heritage. The generations of Chinese who came of age in the 1920s, 1930s, and 1940s worked hard, led frugal lives, and hoped for a better future, especially for their children. At the same time, they persevered against persistent prejudice and discrimination.[5]

World War II and the postwar years hastened the decline of Phoenix's Chinatown. The lessening of prejudice and the increasing mobility of a rising Chinese middle class during the 1940s helped motivate Chinese to move away from or avoid Chinatown. China became an ally in World War II, and in 1943, although quota restrictions remained, the United States government repealed all Chinese immigration exclusion laws as well as many naturalization barriers. Small Chinatowns throughout the nation collapsed as populations shifted and the Americanization of Chinese increased; between 1940 and 1950 twelve Chinatowns disappeared. Chinese in America and in Phoenix enthusiastically contributed to the war effort at home and abroad. Many Phoenix Chinese not only served in the military but also worked in defense plants, joined war bond drives, and took care of Chinese pilots training at local air bases, often providing them a home away from home. Younger Chinese increasingly lost interest in the old ways, while Chinese patriotism during the war and Chinese achievement in education and other areas of American life improved on past images held by the general population. Many new doors opened to mainstream society, including occupational and residential mobility. Differences in the degree of acculturation occurring among Chinese were evident, but in general they accepted more American traits and rejected more traditional Chinese ones. As Chinese Americans, they led dual lives, and for the most part, they thrived.[6]

In contrast, the Japanese American population in the Valley of the Sun encountered worse times after Japan attacked Pearl Harbor in December 1941. While China became a friend of the United States, Japan became its enemy. The Japanese and Chinese populations in America and Arizona were treated accordingly. Following Pearl Harbor, persons of Japanese ancestry in California, Arizona, and several other Western states were placed under restrictions and eventually removed from "prohibited zones" near "vital war industries and military establishments." In May 1942 hundreds of Phoenix-area Japanese were relocated to distant detention camps in the Arizona desert, where they suffered deprivation and dishonor. Located at Sacaton on the Gila River Indian Reservation and Poston on the Colorado River Indian Reservation, the two camps housed 31,000 Japanese from California and Arizona. The internment policy not only seemed necessary as a defense measure, it also pleased perennial "Jap haters" and economic competitors of the Japanese. Pleased with the entire operation, the Arizona Farm Bureau Federation praised the government's action in furthering "the safety of the United States." The attitude of many valley residents was summed up by a leading local grower when he declared, "We don't want them."[7]

Not all valley Japanese were evacuated to the relocation camps during the war. Those not living in "prohibited zones" were allowed to pursue their farming and other endeavors. Limited to "free zones," they were restricted from entering parts of Phoenix and other prohibited areas. Upon their release from the camps, those Japanese not entering the military service returned to their former homes in California and Arizona. Those who had engaged in farming in the free zones during the war had prospered, and they helped many of the returning Japanese resume their places in the community. In the meantime, the Phoenix Chinese American community made substantial gains.[8]

In November 1946, Wing F. Ong, Phoenix attorney and businessman, became the first Chinese American in the nation's history to be elected to a state legislature. His election to the Arizona Legislature was hailed in San Francisco's Chinatown as "a signal honor to the Chinese." In California, Oregon, and Washington, states with large Chinese populations, no Chinese had ever been elected to legislatures. As a result, Chinese-language newspapers on the West Coast devoted major stories to Ong.[9]

Ong was born in the Hoiping District of Guangdong Province, but was a citizen because his father, a Chinese laborer, had been born in the United States. He came to Phoenix via China and San Francisco in 1919 at the age of fourteen on the advice of his uncle, Henry Ong. Henry Ong had arrived in Phoenix in the 1890s from the Hoiping District, where the Ong family was concentrated, under the sponsorship of an uncle, Shung Yip Ong. Henry worked in a family grocery store until he opened his own store, where he worked long hours, seven days a week, fifty-two weeks a year.[10]

In time, his sons, Henry Jr. and Fred, worked with him after school. "We work, work, work, all the time, that's why we got ahead," Fred Ong later recalled. "At that time, a lot of Chinese went into the grocery business because it didn't require a knowledge of English—you just put out your food displays and put the price there. Instead of borrowing from a bank, the relatives and sometimes friends would pool their money, everybody chip in $100, to help someone start a business. It was like a credit union, only for family and friends." Reimbursement was expected, and few defaulted on loans. "To fail to repay a loan would mean a loss of face, not only for yourself but for your whole family," according to Henry Ong, Jr. "If it looked as if someone was not going to make it, the head of the family would step in and repay at least the friends to prevent the family from losing face." The family/clan associations and other Chinese organizations helped the Chinese endure outside criticism as well. Acting as roots, the Ong, Yee, and Wong group affiliations served as economic generators, social agencies, and protective forces.[11]

In 1991 an unpretentious building named Ong Ko Met, located on north Sixteenth Street in Phoenix, served as the headquarters, or "family home," of the Ongs. Occupying leadership roles in the Phoenix Chinese community since the late nineteenth century, the Ong family could trace its roots back to the Han dynasty, a Chinese empire that was "more than two hundred years old when Christ was born." In the family home hung a portrait of Ong Ko Met, the founder of the Ong clan. "He helped the emperor establish the Han dynasty and for this was rewarded with a very high post in the government," according to Fred Ong, a past president of the Ong Family Association. He "was made administrator for the Kingdom and given the title 'Ko Met,' which means the same as 'duke' or 'lord' in English." When the Ongs first arrived in Phoenix, China was under the control of the unpopular Manchu dynasty (1644–1912), and Guangdong Province, home of the Ongs, was suffering from economic and political turbulence. Drawn by the promise of America, the Ongs made their way to Phoenix, where they became the dominant clan. Utilizing their cultural values and institutions, they created a vital community. Their struggle was difficult, but through hard work, self-help, and educational attainment, the Ongs in a few generations became an outstanding example of Chinese American success.

In overcoming barriers and achieving success, the Chinese family associations in Phoenix proved crucial. As elsewhere, they were modeled on associations created by the same clans in China. For example, the Ongs' family home in China "was established by relatives in a city such as Canton, the capital of Guangdong, and served as a boarding house, mail drop, counseling center and social hall for family members arriving in the city to go to school, do business or visit."[12]

Arriving in Phoenix in 1919, after being incarcerated in San Francisco for three months while authorities double-checked his citizenship, Wing F. Ong worked in the family grocery store, learned English, and quickly moved through the school system, graduating from Monroe Elementary School in four years and Phoenix Union High School in two years. In high school he also worked as houseboy for Arizona Governor Thomas Campbell and his wife, Gayle. The Campbell family helped Wing with his studies and encouraged him to go to college. After graduating from Phoenix Union in 1925, he attended the University of Arizona, but because of financial problems, was forced to drop out. Returning to Phoenix, he invested in a failing grocery store and saved it through good management and hard work. Soon established in the grocery business, Wing married Rose Wong, also from Guangdong Province, in December 1928. Born in China, Rose lived several years in Yakima, Washington, but upon her father's death she returned to China at the age of fourteen to live with remaining family members. Married in Phoenix, the couple lived in the back room of Wing's grocery store at Sixteenth and Van Buren streets, where in 1929 Rose gave birth to the first of their six children.

The Ongs, dedicated and ambitious, diligently forged ahead. "We were poor, but we had confidence," Rose later recalled. Many of the small grocery stores in Phoenix, including the Golden Gate Grocery operated by Ong, were located in black and Mexican neighborhoods, and their owners made special efforts to meet the needs of their customers. They made credit available and kept food favorites in stock. The stores gave Chinese an independent source of income, but long hours and low profits made life difficult.

Wing sold his store in 1930, and he and Rose went to China. On their return to Phoenix, the Ongs opened another Golden Gate Grocery not far from the old one. Wing was determined to acquire a college education, but during the Great Depression it was difficult to support a wife and children on the income from the store and go to school too. Rose's brother, Ben Wong, arrived in Phoenix in 1938 and helped run the store while Rose cared for the children and Wing attended Phoenix College; concentrating on business courses, he graduated in 1939. Leaving the store in the capable hands of his family in September 1941, Wing enrolled in the University of Arizona Law School. During the week he lived in Tucson with the Thomas Campbell family, and weekends he spent with his family in Phoenix. To Wing, education was the key to success in the United States, and he was determined to achieve his ambitions. In 1943 he graduated from law school at the top of his class, passed the Arizona bar exams with the third-highest score, and became one of only eight Chinese lawyers in the United States.[13]

In Phoenix, Wing practiced law, operated a grocery business, and sold insurance. He was kept busy, for he knew many people inside and outside the Chinese community; at the same time, the Ong clan made up nearly half of the total Chinese population in Phoenix, and Wing was a natural leader. According to supporters, he served the Chinese and the larger community well as a lawyer, businessman, and legislator, but he had moments of frustration and defeat. Re-elected to the Arizona House of Representatives in 1948, Wing lost the 1950 Democratic primary election to African American Hayzel B. Daniels. Ong pulled less than 30 percent of the vote, coming in last behind Daniels and S. C. Boyer, a black businessman.

In that election incumbent Ong ran from District 8, a new legislative district containing a large African American and Mexican American population. Black leaders questioned his qualifications, pointing out that Ong did not actually live in District 8. Moreover, according to critics, he spent too much time in San Francisco pursuing immigration law cases, and not enough time in Phoenix representing his constituents. The *Arizona Sun,* speaking for many African Americans and reflecting the suspicion and tension often present when minority groups competed for limited rewards, accused Ong of past racist practices in his business and personal life. It stated Ong "probably believes now as he did when he operated a restaurant in connection with his grocery store at 1246 East Jefferson that Negroes are not good enough to eat in his restaurant but are 'good enough' to buy his groceries." The *Sun* declared that Ong felt "superior to his electors." An example of his attitude was indicated, the paper asserted, "when a Negro youth from the neighborhood, who returned in uniform from fighting to make the world safe for Democracy, and was shaking hands with one of Ong's daughters was informed that he, the Negro soldier, did not have such privileges in the Ong family."

Nasty accusations came from both sides. On September 8, 1950, the *Sun* reported that it had learned from "reliable sources" that Ong was injecting a "racial issue" into the campaign by personally requesting white voters "not to vote for his two opponents . . . because they are 'N . . . gers' and neither one could help the district if elected." Daniels went on to win the general election, and Ong and his family moved to San Francisco, where they lived for several years.[14]

Returning to Phoenix in 1955, Ong resumed his law practice and other interests. In the 1950s barriers remained, and even an educated, affluent family like the Ongs could not always live where they wanted in Phoenix. As they progressed and prospered, the Ongs and other successful Chinese American families sought to move into select neighborhoods but were turned away. Ong's daughter Madeline Ong-Sakata later recalled that in 1956 her parents were looking for a house for the family, and "I kept saying, 'Ooo, let's live in the Phoenix Country Club, let's buy a house on East Camelback.' My mother would just drop the subject. Years later I found out it was because these neighborhoods all had deed restrictions prohibiting Chinese. Now they aren't enforced but a lot of them are still on the books." The Ongs eventually found a home they wanted in a predominantly white middle-class neighborhood in north Phoenix. In 1958 he ran again for the Arizona House of Representatives from District 31. He won the Democratic primary but lost to Republican David H. Campbell in the general election; he was unable to win enough white votes in District 31. In 1964, Democrat Ong lost a run for the Arizona Senate to Republican B. C. Rhodes, but in 1966, running again for the Senate, he was elected. In 1968, Ong ran for his second term in the Senate but lost in the primary election.[15]

During the Cold War most Chinese Americans held anti-Communist views and opposed the Communist takeover of China. In Phoenix members of the local chapter of the Chinese Nationalist Association and of Chinese American Legion Post No. 50 expressed their commitment to Chiang Kai-shek's Nationalist government in Taiwan and their gratitude to the United States for supporting it. In October of every year, Chinese Americans in Phoenix held Double Ten celebrations honoring the anniversary of the Chinese Republic's founding by Sun Yat-sen.

Chinese Americans in Phoenix also continued to take care of their own, although most of them benefited from postwar progress and prosperity. In November 1948, for example, local members of the San Francisco–based Ying On Benevolent Association, a fraternal order, led by Tom Yee, Walter Ong, Fred Wong, and other officers of the organization, opened the Chinese Civic Center at 120 South Second Street. It was to be the "headquarters for welfare activities among needy Chinese families"; the *Gazette* called it an "impressive building." Over 300 members of the association from Arizona and California attended the dedication ceremonies, with many staying in the city for a convention featuring traditional Chinese festivities in the civic center area and a banquet at the Hotel Westward Ho. Remnants of Phoenix's Chinatown remained in the area, but it no longer had a future as the center of Chinese life in the city.[16]

The Chinese population in Phoenix increased from 431 in 1940 to

1,092 in 1960, but their percentage of the total population actually decreased. During this period the Chinese population decentralized and Chinatown disintegrated. The rapid, low-density growth and expansion of Phoenix after World War II brought new, affordable neighborhoods into being, and Chinese Americans found their way into a number of them. Located throughout the urban area, the Chinese worked diligently to achieve economic status; a number of them graduated from college and went on to professional school. Associations, offering a sense of security, identity, and community, continued to play a vital role in the success of the Chinese; for example, the large Ong, Yee, Wong, and Lung Kong family associations provided support to newcomers and care for sick or elderly relations and raised permanent funds to subsidize new family enterprises. Other organizations also served social and cultural purposes; the First Chinese Baptist Church, formalized in 1957 with eighty members, was particularly active.

In the years after the war, Chinese Americans were more a part of the general community than at any time in the past. In the 1950s, for example, Thomas Tang, son of Tang Shing, was elected to the Phoenix City Council, and Wing Ong was re-elected to the Arizona Legislature in the 1960s. At hearings before the United States Commission on Civil Rights, held in Phoenix in February 1962, Tang noted that "there was a time when, in the area of swimming pools, places of recreation, and housing, there was a definite restriction," but "today, here in the City of Phoenix, here in the State of Arizona, the Oriental enjoys a very fine position. I believe that the feeling here of Oriental people is that they enjoy as good a position as any in the United States."[17]

Tang mentioned several prominent Chinese Americans as examples, including Walter Ong, a successful businessman who had been named Phoenix Man of the Year in 1956 for his activities in the Chinese American community, especially his efforts to get more Chinese people naturalized. Ong supported a small school where he and other volunteers taught potential citizens English and the United States Constitution so that they could pass the required tests. He appreciated the recognition but remembered the difficult times for Chinese Americans in an earlier Phoenix. As a small grocery store owner in the 1930s, Ong had experienced the racist attacks of the supermarket chains, the prejudice met at movie theaters and swimming pools, the neighborhoods where Chinese Americans were unwelcome. Over the years many neighborhoods tried to keep the Chinese out, Ong later declared, but once they moved in and proved to be good neighbors, opposition dwindled. In fact, some Phoenix leaders welcomed them as neighbors. Barry Goldwater, for example, supported Walter Ong when his neighbors in the Camelback foothills objected to the Chinese American building a home there; as Goldwater remarked to one complainer, "I think we ought to go ask Walter, see if he wants us for neighbors." Goldwater's reaction silenced the protester.[18]

6 PROGRESS AND PROBLEMS, 1960–1992

By the time of the 1962 civil rights hearings in Phoenix, Chinese Americans had achieved considerable progress and prosperity. City Councilman Thomas Tang, in his testimony at the hearings, pointed out several outstanding examples. He also attributed Chinese American success to their small number in the Phoenix area and to the fact that "there is no such place as a Chinatown anymore. The Chinese people have decentralized, and have lived in the community with their neighbors, so that their neighbors get to know them as people, as individuals." Their economic position helped them; as Tang stated, "They have not been in positions of threat to the general economy, there being generally in the area a prosperous economy." Tang, a lawyer and future judge, emphasized the importance of "standards" and "educational status" to the Chinese. "Through their cultural background there has been a desire to learn, and so you will find that most of them in school apply themselves diligently to their studies, so that they do have a fair standard of education in comparison with the average." Also, Tang continued, "They tend to go in for professional education." He noted the increasing number of lawyers, doctors, engineers, architects, teachers and other professionals in the Phoenix Chinese American community.[1]

The native-born, highly educated Chinese Americans, although not totally assimilated, showed signs of increased acculturation. The foreign-born also advanced in that direction, especially after the Communist takeover of China, which made returning to their homeland impossible and caused many Chinese to adapt to a permanent stay in the United

States. Many of them belonged to the Chinese Anti-Communist League and the Kuomingtang, Phoenix Chapter. The Chinese American community in Phoenix was scattered, but its institutions held it together to an extent; they ranged from the Phoenix Chinese United Association, made up of leaders of the various special-interest organizations, to the Desert Jade Women's Club, a group known for its scholarship awards, to the Phoenician American Legion Post 50, a veterans' group.[2]

As the Chinese population increased, due in part to more liberal but selective immigration policies after World War II, changes in the sex ratio occurred, leading to more families. More foreign and American-born Chinese women added to the female population, making possible a more equalized sex ratio. In 1970, reflecting the national ratio, the sex ratio in Arizona was nearly equal. The 1970s and 1980s also witnessed record numbers of Chinese women in the nation's colleges and universities, and more than half of the Chinese women in America worked outside their homes; in 1991, Fred Ong noted with pride that "all five of my daughters are professionals." Influenced by the women's movement, Chinese women in the nation and in Phoenix gained more independence; many of them insisted that parental arrangement of marriages and other traditional Chinese customs fall by the wayside.[3]

The Chinese American women's movement in Phoenix and other urban centers consisted of young, college-educated, middle-class women. Like Mexican American and African American women of the same circumstances, they borrowed ideas from the white women's movement but seldom joined white-dominated organizations. Active in the drive for civil rights and social justice, Chinese American women fought the special oppression of minority females and provided a variety of services conducive to improvement. At the same time, they remained attached to their ethnic, cultural community.[4]

In the 1940s and 1950s many Chinese Americans took advantage of new educational and career opportunities and joined mainstream American society; in fact, some journalists in the 1960s and 1970s began calling the Chinese Americans an integral part of the "model minority" of Asian Americans. Others accused them of harboring a superiority complex. Critics quickly pointed out that not all Chinese Americans were successful, particularly language-deficient, poorly educated, often-exploited recent arrivals. Moreover, although impressive progress had been made by Chinese Americans and other Asian Americans, anti-Asian attitudes and actions remained.[5]

Geographic dispersal made it particularly difficult to keep the Phoenix

Chinese American community together. The Chinese Chamber of Commerce, for example, continued to hold Fourth of July celebrations with a dual purpose: to demonstrate the Chinese American community's integration with the larger society while also promoting the Chinese culture by presenting Chinese food, Chinese films, Chinese fashion shows, and other Chinese delights. In the 1970s and 1980s, however, few Chinese American young people understood the Chinese language or wished to practice, perpetuate, or promote traditional Chinese culture. The increasingly self-confident Chinese community no longer reflected the image of the Chinatown past; a more positive image had evolved as it established families and businesses across the city. With the demise of Phoenix's Chinatown, the rise of the native-born, and the decline of the sojourner population, the Chinese American community became more American, more reflective of America's progress and problems.[6]

At the same time, all the progress made by Chinese Americans and other Asian Americans often caused others to overlook their problems. For example, Chinese American and other Asian American students at Arizona State University occasionally complained of being "invisible" on campus as a minority group. Although they suffered from prejudice and discrimination, as did other groups, university studies and polls omitted them and their problems, no doubt considering them successful members of the "model minority," individuals free from the many difficulties faced by African Americans and Hispanic Americans. Asian American faculty at ASU also expressed their dissatisfaction with the "model minority" depiction. As one of them said in 1991, regarding subtle racial animosity:

> You enter a profession and run into this invisible ceiling. You won't find Chinese at the top in City Hall; you'll find very few [ASU] deans or department heads who are Asian. . . . When we complain, the attitude is like, "They have education, they have a profession, what more do they want?" We wear the label "successful," but what does that really mean? What kind of success is it when you are not allowed to rise to the natural level of your abilities?[7]

Nevertheless, times had definitely changed. In the 1970s and 1980s, for example, few Chinese Americans worked in small grocery stores. As Fred Ong recalled in March 1991: "From 1920 to the 1950s, there were maybe 200 or 300 Chinese grocery stores in Phoenix. Right now there are 40 or 50 left, maybe not that many." For many Chinese, a grocery business was their door to the American dream. "There were no Circle Ks then," Ong remembered. "There would be no other store available in the neighborhood. Those stores really served a need for the community."

The proliferation of supermarket and convenience store chains caused many of the groceries to close. At the same time, Americanized, college-educated sons and daughters of the store operators did not want to work in the family stores. Young people, an observer noted, "grew up and got a good education, an American education, and they don't want to work 14 hours a day in a grocery store." Moreover, many of the neighborhoods where the grocery stores were located fell into decay and decline over the years and became centers of violence and crime.[8]

Beginning in the 1980s, incidents of violence against Chinese Americans in Phoenix, as elsewhere in the nation, escalated, culminating in the March 1991 shooting deaths of a grocery store owner and his daughter. "A lot of people in the small grocery stores are scared," reported Fred Ong, president of the Chinese Chamber of Commerce, who declared he would "work with Phoenix police to set up crime prevention sessions for small grocery store owners, who, for whatever reason don't want to leave their neighborhoods." Ong noted that "many of them don't have the kind of money to move the store, or the children are gone and the parents are at retiring age, just waiting to quit."[9]

Despite problems, some grocers continued to take pride in serving their neighborhoods. Hyland Woo worked long hours for little profit in his small store on Buckeye Road. "We're here to serve the community. We give people what they want," Woo asserted a few weeks after the murders. "Look at this—catfish, buffalo fish, pork ribs, pig's feet. If a supermarket carried these things, they'd have to sell it at a higher price to make it pay. I sell a lot of it, so I can sell it cheaper." The "profit is not that great and the area is rough, but our customers have been good to us." Nevertheless, there were fewer Chinese-owned stores, according to Ong. The "Vietnamese and the Koreans are taking our place now. They're coming in, and we're selling to them. They're the new immigrants, the same boat we were in once."[10]

As useful as they were, Chinese-operated groceries in some poor neighborhoods generated criticism. Black critics, for example, accused Chinese grocers of manipulating customers. They "often let the people charge purchases until the checks from the government come in," one observer noted. "The people come into the store, cash their checks and pay what the store owner says they owe. But many times, he just gives them back what he wants them to have." "Some store owners charge them 10 percent for cashing the checks or interest on the credit accounts," he added. "Sometimes, they only get a few dollars from their checks and they're right back to charging at the store the same day." In

1980 a *Gazette* reporter toured several stores and found some of them selling poor-quality food. "Wilted lettuce, cabbage and other vegetables would have been discarded days earlier in supermarkets on the north side of Phoenix," she declared. "Some meat counters contained gray-green slices of ham or steaks." Some black leaders resented the lack of black businesses in black neighborhoods. Outsiders operated many of the businesses, but they hired few black people. African Americans "were good enough to sell to, but not good enough to hire," asserted one critic. "They don't hire you; they don't socialize with you; they take money out of the community, but they put very little back in." [11]

Incidents of vandalism and violence against Chinese Americans were of particular concern to community leaders, especially "hate crimes" motivated by economic and cultural resentment. Increased gang activity also contributed to increased crime in the Chinese community and in other sectors of the Asian population; in April 1990, for example, several Vietnamese gangs were identified in the Phoenix area. The number of Asians in the city jumped to about 16,303 (4,254 Chinese) by 1990, up from 6,863 (2,493 Chinese) in 1980, mostly the result of an influx of refugees from Vietnam, Cambodia, Laos, and other parts of Southeast Asia. It should be noted that the top concerns of most Southeast Asian newcomers, regardless of nationality and background, appeared to be hard work and the pursuit of education. [12]

In the 1980s many new arrivals from Taiwan, Hong Kong, and mainland China settled in Phoenix. Unlike most of the earlier immigrants from Guangdong Province in southeastern China, who spoke Cantonese and were uneducated and poor, the newcomers included many educated professionals who not only were fluent in English but also spoke Mandarin rather than Cantonese. Many of them were engineers or other high-tech professionals employed at plants like Motorola, Honeywell, and Intel, or medical doctors or faculty at Arizona State University. Differences in language, place of origin, and economic activity often determined status and class in the Chinese American community. "They have their separate little groups, and there isn't much intermingling between the people that speak Cantonese and Mandarin," noted an observer in 1978. [13]

Diversity existed in the Chinese population of Phoenix. In another example, elder members of the newer groups who sought out companions of similar background and language often found them at the Phoenix Chinese Senior Center. Yuk Lan Cheng, a member of the Phoenix Chinese Senior Citizens Association, declared in August 1990 that Cantonese and Mandarin "are so far apart they are essentially foreign languages to each other," so at the center "small groups tend to form around common dialects." Cheng had "found her own circle of friends" and visited the center every day. Local Chinese restaurants also became more diverse. "For many years the only food served in Phoenix restaurants was Cantonese food," a long-time resident pointed out in 1978, "but now there are all kinds of restaurants that serve Mandarin food or Northern style cooking." [14]

The more diversity the Chinese community acquired, the more complex it appeared, but at times a sense of unity expressed itself in common institutions and celebrations. For example, the *Arizona Chinese Times*, published by Manny Wong, featured news about the Chinese community in and beyond Phoenix. First published entirely in Chinese, it added an English-language page after numerous complaints from English-reading-only Chinese. "We do need a newspaper, but it being in Chinese keeps a lot of us out," lamented one commentator who was born in Phoenix and did not speak or read Chinese. But William Ong, president of the Phoenix Chinese United Association in 1990, said he hoped the *Times* would "motivate young Chinese-Americans to learn the first language of their grandparents." Ong, a retired grocer who was born in Canton, China, but had lived in Phoenix since age twelve, also noted the newspaper was used by students of Chinese. Early in 1991, Wong began publishing two community newspapers, one in Chinese and one in English. [15]

In 1990 the Chinese Linguistic School of Phoenix expanded and Chinese leaders expressed approval. It taught major dialects and inspired publisher Wong to proudly proclaim, "We now have a school and a newspaper." Evenings benefiting Chinese artists and musicians occurred regularly at the China Doll Restaurant, and picnics at Encanto Park were attended by Chinese groups and individuals. Tennis, golf, volleyball and other athletic competitions engaged many, as did Chinese culture and cuisine. The Phoenix Chinese United Association, in cooperation with the Phoenix Sister Cities Commission, presented the first Chinese Week early in 1991. Planned as an annual affair, it offered a series of events celebrating the rich and diverse Chinese social and cultural heritage. Clarence Tang and other outstanding Chinese American community leaders were honored, as were Phoenix's sister cities in China and Taiwan—Chengdu and Taipei. Involved individuals and groups called it a successful and rewarding series of experiences, topped off with a Chinese New Year banquet. The Chinese American Professional Association of Arizona, the Chinese Restaurant Association of Arizona, and other statewide organizations promised their continued support for such memorable occasions.[16]

Most important, the Chinese American population continued to share certain feelings. Hard work, the family, and education persisted as values of high priority. The Chinese belief in hard work comes from the philosophy of Confucius, who taught that perfection could be achieved through practice; this belief is part of their cultural heritage. Confucius also taught that people should work not just for themselves, but for the honor of the family. In America and in Phoenix, Chinese parents, often sacrificing much themselves, encouraged their sons and daughters to reach high levels of educational attainment for the benefit of all concerned, and their progeny, imbued with a strong motivation for achievement, usually met their expectations. The Chinese struggle brought gains, but not all benefited. Although problems existed, concerned observers continued to be hopeful that the Chinese American experience would remain largely a forward-moving one.[17]

PART 3   THE AFRICAN AMERICANS

7 COMMUNITY DEVELOPMENT TO 1930

African Americans have lived in the West since the beginnings of Spanish settlement and were among the founders of Los Angeles. During the California gold rush, many of them arrived with the same expectations as other gold seekers, although their efforts were hampered by prejudice and discrimination. African Americans are recognized for playing an important role in the history of Western development. The rise of black communities in San Francisco, Los Angeles, Portland, Seattle, Denver, and other cities in the West, as well as in Texas, has received considerable treatment. Within that history are numerous accounts of antiblack attitudes and actions as well as black resistance on the urban frontier. Cities in the American West hardly served as ports of paradise for African Americans, but they and their supporters actively worked to overcome barriers to equality and opportunity.[1]

The 1870 United States census listed twenty-eight African Americans (five of whom were women) in Arizona. Most of the men engaged in mining and ranching in the southern part of the territory. Not counted were African American soldiers, who were first stationed in Arizona in the late 1860s at Fort Huachuca, south of Tucson. African Americans began arriving in Phoenix at the same time, the first being Mary Green, a servant who came with the Columbus H. Gray family in 1868. They continued to trickle into Phoenix until by 1900 they numbered 150, or 2.7 percent of the total population of 5,544. Some were former soldiers, some were health seekers, but most of them, like others in the general population, were opportunity seekers.[2]

Table 7.1. Occupational Structure for African Americans,
           1870–1900[a]

Occupations	1870	1880	1900
Unskilled	—	2	57
Semiskilled	1	—	11
Skilled	—	1	10
Farming/Ranching	—	—	2
Mercantile	—	—	4
Professional	—	—	1
Totals	1	3	85

SOURCE: Federal manuscript census schedules, 1870, 1880, 1900.
[a] African American populations derived from enumerator classification of "B" for
   Blacks.

As in the case of other minority groups, African Americans were no
doubt undercounted by census takers in the nineteenth century. Although
a small black middle class was emerging, the majority of males worked
in unskilled and semi-skilled occupations; women were employed mostly
as domestic and service workers (see Table 7.1).

African American leaders emerged in the 1890s to encourage community development. Frank Shirley, after arriving in Phoenix in 1887,
opened the Fashion Square Barber Shop; the popular shop serviced
whites but employed several blacks. Active in the community, Shirley
founded the Afro-American Society, a leading social group, in 1893.
Richard Rosser arrived in Phoenix from Georgia in 1893 and bought a
small farm. He prospered and acquired property, donating some of it to
African American causes; in one example Rosser, a deeply religious man,
deeded land in 1905 to his congregation so that it could build the Second Colored Baptist Church at Fifth and Jefferson streets, completed
in 1908.[3]

After arriving in Phoenix from West Virginia in 1897, William P.
Crump started as a waiter at the Ford Hotel but eventually became owner
of a highly profitable fruit and produce business near Central Avenue and
Jefferson Street. Crump became the best spokesman for the Phoenix African American population; according to the *Republican*, "Mr. Crump's
diction was elegant, his manner attractive and his reasoning clear." He

not only resisted second-class citizenship for African Americans but insisted members of the community act in a responsible and moral way; for example, he opposed the sale or consumption of alcohol on Sunday. By the turn of the century, Shirley, Rosser, Crump, and other successful African American leaders lived on East Jefferson and East Washington streets in the heart of the small Phoenix African American community. Numerous black residences and businesses dotted the area within Van Buren and Madison streets, Central Avenue and Seventh Street.[4]

African Americans in the 1890s participated in a variety of activities. They watched and listened to local and traveling black musical and dramatic groups. They attended black baseball league games and joined black art and literary clubs. Fraternal lodges provided companionship as well as help when needed; the Colored Masons, the Colored Odd Fellows, and the Colored Knights of the Pythias led the way. For the politically inclined, the Colored Republican Club proved to be the most appealing group. Shirley, Rosser, Crump, and others belonged to the club, although they personally felt Republicans did little for blacks. The "right politics" in Phoenix, however, meant city jobs for blacks and city favors for black entrepreneurs.

Blacks wanted more recognition and attention, but they always supported national and local Republican candidates. The Good Citizens' League, a black organization led by business partners Frank Shirley and John E. Lewis, wanted to "better the conditions of the colored race in the city, both material and moral, and restrain influences for their undoing, whether fostered by whites or blacks." Said to be nonpolitical, the league expected to "take no part in political questions unless some candidate appears to be inimical to their material interests. Their opposition then would not be on the ground of politics, but that of racial prosperity." The Good Citizens' League also encouraged African American participation in parades, celebrations, and other community activities.[5]

For the religious-minded, the dedication of Phoenix's first black church, the African Methodist Episcopal (AME) Church, at the corner of Jefferson and Second streets in 1899, was impressive and welcome. The new structure, called Tanner Chapel, not only held church services but also provided for the Colored Sunday School. Black churches experienced financial difficulty during their early years, but support from the community was forthcoming, and energetic ministers provided leadership. The churches served as centers for African American community life. They offered not only spiritual but also secular services. The AME Church, for example, presented lectures such as "The Future of the

American Negro" and plays such as *Thirty Years of Freedom,* as well as birthday celebrations honoring Abraham Lincoln, Frederick Douglass, and Richard Allen. Orations by William P. Crump and other church members were well attended and always followed by good fellowship, food, and music. Following the construction of the Second Colored Baptist Church and the African Methodist Episcopal Church, a third house of worship, the Colored Methodist Episcopal Church, South, organized in 1909 and completed its building at Seventh and Jefferson streets in 1911. A number of smaller religious congregations also served the Phoenix African American community.[6]

Churches and other African American voluntary associations helped encourage a sense of community in the Phoenix black population. The variety of organizations attracted people from all elements of African American society; needs could be addressed and identities established. "Rowing Not Drifting" was the motto of a local black women's club. As Geoffrey Mawn, a student of black associational life in early Phoenix, put it: "All these groups sought to assist blacks to develop materially, morally, and socially. Through lectures, discussions, and debates individuals exchanged and disseminated ideas and arguments on topics of contemporary importance to the black community." The "list of speakers to these forums included white civic leaders and governmental officials as well as black intellectuals and visiting black religious and educational dignitaries."[7]

By 1910, African Americans in Phoenix numbered 328, or 2.9 percent of the total population of 11,134. Most of them came from Oklahoma and Texas, with a smaller count from Kansas, Missouri, and other Southern states. The men continued to work mostly as field hands, common laborers, or in unskilled service jobs, but many owned small businesses, and some functioned as professionals; women usually worked as domestics. A high percentage of black Phoenicians owned their own homes. Although most of the houses were modest, those of Shirley, Rosser, Crump, and other leaders ranged as high as $10,000 to $15,000. African American institutional life remained centered in the churches, and other black voluntary associations multiplied. Outside their community, however, African Americans still faced a generally unfriendly and hostile population, which made life difficult for many of them.

Hotel accommodations, for example, were a problem. When John E. Lewis, black owner with Frank Shirley of the Fashion Square Barber Shop, opened a "hotel for colored people" on Seventh and Jefferson streets in July 1912, he declared that in Phoenix "all the better class of hotels and rooming houses cater exclusively to white people. There are a few cheap places where a colored man can find accommodations, but there are many colored men who do not care to patronize such places, both because the accommodations are poor and because of the low class of humanity often met there." The intersection where the hotel was opened was a major center of African American life in Phoenix. The Horseshoe Athletic Club, a social organization with two hundred members, was located there, along with the Lewis Apartments, an eighteen-room hotel run by blacks for blacks.

The local press dutifully continued to mention the business and social life of the African American community in the city. It noted lectures delivered to the Colored Forum, concerts given by the Colored Band and the Colored Glee Club, and games played by the Colored Cubs, a Phoenix baseball team, but at times the press emphasized what it considered to be the negative side of black life in the city. In March 1912, for example, the Afro-American Club was called a "moral sink," a "vehicle for the exercise of license and debauchery," a "lawless nigger club," and a "disgrace to the city of Phoenix."[8]

African American leaders and organizations resisted second-class citizenship in Phoenix, but to no avail. School segregation, for example, did not prevail without protest. In March 1909 the territorial legislature passed a proposal allowing Arizona school districts, when they deemed it advisable, to segregate students of African ancestry from students of other racial backgrounds. Few white Arizonans opposed the measure, but one who did was Governor Joseph H. Kibbey, who promptly vetoed it. Kibbey had already served as chief justice of the Arizona Supreme Court and as a prominent Phoenix lawyer of the Salt River Valley Water Users' Association when he was appointed governor of Arizona Territory in 1905 by President Theodore Roosevelt. Kibbey opposed the segregation proposal on economic and moral grounds: "It would be unfair that pupils of the African race should be given accommodations and facilities for a common school education, less effective, less complete, less convenient or less pleasant so far as the accessories of the school and its operations are concerned than those accorded pupils of the white race in the same school district; and the bill in terms contemplates nothing less." The territorial legislature reacted by overriding Governor Kibbey's veto, and school segregation became legal on March 17, 1909.

Few districts in Arizona adopted school segregation, but Phoenix did.

In April 1910 the Phoenix School Board, supported by the majority of the white population in the city, adopted a segregation policy. In protest, African Americans hired Kibbey, who had returned to private practice in Phoenix, to initiate injunction proceedings against the school board to prevent the segregation of white and black students. The injunction suit on behalf of African American plaintiff Samuel F. Bayless, who contended that segregation imposed an unfair burden on his children, against defendants L. D. Dameron, Sims Ely, and W. G. Tolleson, all board members, asked that the board be enjoined from segregating black children from those of other races and requiring them to attend a school for black children. Kibbey argued that separate could never be equal. To provide "separate but equal" facilities was "impracticable," but "if it is not done, this law is unjust and unfair, and justified by no just consideration whatever." In July the injunction suit was set for trial in December; in the meantime, the construction of what would become Frederick Douglass Elementary School for "colored children" on Madison Street between Fifth and Sixth streets, in the midst of the predominant black neighborhood in Phoenix, proceeded (see Map 7.1).

In August 1910, District Attorney George Bullard contended that African American citizens favored a separate school for their children. He stated that a group of black parents indicated to him that their children did not receive an "even break" with white students in integrated schools and that in segregated schools they would not "suffer from ostracism." The Good Citizens' League and other African American organizations immediately objected to Bullard's contentions. Reacting quickly and strongly to his comments, African American leader William P. Crump denied that a basis of black support for segregated schools existed. Noting that 98 percent of the African Americans he knew in Phoenix bitterly resented the policy, Crump declared:

> We do not oppose it from any desire for social equality, for that is foreign to our thoughts. We fight it because it is a step backward; because there are not enough colored children here to enable them to establish a fully equipped school; because it is an injustice to take the money of all the taxpayers to establish ward schools and then force the colored children to walk two miles to school while their property is taxed to provide ward schools for all other children; because from the organization of the territory to the present time the children of all classes of its cosmopolitan citizenship have gone to school together and there has been no friction or trouble of any kind, and as a result there is not a community in America where the relations of the black and white are more amicable and peaceful than in Phoenix.

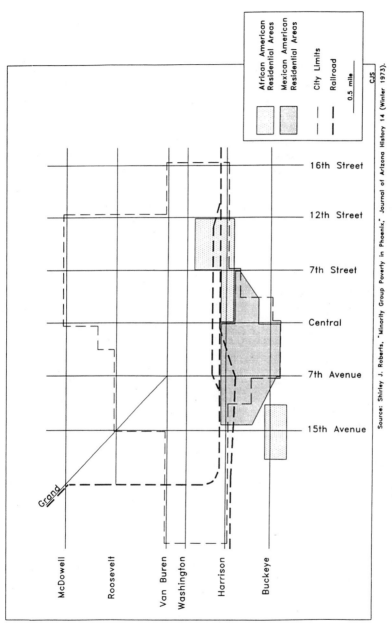

MAP 7.1 Minority Neighborhoods in Phoenix, 1911

Source: Shirley J. Roberts, "Minority Group Poverty in Phoenix," Journal of Arizona History 14 (Winter 1973).

African American Residential Areas

Mexican American Residential Areas

City Limits

Railroad

0.5 mile

CJS

16th Street

12th Street

7th Street

Central

7th Avenue

15th Avenue

McDowell

Roosevelt

Van Buren

Washington

Harrison

Buckeye

Grand

Crump resented being the victim of Jim Crow restrictions in hotels, theaters, restaurants, and other gathering places in Phoenix. Race restrictions precluded the entry of blacks in white neighborhoods; indeed, even the cemeteries in Phoenix were segregated. Segregation made the whole Crump family angry, as one of his daughters, Emily, later recalled; "we felt it deeply, that we were treated so differently." Rather than send Emily and her sister Elizabeth to the "colored school," Crump enrolled them in St. Mary's Catholic Church School, where they were among the first of their race to graduate in 1916.

The idea of school segregation infuriated Crump, and when he called on the African American population to protest "this unnecessary and uncalled for outrage," white Phoenix reacted. "The Negroes who protest against the segregation law are doing their race a great injury," asserted the *Arizona Democrat,* a local newspaper. It stated that "colored people in Arizona are nicely treated," and it suggested that "they conduct themselves in such a manner that this kindly feeling will continue." The "people of Arizona are in favor of this segregation of the races in our public schools and they propose to have such segregation; and protests will only result in making the demand for it persistent."

In September 1910 sixteen African American children enrolled at Douglass School to study under African American principal J. T. Williams and African American teacher Lucy B. Craig; by December fifty-four had enrolled. In that month the trial of *Bayless v. Dameron et al.* unfolded, and Kibbey presented his case. At this time, Bayless had two daughters aged six and ten years, who prior to segregation had walked five blocks to school. After Douglass School opened, the girls were forced to walk two miles and to cross the railroad tracks of both the Southern Pacific and the Santa Fe railroads, an act that imperiled life and limb. Kibbey argued that to impose this unequal and dangerous situation on the black students was unfair. He also called upon Crump, who had once taught school in West Virginia, to testify that ungraded schools were not as good as graded ones. On the other side, Phoenix Superintendent of Schools John D. Loper declared that black schools were equal to white schools.

Judge Edward Kent commented that he could not understand why "Africans" would want to attend white schools when they would be happier "with their own." He also believed the territorial legislature had the power to segregate on the basis of race where "equal facilities for each are afforded." Kent agreed with the *Republican* assessment that the black students were actually better off than the whites in their new school building, and he felt they would especially benefit from close attention in small classes. On the other hand, Kent agreed with Kibbey that unjust discrimination did exist in the distances and dangers the children had to overcome, and he exempted black students in the first four grades from attending Douglass School.

District Attorney Bullard appealed Kent's decision regarding the exemption in January 1911, but the case did not reach final settlement until after Arizona was admitted to the federal union in February 1912. The Arizona Supreme Court, after citing the "separate but equal" doctrine enunciated in the famous 1896 United States Supreme Court case of *Plessy v. Ferguson,* confirmed the constitutionality of the segregation law. As for the distances traveled and dangers encountered by black students that had led Judge Kent to exempt the first four grades from attending Douglass School, the Arizona justices concluded that they furnished "no substantial ground of complaint." The case was dismissed, and under the segregation law Douglass School continued to provide classes for all African American school students in the public system; at the same time, the majority of African American students in Phoenix in 1912 lived in the area east, south, and west of Douglass School and probably would have attended the institution without the law. For the few African American students who managed to reach the secondary level of public education, Phoenix Union High School provided a "colored room."[9]

The creation of Douglass School did, however, clear the neighborhood of some unwanted residents. The growth of prostitution in Phoenix had concentrated in south Phoenix. African American leaders were especially annoyed by Block 41, bounded by Jackson and Madison, Fifth and Sixth streets, an area that had specifically been set aside in south Phoenix to confine prostitutes to a certain locality within the city. Critics called Block 41 "a scandal and a disgrace," but those in favor of a "reservation" policy pointed out that the prostitutes were kept removed from "respectable" neighborhoods and under "constant" supervision. In September 1910 the opening of Douglass School for black children in the block next to Block 41 forced the city fathers to eliminate houses of ill fame in the neighborhood by invoking a 1903 territorial law that stated they could not be located within four hundred yards of a public building, including schools. The displaced prostitutes moved farther east in south Phoenix to a new location in the vicinity of Sixteenth and Jefferson streets. Black leaders expressed relief that Block 41 would no longer function as the "unofficial" headquarters of prostitution in the city, but as Geoffrey Mawn has noted, "While there appeared to be no direct participating connections to blacks to prostitution, whites certainly considered the neighborhood 'less desirable' and thus opened it to black settlement without notice or protest."[10]

Holidays and other special occasions provided welcome relief for members of the African American community. Especially popular were those times when a national figure visited Phoenix. When Booker T. Washington arrived on September 22, 1911, to participate in "The Great Emancipation Jubilee," he was greeted mainly "by his own people," who escorted him from the Santa Fe depot to Eastlake Park at Sixteenth Street and Jefferson. Following a reception hosted by members of the Second Colored Baptist Church, Washington delivered a speech in which he rejected social equality for African Americans but insisted they receive equal protection under the law. He also stressed to them the importance of work and the dignity of labor:

> Every colored citizen should be made to feel that it is just as honorable, just as dignified to work with his hands in the field, in the shop, in the mine, as it is to preach the gospel, teach school, or write poetry. There is no disgrace to working in the kitchen, in a dining room, in a laundry, provided good service is rendered. The masses of all races live by the labor of their hands, and the Negro can be no exception to the rule. Just in preparation as we learn to dignify good labor in this generation, will we lay a foundation on which to rise and grow in what the world calls the higher and more important things in life, but without the foundation in proper habits and methods of labor it is impossible for any race to rise to a higher degree of efficiency.

Washington delivered several speeches on the same theme during his three-day stay in the city, and all were well received by whites as well as blacks. His moderate views did not threaten whites, and he inspired blacks. Following a special service in his honor at the Second Colored Baptist Church on Sunday morning, he attended a concert at Eastlake Park featuring the music of the Colored Band, the Mexican Band, and the Indian School Band. Shortly after Washington left Phoenix on September 24, local black leaders formed the International Council to foster better understanding between blacks and "all other peoples." Members of the organization hoped "to help develop the resources of Arizona, and to assist in making a greater Phoenix."[11]

African Americans worked hard at being good, constructive citizens. Although most were employed as unskilled workers, there were also several small black-owned businesses. Self-improvement societies continued to blossom. The Colored Literary Society sought "to develop the various interests and talents of its members as well as to stimulate civic pride and righteousness." The Colored Forum, sponsored by the African American churches in the city, wanted "colored citizens" to meet regularly to "discuss religious, moral, educational and civic questions and to seek ways of bettering themselves." Speaking to the Forum in March 1913, a local minister addressing the question of "How to Help the Negro Youth of Phoenix," insisted on "proper example on the part of parents" and the provision of "wholesome amusement."

The Forum, which held meetings every Sunday afternoon in one or another of the "colored churches," hoped "to dissolve what there were of factions among the colored people of the city." Speakers lashed out at lynching and oppression, but they also celebrated gains; it was pointed out, for example, that Elizabeth Harrison, the first "colored person" to graduate from Phoenix Union High School (class of 1913), had "worked nights and mornings to remain in school," and others would do well to follow her path. At the same time, first-class citizenship continued to be denied to African Americans in Phoenix. Segregation and discrimination remained the norm. Race-restrictive covenants, for example, kept African Americans out of select white neighborhoods; in November 1913, a *Republican* ad for "high class" Bella Vista Place on north Central Avenue mentioned "appropriate building and race restrictions." A 1927 deed restriction read:

> No lot or any part thereof within a period of ninety-nine (99) years from the date of the filing for record of the plot of Palmcroft shall ever be sold, transferred or leased to, nor shall any lot or part thereof within said period, be inhabited or occupied by any person not of the White or Caucasian race.[12]

In August 1913 second-class citizenship for blacks as well as other minority groups in Phoenix remained in place when the structure of government changed from a mayor–city council to a city manager–city commission political system with at-large rather than ward elections. The change struck white voters as "progressive," but blacks and other minority group members lost influence, and it proved to them that the term *progressive* was in reality a gross misnomer. Under the new system, south Phoenix would wield even less power than it had in the past. It would take another fifty years before Phoenix instituted a district system that would allow that part of the city any meaningful representation. The 1913 change made white people from north Phoenix more powerful than ever in Phoenix political life.[13]

African American leaders and organizations kept protesting their position in white-dominated Phoenix. For example, nothing aroused the opposition of William P. Crump and other blacks more than the proposal to show the movie *The Nigger* in Phoenix at the Lamara Theater in March 1915. The title alone was "an insult to every law-abiding and self-respecting colored man," Crump declared. Officials in many American cities had prohibited its showing because of its potential as a "riot breeder," if not because of its racial prejudice.

Crump, quoting Booker T. Washington, noted that no matter how many "artistic and historical features" it might have had, the movie's "ultimate result would be to intensify race prejudice and there do great and lasting harm to both races." The city commission, not wanting to "excite race hatred or prejudice," quickly passed an ordinance censoring movies that did, and *The Nigger* was not shown in Phoenix. Perhaps commission members also were influenced by the following letter written to the *Republican* by Frank Smith, a local black:

> There is more race hatred right here in Phoenix to the square inch than in any city I have lived in, and we do not think this picture will make the negro haters feel more kindly toward us. We, however, are doing the best we can, causing but little trouble to the authorities, taking such employment as we can get, and only ask civil treatment and protection from such defamatory photoplays as "The Nigger." [14]

Less than a year later, in March 1916, the city commission banned the showing of *The Birth of a Nation,* another movie opposed by African Americans. This time Ella S. White, president of the Phoenix-based Arizona Federation of Colored Women's Clubs, led the protest. Her organization, in conjunction with the African American churches and other African American associations in Phoenix, petitioned the commission to ban the presentation. As White argued: "We are working for the uplift of our people. Cannot the public sacrifice its desire to view a production for the general good? All we ask is fair play." The "terrible effect of that picture, which is not historically correct, has been demonstrated. It has created prejudice against the colored man."

To support her arguments, she noted the riots, denouncements, and bannings resulting from the impact of the movie elsewhere in the country. She stated that "it means everything to us to keep it out of Phoenix. It does not portray the true character of the colored man, and it is not right that it should be shown." She reminded white Phoenix once again that "we do not ask for social equality—that has never been our aim, but in a time like this we want fair play. We are good citizens, property owners and taxpayers." This time, in the end, the blacks lost. Ignoring the commission's ban order, the public-backed promoters of *The Birth of a Nation* brought it to Phoenix, complete with a thirty-piece orchestra, for a twenty-week run at the Elk's Theater. Finally, on May 9, the film was withdrawn when the theater manager was arrested for continuing to show it and fined fifty dollars.[15]

The Ku Klux Klan played a leading role in *The Birth of a Nation.* It also showed up in the flesh in Phoenix a few years later and posed problems for African Americans and other racial and religious minority groups. The KKK made its presence known in the city in March 1922 when it began, in the name of law and order, a brief reign of terror. KKK pamphlets insisted the organization was only trying to "assist law enforcement," but a number of innocent people were abused. By May 1922 three hundred Phoenicians belonged to the Klan, more than one-third of the state enrollment. Many of them were prominent citizens, including the mayor, members of the city commission, and the publisher of the (Phoenix) *Arizona Gazette.*

Prominent local organizations, such as the Masons, also supported the KKK. In July 1922, for example, when two Klan members were accused of beating Ira Haywood, an African American shoeshine stand operator, for showing disrespect to a white woman, the Masons came to their defense. The *Independent,* a Masonic paper, asserted that by beating Haywood the KKK had detained him from eventually committing an "unspeakable act." The woman's husband had threatened to kill Haywood, but Klan friends had advised him that they would take revenge. According to the *Independent,* here was a case where the Klan had helped to enforce law and order. Instead of blaming KKK members who tried to teach Haywood a lesson, the community should have been grateful. "A killing has been averted, racial disturbance was obviated, a good woman's name preserved untarnished, a dangerous and menacing condition was dissipated," posited the *Independent.* If the Ku Klux Klan "actually did accomplish all this good, then thank God for their courageous and praiseworthy act." The paper concluded that no "true American citizen will oppose what the Ku Klux Klan stands for if they fully understand them." People "should not discredit this 100 percent American organization which comes closer each week to the attainment of that wholly desirable goal, the making of this country a White Man's country for White Men."

While individuals and organizations in favor of the Klan were stating their case, more African Americans were being "taught a lesson" in Phoenix. At about the same time Haywood was beaten, Aubrey Carter, a black elevator operator in the Fleming Building, was undergoing a similar experience. Klansmen alleged that he paid undue attention to a white woman passenger on his elevator and that he had to be punished. The Klan members responsible for Carter's beating left three crimson letters on his chest and gave him a message to deliver: "Report to the police, the sheriff's office and the newspaper, and let them know that the Ku Klux Klan has been active." A local black newspaper, the *Phoenix Tribune,* and several black leaders protested the activities of the local KKK and condemned its prejudices, but little was done to eradicate the organization, which continued to parade openly in the streets of the city.

As in the rest of the country, the Phoenix Klan did not discriminate only against blacks. In Phoenix, spokesmen for the organization made "foul-mouthed attacks on Catholics, Jews, Mormons and Negroes." Dr. H. A. Hughes, a Phoenician and editor of the KKK newspaper, *The Crank,* asked citizens to consider the opposition:

> Every criminal, every gambler, every thug, every libertine, every girl-ruiner, every home-wrecker, every wife-beater, every dope peddler, every moonshiner, every crooked politician, every pagan papal priest, every shyster, every K. of C., every white slaver, every brothel madam, every Roman controlled newspaper is fighting against the Ku Klux Klan. THINK IT OVER. WHICH SIDE ARE YOU ON? GET OFF THE FENCE!

In time, most Phoenicians and Arizonans lost interest in the Klan. In the elections of 1924, Klan candidates lost at all levels. After the defeats, the KKK faded into the background for a time in the city and the state, but it would rise again in another era.[16]

Although the Ku Klux Klan failed to achieve its goals, African Americans still suffered in many ways from second-class citizenship. During World War I, for example, a number of African Americans joined or were drafted into the armed forces. They received warm farewells from the African American community and served well, only to come home to second-class citizenship. They were allowed their place in the victory parade but were encouraged to celebrate "with their own people" at Eastlake Park. African Americans at home during the war joined Liberty Bond drives, formed a chapter of the Colored Red Cross, and supported the war effort in many other ways. At the same time, their leaders called for more justice for African Americans after the war. They contrasted the war efforts of African Americans with lynchings and oppression in the United States.

William P. Crump and other community stalwarts emphasized the need for better schooling for young blacks to help them progress in life. "The Negroes do not seek social equality, but they do ask to be treated more like other citizens, legally and civilly." He noted that "inferior education hurts everybody," and his plea was that "poor education tended to drive blacks out of school before they had acquired the basic rudiments of education." He asked that "white citizens open their eyes to the great advantages which will follow the complete education of the colored children of this state and every other state, and instead of having a population which is lacking in education and love of country, produce instead a race which has been taught to love and respect the government under which it is living." [17]

In 1926 the state's only segregated high school opened in Phoenix. How the Phoenix Union Colored High School came about further mirrors the situation of African Americans in the city. Unlike other racial minority groups, African Americans had to live with an official policy of racial segregation in the Phoenix school system. The state constitution, reflecting a Southern influence, was created by men who wanted segregated schools. "I won't send my children to school with niggers," declared former Texan B. B. Moeur, chairman of the committee on education at the state constitutional convention in 1910. A future governor of Arizona, he reflected the attitude of most Arizonans.

In turn, Arizona law from the time of statehood required "children of African descent" to attend separate elementary schools. In very small schools "a screen around the desk of a Negro child" was ruled to be separation in terms of the law. Arizona law stated that once a high school had an enrollment of twenty-five students of African descent, a district could vote to establish "a separate Negro high school." Although the high schools for blacks and whites were to be separate, the law required that they be equal, in that "provisions in the Negro school should always be the same as those in the white school." A black critic later found it "amusing to contemplate that anyone could ever believe that conditions can be provided for twenty-five children that are equal to the facilities provided for several hundred children in another plant." He noted, however, that "the people who made such laws in Arizona had come from states with experience in piously making such meaningless statements into laws affecting Negroes."

In Phoenix, citizens voted to establish Arizona's first segregated high school. Successive classes, under the direction of the "colored department," moved from the "colored room" to the "colored cottage" on the Phoenix Union High School campus, and then to rented quarters in

1925 and finally to a campus of their own in 1926, located at 415 East Grant Street. White pressure, particularly from "some prominent Phoenix people who came from the South" and "objected strongly to Negro children attending classes with their children," helped create Phoenix Union Colored High School, but the unfortunate circumstances of blacks in the city also contributed. From the time of the "colored room," school segregation in Phoenix proved to be a humiliating and limiting experience for African Americans. What little protest existed failed to put black students back into classes with whites. It was "a 'David and Goliath' contest," asserted African American educator W. A. Robinson; thus "the prospect of a school of their own such as they had known back in Oklahoma or Texas, where they came from, seemed to Negroes to be the height of reason and good fortune."[18]

Segregated from the white community in restaurants, theaters, hospitals, hotels, swimming pools, buses, and other public places, African Americans were left out of the larger, racist white society of Phoenix. At the same time, they continued to develop their own community. Black businesses, from barber shops to hotels, continued to serve the black population; by 1925 there existed two black-owned hotels, the St. Louis Hotel at Sixth and Jefferson streets and the Rice Hotel at Fifth and Jefferson streets. Eastlake Park served black residents; black neighborhood elementary schools served black students; and after 1926 the new Phoenix Union Colored High School provided secondary education.

Health facilities also emerged in the African American neighborhoods, since Phoenix hospitals remained closed to blacks. To provide medical services, Dr. Winston C. Hackett and his wife, Myrtle, opened Booker T. Washington Hospital at Jefferson and Fourteenth streets in 1921. The small hospital, with the help of black support organizations, kept expanding to meet the demand for care; in 1927 the *Republican* happily called it "the finest and most completely equipped hospital owned and devoted to the welfare of colored people west of the Mississippi." Legal aid was available from a few lawyers, including William Watkins, who became the first "colored lawyer" in Arizona when he arrived in 1921. The churches remained centers of vitality in African American Phoenix, particularly the Tanner Chapel African Methodist Episcopal Church and the First Colored Baptist Church (its name changed from Second Colored Baptist Church in 1927), but other groups, ranging from fraternal orders to branches of the National Negro Business League, the National Association for the Advancement of Colored People, and the National Urban League, served the black population.

Because many African American groups, such as the black YMCA, the black YWCA, the black Boy Scouts, the black Campfire Girls, the black American Legion, the black Veterans of Foreign Wars, the black Elks, and the black Masons, had few adequate facilities of their own, they supported the Phoenix chapter of the Arizona Federation of Colored Women's Clubs in their fund drive to build the Phyliss Wheatley Community Center. It opened in March 1927 at Jefferson and Fourteenth streets.[19]

Community leaders were aware of the national scene and knew what their counterparts were doing elsewhere in the country. At J. W. Snell's restaurant at 27 South Second Street, they bought the *Chicago Defender, Dallas Express, New York Age,* the *Crisis,* and other African American newspapers and journals. For a few years the *Phoenix Tribune,* a black newspaper published from 1918 to 1925, helped keep them informed. Editor Arthur Randolph Smith demanded better schools for blacks; he fought, for example, against locating the Phoenix Union Colored High School in the factory and warehouse district. He urged the black population to vote for political candidates who would help it progress. He applauded Phoenix African American leaders like Crump, George Caldwell, James A. Green, W. C. Hackett, M. H. Shelton, and others who were active in the political, economic, and cultural life of the community. He called for the establishment of more black businesses that would provide better jobs for blacks than the usual ones of janitor and maid.

The African American community needed more business and professional services; in the meantime, Smith advised, "do business with merchants who invite our trade." The editor appreciated the aims of the Phoenix branch of the National Negro Business League because it emphasized "race solidarity, race pride, and race loyalty." The prime object of the League, he declared, "is to bring about a closer relationship among the business and professional men of our group, and cement them into one common mass of friends and brothers." Smith also praised the African American women of Phoenix who organized and supported the many voluntary associations in the city devoted to community social and cultural development.

African Americans kept migrating to Phoenix. How many of them read the booster organization brochures describing Phoenix as the "city where diligence and industry will bring you the best of the worldly goods" is unknown, but the majority who came from Oklahoma, Texas, Arkansas, Louisiana, and other Southern states looked upon Arizona and Phoenix as places "holding more opportunities for their social and economic betterment." Many of them improved their economic position, participated in local politics, and joined social and cultural organizations. Despite the obstacles confronting them, they actively sought to better themselves and their community. That some of them were disappointed is a matter of record, but it could have been worse. As one black who came to Arizona in 1916 after stays in Georgia and Oklahoma later observed, "At least they didn't lynch you here, like they did back there."[20]

Nevertheless, exclusion took its toll in the African American community, especially on the children. For example, the first Children's Free Picnic, sponsored by the *Republican* in July 1921, drew thousands of Salt River valley youngsters to Riverside Park, but black children were refused admittance. "Humiliated to find that they could not be admitted to the park," the *Tribune* asserted, they would stay away from the annual picnic. In August 1925 the *Republican* announced that a separate party would be held for black children at Eastlake Park. "*The Republican* has long recognized that some form of entertainment should be given to the colored children of the city and valley as well as to the white children and it was decided that this entertainment should take the form of a picnic with all the trimmings which generally accompany the annual kiddies frolic held each year at Riverside Park for the children. Arrangements have been completed for the use of Eastlake Park by *The Republican*." The newspaper reported on August 18 that "with faces wreathed in smiles that wouldn't come off, and in their best 'bibs and tuckers,' over 500 colored boys and girls . . . assembled at Eastlake Park . . . to participate in the First *Arizona Republican's* Colored Children's picnic and frolic."[21]

African Americans continued to sponsor their own celebrations during the 1920s and 1930s. Various festivals and colorful carnivals drew large crowds. In November 1928, for example, Troop 17 of the Boy Scouts of America, William F. Blake Post of the American Legion, and the Knights and Daughters of Tabor held a carnival at Eastlake Park that lasted for five days and nights. The carnival raised money for the scout band, the American Legion post community fund, and for a convention of the Grand Lodge of the Knights and Daughters of Tabor to be held in Phoenix the following year. Phoenix members of the Grand Lodge of Tabor, the "strongest lodge in the west for colored people," hoped to draw at least one thousand delegates to the city.

Emancipation Day, or "Juneteenth," an annual holiday gathering in June, was especially popular. Supported by African American churches and voluntary associations in the city, it featured parades, speeches, food, and music to commemorate the day in 1865 (June 19) when General

Gordon Granger landed with the first Union soldiers at Galveston and announced that all the slaves in Texas were free. Although the Emancipation Proclamation, issued in September 1862 by President Abraham Lincoln, had become effective on January 1, 1863, word did not reach the slaves in the Southwest until Granger arrived in Texas in June 1865. The celebration in Texas caught on, and over the years, it spread throughout the Southwest, including Arizona. In June 1921, for example, more than five hundred African Americans turned up at Eastlake Park to celebrate.[22]

8 DEPRESSION, WAR, AND PEACE, 1930–1960

For many African Americans, the years of the Great Depression brought more hardship. They had more than tripled in population from 1920 to 1940, but most of the newcomers were of low economic status. Denied adequate educational and job opportunities, they were forced to endure a lower standard of living than most whites. Marginal black men, employed mostly as unskilled service workers downtown or as common laborers or farm help, along with black women, usually employed as domestic workers, faced rising unemployment in the 1930s. By 1940 it was established that "the average black family in Phoenix was living under crowded conditions in a poorly furnished home." In that year federal census workers canvassed the neighborhoods in which blacks lived and found "only a few modern homes, and many wooden shacks, trailers, tents, sheds, and abandoned stores." They reported "most homes are one to four room structures without benefit of running water or sewage."[1]

As in the past, many white Phoenicians in the 1920s and 1930s looked upon African American neighborhoods as "notorious dark-towns." Some blacks, like members of other groups, engaged in illegal activities; drugs, alcohol, gambling, and prostitution were all part of the irregular economy in the city. The Phoenix police and press reports noted black participation, but also pointed out that it constituted only part of the problem. At the same time, as in many other cities, much of the more publicized illicit trade was conducted in the poorer minority neighborhoods. The African American majority disapproved the presence of "undesirable elements" in their neighborhoods and did what they could to discourage them. At a mass meeting at the Tanner Chapel African Methodist Episcopal Church in 1930, spokesmen declared that "colored people are for law and order" and called for police action to rid the neighborhood of criminals, but the Phoenix police offered little cooperation. Without official help, scant progress occurred.

To add to the plight of Phoenix blacks, poor blacks from throughout Arizona moved to the city during the early 1930s in search of relief. Many of them lived under the Central Avenue bridge, along the bed of the Salt River. Their "abodes consisted of hastily thrown up cardboard shacks, lean-to's and anything that would help protect them from the elements," noted an observer. The arrival of more poor children increased the burden on Douglass, Dunbar, and Booker T. Washington elementary schools for blacks and on Phoenix Union Colored High School. White-dominated relief agencies in Phoenix offered little or no help early in the decade, and so the black community utilized their own organizations to combat the situation. In 1931 the Phoenix Protective League, headed by Sidney Scott, H. D. Simpson, James L. Davis, and other African American leaders, collected and distributed food and clothing to unemployed blacks; it also tried to find jobs for them. The Phoenix branch of the National Urban League and the local chapter of the National Association for the Advancement of Colored People also provided relief to the "colored needy."

The black Masons, the black Elks, and members of other black fraternal lodges made an effort to take care of their own jobless members and their friends. All of these organizations demanded and succeeded in getting an "all Negro Division" of the Phoenix Community Chest during the 1930s, and they also welcomed the arrival of federal funds and programs designed to help all Phoenicians in need of aid. Black voters, like the majority of white voters, were grateful, and throughout the decade they supported Franklin D. Roosevelt and his New Deal.[2]

In 1940, African Americans continued to make up about 5 percent of the total Phoenix population; in that year they numbered 4,263, up from 2,366 in 1930 and 1,075 in 1920. Most of them resided south of Washington Street and north of Buckeye Road, from Central Avenue to Sixteenth Street. Other African Americans lived in a poorer neighborhood located between Seventh and Seventeenth avenues, from Madison Street to the south side of Buckeye Road (see Map 8.1). Segregated housing for blacks was strongly supported in Phoenix by white institutions. Banks and other lending agencies refused to give mortgages to blacks on homes in white areas, while the building and real estate industries would not

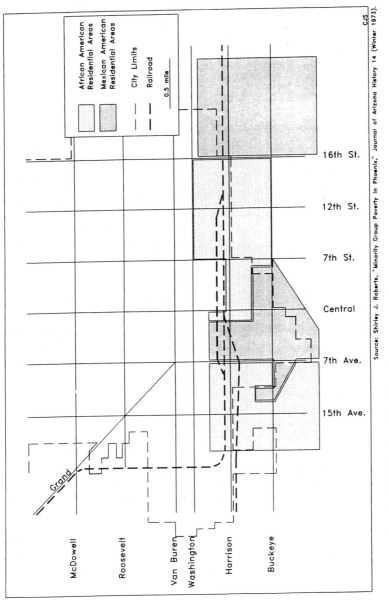

MAP 8.1 Minority Neighborhoods in Phoenix, 1940

Legend:
- African American Residential Areas
- Mexican American Residential Areas
- City Limits
- Railroad
- 0.5 mile

16th St.
12th St.
7th St.
Central
7th Ave.
15th Ave.

McDowell
Roosevelt
Van Buren
Washington
Harrison
Buckeye
Grand

Source: Shirley J. Roberts, "Minority Group Poverty in Phoenix," Journal of Arizona History 14 (Winter 1973).

CJS

sell homes to blacks in white neighborhoods. Firms vied with each other in offering for sale property with the most rigid race restrictions in Phoenix.[3]

Living conditions for many African Americans in south Phoenix during the 1930s proved to be as depressing as any in the nation. Father Emmett McLoughlin, a Catholic priest from California assigned to Phoenix in 1934, was appalled by what he observed. One poor area inhabited by African Americans, located between the warehouse district and the city dump in southwest Phoenix, was, according to Father McLoughlin, "permeated with the odors of a fertilizer plant, an iron foundry, a thousand open privies, and the city sewage disposal plant." According to the clergyman: "Its dwellings for the most part were shacks, many without electricity, most without plumbing and heat. They were built of tin cans, cardboard boxes, and wooden crates picked up by the railroad tracks."[4]

Father McLoughlin's vivid descriptions of the horrid physical conditions in southwest Phoenix, inside and outside the city limits, left little to the imagination. He was sensitive to the health as well as the housing problems existing in the area. "In these shacks," McLoughlin asserted, "babies were born without medical care; they often died because of the extreme temperatures (up to 118 degrees) in the summer or froze to death in winter." Conditions in "southwest Phoenix helped Arizona attain the highest infant death rate in the nation," and "officials of the United States government awarded it the distinction of being the worst slum area in the United States." To a social worker the neighborhood was "a cesspool of poverty and disease, of syphilis, of gonorrhea, of grotesquely deformed venereal babies, of blindness arising from contamination in the birth canal, of women being delivered in one-room shacks by untrained midwives and neighbors, while their children looked on."[5]

A spirited Irishman, Father McLoughlin had never before in his life observed such tragic scenes as he did in the capital of Arizona. In the course of his duties at St. Mary's Church, the young priest was called into a black neighborhood in southwest Phoenix to minister to a boy dying of tuberculosis. The more he became acquainted with the dismal living conditions of the black poor in the area, the more determined he became to do something about them.[6]

Shocked by life in the poorer neighborhoods of south Phoenix, the priest viewed them as "an opportunity and a challenge." With funds he acquired from "dinners, bazaars, barbecues, gambling, panhandling, and begging," in 1936 he bought an abandoned grocery store building located in one of the most depressed black neighborhoods and remodeled it into a church and social hall. Called St. Monica's Community Center, it was located at Seventh Avenue and Sherman Street. White Catholics in Phoenix contributed well, McLoughlin noted, but he felt many of them only "wished a separate Negro church lest they might have to worship together before a common alter." Some of them advised McLoughlin to stay out of "Nigger-town." He recalled the opposition from priests, nuns, and laity when he had "tried to gain acceptance of Negroes in the Knights of Columbus, parish societies, the parochial school (where only a token few were taken), and the Catholic school of nursing."[7]

The social hall fared better than the church, especially after Father McLoughlin installed a jukebox. It "packed the social hall more effectively than the Pied Piper of Hamlin. Many youngsters played and danced till they were too tired to fight or steal or molest. Juvenile delinquency dropped." Health problems especially interested the priest, and when the owner of an adjoining barber shop donated his property in 1937, McLoughlin remodeled it into a maternity clinic, the first in Arizona. Free care was administered by volunteer doctors and nurses, many of them from St. Joseph's Hospital. Other free clinics followed, including a venereal disease clinic, another first for Arizona. It became necessary because "too many babies had gonorrhea of the eyes, or congenital deformity due to syphilis."[8]

St. Monica's Community Center, also known as Father Emmett's Mission, became an institution in south Phoenix. Despite his critics, including some black religious leaders who felt he was competing with them, the white priest continued to pursue his goals. "I had to humiliate myself, to beg, to accept insults, to wait in offices, to explain the needs of the poor, to be brushed off like an unwanted salesman and to persist for the sake of my people till I was tossed the crumbs that would send me on my way." In the process he won the admiration of black leaders, and he expanded his operation in many positive directions, from playgrounds to housing projects.[9]

Federal funds and programs played a crucial role in the improvement of housing conditions in south Phoenix. In 1938, Father McLoughlin began emphasizing in public the large number of substandard dwellings in the area. Time and again he called for New Deal programs to change the situation. With the aid of *Gazette* reporter Bob Macon, who ran headline stories with photographs, the priest further documented his case by taking motion pictures of "the leaning shacks, 'one-holers,' and congested fire-traps. One of them was actually a horse stable on a fifty-foot lot, which had been converted into one-room shelters housing twenty families—of people, not horses—at $20 per month per family." The priest "showed the pictures to and pleaded with Catholics, Baptists, Methodists, Presbyterians, Orthodox and unorthodox Jews, Kiwanians, Rotarians, Lions, the PTA, the YMCA, the YWCA, and the man on the street."[10]

When state legislators met in Phoenix in January 1939, Father McLoughlin and his supporters lobbied hard to convince them to approve public housing under the United States Housing Act of 1937. The priest had managed to be appointed a chaplain at the session, and he quickly violated the nonpolitical nature of his appointment by arguing public housing with representatives from every part of the state. At the end of the session, the legislators finally passed the enabling law that allowed federal funds for the eradication of slums in Arizona.[11]

The Phoenix City Commission soon appointed a housing authority and named Father McLoughlin as chairman. As chairman of the Phoenix Housing Authority, he realized that "the fight had just started." Three sites, all located in decaying areas, were chosen for housing projects, but according to Father Emmett, "The cries that rose to the city commission would have led bystanders to believe that we were about to tear down the country club." The property owners led the protest, but the Phoenix Housing Authority backed the priest and the sites were approved.

Condemnation of the properties followed, and the odious shacks were demolished. After receiving a grant of $1.9 million from the federal government, Phoenix officials ordered the construction of three housing tracts, and homes for six hundred low-income families were completed in 1941. Built without graft, the projects had construction costs that turned out to be the lowest in the nation; rents were as little as ten dollars per month. The developments were the Marcos de Niza Project for Mexicans and the Matthew Henson Project for blacks, both located in south Phoenix, and the Frank Luke, Jr. Project for Anglos, located in east Phoenix. These projects proved popular and quickly filled with residents. Thus some progress was made on the housing front largely as a result of New Deal programs and the persistent leadership of "the people's padre," Father Emmett McLoughlin.[12]

Father Emmett also became the driving force behind the construction of St. Monica's Hospital, a new hospital to serve south Phoenix. In the early 1940s the influx of military personnel and defense workers strained health care facilities in the valley, and the poor minorities often were the last to receive medical treatment. At the same time that Father Emmett was contemplating a hospital for the south side, military authorities were complaining of the high rate of venereal disease among post personnel. Air field commanders blamed "the promiscuous women of Phoenix" for the outbreak of syphilis among the flyers, while angry Phoenix officials claimed that the "lecherous" flyers and soldiers stationed in the area were "contaminating the purity of Phoenix womanhood."

Father McLoughlin discussed the matter with the commander of Luke Field, who recommended that the federal government, under the Lanham Act, approve and fund a new hospital "on condition that the proposed bed capacity be doubled and that half the beds be reserved for the treatment of the female syphilitics of Phoenix." The priest quickly agreed, and in August 1942, President Roosevelt approved the hospital and the financial appropriation needed for its construction. Fund-raising events and personal donations allowed Father McLoughlin to purchase a hospital site in a "slum area" one mile south of the railroad tracks at Seventh Avenue and Buckeye Road, but the material demands of World War II delayed the completion of the project.

Senators Carl Hayden and Ernest McFarland exerted pressure in Washington, and it helped. Finally, in February 1944 the 230-bed nonsectarian St. Monica's Hospital opened, and it reflected Father Emmett's influence. The first integrated hospital in Phoenix, it soon introduced the first interracial nurses' training program west of the Mississippi River. Father Emmett had once asked St. Joseph's Hospital nurses' training school officials to accept a black student, but they refused. Eleanor Roosevelt visited Father Emmett at St. Monica's Hospital in 1946 and later wrote that she was "particularly interested in the training school for nurses. Here they have eliminated all discrimination of race and color. They all study and work together. The hospital has a wonderful atmosphere."

A clinic for poor schoolchildren, under the direction of Father Emmett's friend Dr. Trevor Brown, also opened in 1946. Father Emmett, often at odds with the hierarchy of the Catholic Church, resigned from the priesthood in 1948 but continued to work for the betterment of south Phoenix. The neighborhoods of that section of the urban center benefited greatly as St. Monica's, a haven "for all races," evolved into Phoenix Memorial Hospital by 1951, and during the following decade its reputation as "the hospital with a heart" increased.[13]

Rather than leave Phoenix and his beloved hospital, Father McLoughlin resigned from the priesthood when his religious superiors notified him that he was to be transferred. He remained head of Memorial Hospital until his death in 1970. His autobiography, *People's Padre*, published in

1954, received mixed reviews; in it he accused the Catholic Church of not understanding his mission in Phoenix. Admiring Phoenicians, however, understood. As one observer declared at the time, "It is not so much that Emmett has helped minority groups; the truth is, he has simply refused to recognize any group at all, except the one family of humanity." Emmett McLoughlin's greatest accomplishments were in housing and health, and by 1950 he was widely known as the "Guardian of the Southside of Phoenix." His work on behalf of Phoenix African Americans was especially appreciated. The *Arizona Sun,* a black newspaper, declared in 1950 that "he always will be remembered by thousands of Phoenicians." He "more than any other person is responsible for better living conditions for the poor and underprivileged in our community." At a civil rights rally in 1963, African American leader Lincoln Ragsdale called him "the man who has done more to further equal opportunity than anyone else in Phoenix." The *Arizona Republic,* upon McLoughlin's death in 1970, stated that he "worked endlessly to improve the health and living conditions of the poor." Mary Bennett, a co-worker at Memorial Hospital and a good friend, added, "Emmett was doing things for the Inner City long before it came into vogue." [14]

During the 1930s and 1940s, medical care for African Americans and others in Phoenix was also provided at the Colored Child Welfare Clinic, run by Dr. J. A. Merriman at 224 East Jefferson Street, and the Booker T. Washington Hospital, owned by Dr. Winston C. Hackett and located at Jefferson and Fourteenth streets. After going blind in 1943, however, Dr. Hackett converted his hospital into the Winston Inn, which housed and fed hundreds of World War II black soldiers; he died in 1949. [15]

During World War II, African Americans served valiantly in the armed forces. On the home front, military posts and defense plants eventually hired blacks, and they were able to benefit from better wages and working conditions. A protest march in Washington, D.C., in 1941 inspired President Roosevelt to issue Executive Order 8802, which inserted a non-discrimination clause into government defense contracts. As a result, more jobs became available to African Americans, and they came out of World War II determined to achieve first-class citizenship. Having fought a war to defeat racism, they felt that it was time the United States and Arizona recognize their rights. Official and unofficial discrimination and segregation policies had continued to prevail in almost every aspect of life during World War II, and African Americans found their task would not be an easy one.

Intense and unstable times brought problems as well as progress to

Phoenix during and after the war. Explosive situations on occasion led to violence. For example, off-duty black soldiers from the 364th Infantry Regiment stationed at Papago Park frequented the Phoenix "colored neighborhood." On the night of November 26, 1942, in a cafe at Thirteenth Street and Washington, one of them struck a black female over the head with a bottle following an argument. A black military policeman tried to arrest the soldier, but he resisted with a knife. When the military policeman shot and wounded the soldier, black servicemen protested.

Many of them had been drinking, and they were difficult to control. Military policemen soon assembled about 150 of the soldiers at Seventeenth Street and Washington to return them to Papago Park. Buses were brought in, but before the soldiers could be transported back to camp, they became excited and broke ranks when a jeep full of armed blacks appeared. A "lone shot from somewhere" was fired, according to accounts; the source of the shot was never determined, but it ignited a riot. "This does it," an observer declared, "now all hell will pop." Soldiers scattered widely as pistols, rifles, and machine guns suddenly "snapped and barked." There began a "hunt for all who might be involved."

All available law enforcement officers joined the military police, and twenty-eight blocks were cordoned off and searched. A number of hunted soldiers hid in the homes of friends in the area. To flush them out, the military police utilized armored personnel carriers. As another observer later recalled, "They'd roll up in front of these homes and with the loudspeaker they had on these vehicles, they'd call on him to surrender. If he didn't come out, they'd start potting the house with these fifty-caliber machine guns that just made a hole you could stick your fist through." Before the episode ended, three men died and eleven were wounded. Most of the 180 men arrested and jailed were soon released, but some of those who bore arms during the conflict were eventually court-martialed and sent to military prisons. The episode did little to improve community-military or white-black relations in Phoenix.[16]

Following World War II, African Americans began making gains. African American veterans, like others, benefited from the G.I. Bill and other postwar opportunities. Winston Hackett, Wade Hammond, Augustus Shaw, Lincoln Ragsdale, and other black leaders joined with Father McLoughlin and other white supporters to reorganize the Phoenix Urban League in 1945. The League grew increasingly concerned with racial discrimination in employment, housing, and education, as did the local branch of the National Association for the Advancement of Colored People. The Phoenix NAACP, under the leadership of James L. Davis, who served as president for several years, boasted a membership of more than six hundred when it celebrated its twenty-sixth anniversary in Phoenix in January 1947. The Urban League, the NAACP, and other groups worked hard to facilitate change, but it was always a struggle.

While the Urban League and the NAACP often led the way, some groups proved to be more aggressive. In May 1946, for example, members of the Communist Party of America showed up at Woolworth's downtown store to stage a protest. A spokesman noted that "Woolworth's does not allow Negroes at its food counter and does not have any Negro clerks." The placards carried by the demonstrators, an observer declared, "point out the fact that Negroes fought in a recent war for democracy but were denied democracy in their own country."

On Independence Day 1946, at a public meeting at Eastlake Park, the local NAACP chapter called for civil rights laws in Arizona. In a resolution the organization went on record "as protesting the un-American, undemocratic, pro-Fascist actions of the Woolworth store in its policy of not serving meals to Negroes at their lunch counters, notwithstanding they will serve them at the merchandise counters." In another incident a few months later, the Urban League protested a sign reading "This Entrance for Colored," which was posted in a small downtown restaurant. The manager of the establishment claimed he "meant no harm by displaying the sign." He stated, "It was only to inform colored people that they could come inside and eat, since the custom had been to feed them standing up on the outside for many years." [17]

Many black leaders, members of the small black middle class, may not have suffered the worst consequences of discrimination, segregation, and poverty, but they could not avoid being touched by it if they had spent time in Phoenix. Ragsdale, stationed there at the end of World War II, later recalled that "Phoenix was just like Mississippi. People were just as bigoted. They had segregation. They had signs in many places, 'Mexicans and Negroes not welcome.'" [18]

In the 1940s conditions for blacks in Phoenix were generally deplorable. Most black families lived on low incomes in segregated neighborhoods in substandard homes. The majority of black families rented, and more than 50 percent of them resided in dwellings without running water or bathrooms. Unsanitary shacks and inadequate diets caused serious health problems. Except for educational attainment, blacks occupied the bottom ranks in crucial categories; they outlasted Mexicans in school, but they continued to drop out early. Black boys went to work as laborers, while black girls left school to marry or help take care of the family while their mothers worked; others labored as domestics. Blacks were excluded from white unions until the 1950s, and then only a few were allowed entry.

Black children were constantly reminded of their separate status. In July 1941, for example, the *Republic* announced its twenty-fourth annual "Kiddies Picnic." It stated that "Riverside Park will be turned over completely to the white kiddies of Arizona Monday afternoon. On Tuesday the colored children will gather for frolic at Eastlake Park while the Mexican kiddies will have their picnic Wednesday at the same park." Local adults endured the same treatment; for example, big bands always played several nights a week at the Riverside Ballroom: one night for whites, one night for Mexicans, one night for blacks. Even black soldiers stationed in Phoenix during the war received the message. When a labor shortage threatened the 1942 Salt River valley cotton crop, a local grower suggested they pick it. They were, he said, "raised in the cotton fields down South. They know how to pick cotton, like to do it and would rather be in the sunny fields of Arizona than on guard duty." As it turned out, prisoners from the German POW camp at Papago Park helped valley agriculturists save the cotton crop.

With segregation a barrier to equality in Phoenix, the black community continued to develop its own range of attractions and services. Segregated in local theaters, many blacks preferred the "all colored casts" in the films offered occasionally at the Ramona and Westside theaters. Radio station KPHO presented black programs, usually featuring popular Phoenix musician and disc jockey Curtis Gray. The Miss Bronze Arizona pageant and other beauty contests drew large crowds. Zeta Phi Beta and other black sororities awarded "outstanding women" of the community awards. A number of black fraternities sponsored social gatherings, cultural presentations, and charitable events. When prominent black leaders came to Phoenix, they received a warm reception. In September 1946, for instance, when NAACP national leader Roy Wilkins visited Phoenix, he was a guest in the home of local educator Roy Lee and his family and enjoyed an evening of entertainment hosted by Dr. and Mrs. Lowell C. Wormley at the Phyliss Wheatley Community Center. Internationally known blacks also visited Phoenix, including Dr. Percy L. Julian, the world-renowned chemist, who wintered in south Phoenix. In 1950 a school in south Phoenix was named after him. Dr. Curtis O. Greenfield, principal of Julian School for twenty-eight years, later recalled the effort and excellence legendary teachers such as Letha Slaughter, Nannie Owens, and Gertrude Vaughn put into their work.

Black leaders and groups worked hard to improve black community institutions. During World War II the black Phoenix Civic Welfare League, led by John D. Washington, emphasized betterment, especially for soldiers and veterans. It helped form the Negro Soldiers Center on East Washington, an establishment designed to serve black military personnel. Following the war, the Tildon White American Legion Post No. 40 called for patriotism and the integration of the Arizona National Guard. The black Elks, William H. Patterson Lodge, 477, proudly celebrated a "beautiful new $70,000 building" on East Washington, completed in September 1946; both the Elks and the Prince Hall Masonic Lodge remained popular. Moments of accomplishment were appreciated and reported on by the *Arizona Sun,* the only black newspaper in the city, edited by D. F. Benson. Wade Hammond and other black leaders finished remodeling the Phyliss Wheatley Community Center on East Jefferson after the war. Hammond, a retired serviceman and an organizer of the black Arizona Voters' League, often took it upon himself to speak to white leaders about the Phoenix black community; in return, local influentials occasionally offered political appointments and job opportunities to him and other blacks. The Arizona Voters' League, declared the *Sun,* would not "sponsor candidates who practice buying Negro voters with a slice of watermelon and red soda-pops."[19]

At all social levels, however, African Americans suffered from racist policies. Prominent white lawyer and civil rights activist William P. Mahoney, Jr., recalled that in 1947 Dorothy Maynor, a famous black singer and friend of his family, was staying with him and his wife. Before taking Maynor out to dinner, he did "a little checking" and to his dismay found that all the "best" restaurants he called in Phoenix refused to serve his black guest. Infuriated, he called Dr. Fred Holmes, a Phoenix surgeon and acknowledged white supporter of black causes. Holmes recommended Cudia's, a "fine place" owned by Salvatore P. D. Cudia, actor, artist, and promoter of Cudia City. Located near Fortieth Street and Camelback, Cudia City resembled a miniature Western town and served as a movie and television show set. A flamboyant personality, Salvatore Cudia was his own man and told Mahoney when he called his restaurant, "Mahoney, no Ku Klux Klan son-of-a-bitch is going to tell me who I can or cannot serve. Come on out." Mahoney and his black guest went out and "had this delightful dinner featured right in the middle of the dining room."[20]

Mahoney and Holmes became good friends and worked to eliminate racism in Phoenix and Arizona. Holmes invited Louis Wirth, a nationally known sociologist from the University of Chicago, to come to Phoenix and address interested persons on the subject of racism. Several hundred people attended Professor Wirth's lecture on "the terrible injustices that had been done, and were still being done to the black people." According to Mahoney, his words "inspired us all to really go to work." In 1947, Mahoney and others organized the middle-class, multiracial Greater Phoenix Council for Civic Unity and hired a student of Wirth's, John Lassoe, to direct it; within a year it had a membership of four to five hundred. A similar organization formed in Tucson, and soon the Arizona Council for Civic Unity emerged, a union of the two urban groups dedicated to fighting Jim Crowism in the state.[21]

Jim Crowism flourished in Phoenix. Theaters, restaurants, hotels, and other places of public accommodation separated blacks from other patrons, but segregation was official only in the public schools. Black elementary schools and a black high school continued to exist by law in the city. In 1942, Phoenix Union Colored High School became George Washington Carver High School. When W. A. Robinson became principal in 1945, he found the conditions appalling. Twenty years after it opened, he declared, the high school still had "no library, no music equipment, no modern home economics, no shop equipment, no art equipment." Robinson found that "the only athletic equipment in the school consisted of some worn-out parts of football and basketball uniforms marked with the names of other schools in the system."[22]

In the next several years under Robinson's leadership, the school made remarkable strides. He emphasized black accomplishment and pride. Improvements in facilities and faculty brought the institution, according to Robinson, "up somewhere near the legal requirement that a segregated Negro high school be as good as the segregated white schools." Although in many ways it provided "a separate but unequal education," the teachers were capable, committed, and dedicated. Many Carver graduates became constructive citizens, and some made notable contributions. Carver also became an African American community center, with its auditorium offering a variety of programs and presentations. The school also conducted a night school for adults, and its athletic teams proved to be among the best in the state. The 450-student school, however, proved costly to operate.[23]

For several years in Arizona, a growing protest had been developing against school segregation. The Arizona Council for Civic Unity, the NAACP, the Urban League, and other state and local organizations effectively lobbied the legislature in 1951 and secured a law giving local school boards the option of voluntary desegregation. Arizona's first two African American legislators, Hayzel B. Daniels and Carl Sims, both representing predominantly African American Phoenix neighborhoods, "worked their hearts out" to help enlist the aid of white colleagues to rid the state of mandatory segregation. William P. Mahoney, Jr., and other Phoenix liberals pressured influential legislators to obtain passage of the law. Tucson and several smaller communities soon desegregated their schools, but Phoenix balked.

In 1952, lawyers Mahoney and Herb Finn, both white, and Hayzel B. Daniels, a black, filed suit on behalf of three black children seeking admission to Phoenix Union High School, naming its governing board members as defendants. Basing their arguments on recent California cases, which held that the segregation of pupils for ethnic reasons at the discretion of school boards was an unconstitutional delegation of legislative power, the lawyers won. They succeeded by getting a law declared unconstitutional that they had urged the legislature to pass. After hearing the case, Superior Court Judge Frederic C. Struckmeyer, Jr., ruled in 1953 that such segregation laws were invalid; the segregation laws of Arizona were an unconstitutional delegation of powers by the legislature to subordinate bodies. And, he added, "A half century of intolerance is enough." Anticipating that the Supreme Court would ban segregation in the nation's schools, the Phoenix Union High School District board members voted to abide by the court ruling. Daniels and Finn also filed suit in 1953 against Wilson Elementary School District in Phoenix, and Judge Charles E. Bernstein ruled that segregation in elementary schools was unconstitutional. Wilson School board members also accepted the court's ruling. The Phoenix decisions were rendered before the United States Supreme Court delivered its famous ruling regarding the desegregation of America's schools in the *Brown v. the Board of Education of Topeka* case in 1954. In that case, the Arizona experience was taken into consideration.

The costly George Washington Carver High School soon closed its doors, and its students were instructed to attend the high schools in their residential zones, namely Phoenix Union and South Mountain. Phoenix elementary school districts also required all students, regardless of race, to attend schools in their respective neighborhoods. Because of economic and residential patterns in Phoenix, racial integration was not achieved; minority students usually ended up in minority neighborhood schools. As it worked out, the "plan" placed many Mexican American children in the former black schools and many black children in some of the former

"Mexican" schools. Only a few blacks lived in the zones of white schools. There existed in Phoenix, W. A. Robinson lamented, "a sort of belief that desegregation can be carried out successfully without greatly disturbing the former pattern of school attendance and teacher employment." At the same time, he noted, the situation was superior to "the former pattern of complete segregation in the schools."[24]

Although segregation may have been "official" only in the schools, it had to be fought in other sectors as well. In September 1952 the Phoenix City Council received a complaint from band leader Louis Jordan, a Phoenix resident, about the "no Negro policy" at the Sky Chef restaurant at Sky Harbor Airport, a municipal facility. Some city council members thought it best to let Sky Chef management handle the matter "as they might see fit," but others argued that the management should "not discriminate in the matter of service in their restaurant." Sky Chef declared that it "refused to admit Negroes because of local custom." The management felt that if they overlooked "local custom," they would offend white customers and lose business.

City Attorney Jack Hays noted to Mayor Hohen Foster that in the lease agreement between the city and the restaurant, Sky Chef was required to be "open to all of the *general public*." In turn, the city council directed Sky Chef management to end its discriminatory policy; reluctantly, they complied, fearing that legal action would be taken to terminate the Sky Chef lease if discrimination continued. It was a positive ending to an unsavory incident; as the *Republic* noted, the city council "took the only position it should ever have considered taking on racial discrimination applied to property under governmental control." Unfortunately, problems remained.[25]

De facto segregation continued to plague African Americans in the 1950s, and education, housing, and employment continued to pose problems. In 1960 the African American population reached 20,919, up from 4,263 in 1940. The percentage of blacks in Phoenix actually decreased from 6.5 to 4.8 percent of the total population in twenty years, and according to the local chapter of the Urban League, at least 95 percent of them still resided south of Van Buren, in the "worst housing areas in the city." As a report of that organization put it: "Of the 21,000 Negroes in Phoenix, 19,000 live in 9 of the city's 92 census tracts, with 7 of these south of the Southern Pacific Railroad tracks. Three of these seven tracts contain roughly one-half of the city's Negro population."

North Phoenix remained a white preserve during the 1950s, offering its inhabitants the best educational facilities and the best housing developments. The affluent lived in north Phoenix, including the city's political, social, and economic leaders. In the more southern sections of the city, an observer declared in 1960, "It would appear that in almost every instance in education, employment, and housing, the minority-group members are suffering some degree of deprivation—not necessarily civil rights deprivation—but less schooling, less employment, and more crowded housing." The impact of inferior schools, unskilled low-income jobs, and restrictive white real estate practices depressed the African American community. Unsuccessful attempts to open up hotels, restaurants, and theaters also proved hard to take. In Phoenix, deplored African American leader Lincoln Ragsdale in 1962, "not only is the Negro segregated while alive, but even when he is dead, when he goes to his final resting place, and to the sod. Every cemetery in Phoenix has some form of discrimination, either racial or religious. As one man told us, 'So shall you live. So shall you die. Segregated.' "[26]

Ragsdale, a mortician, was speaking from experience. In 1952 he had approached Eugene and Thomasena Grigsby, fellow civil rights activists in Phoenix, and told them the story of Thomas Reed, a black soldier from Phoenix who was killed in Korea. Eugene was a respected teacher at George Washington Carver High School, and Thomasena occasionally wrote news stories about local blacks for national African American newspapers. After listening to Ragsdale, she wrote an article about Reed for the *Chicago Defender*, telling how Ragsdale's mortuary was holding Reed's body because his family could not get him buried with his fellow veterans in the all-white veterans' plot in Greenwood Cemetery. "He was good enough to fight in combat duty along side white boys, why can't they be buried side by side?" asked the *Arizona Sun*. Reed eventually was buried in the cemetery, but the incident caused considerable ill will and illustrated once again the "white problem" in Phoenix.[27]

The housing situation in Phoenix also troubled Ragsdale, a veteran and successful businessman. Despite his military service and economic success, he could not purchase a house in the white neighborhoods of north Phoenix; real estate agents refused to show him houses, and banks denied him loans. Finally Ragsdale bypassed the restrictions by having a white friend purchase a northside house for him at 1606 West Thomas Road. The deal was still in escrow when his friend transferred the title to Ragsdale. As Ragsdale later recalled, he and his family lived in the house for seventeen years and the neighborhood never accepted them. The word *nigger* was spray-painted on his house, and his children were treated badly by white children. Every new police officer who patrolled the area stopped Ragsdale in his car. "I looked suspicious," the affluent mortician remembered. "And all you have to do to look suspicious is to be driving a Cadillac and be black. . . . When I'd see him coming with his lights, I'd get my ownership of the car out and show him my driver's license."[28]

Ragsdale's wife, Eleanor, also served the civil rights movement in Phoenix well. A college graduate and teacher at Dunbar School in 1947, she married Lincoln in 1949. She diligently promoted the value of acquiring a good education and often remembered the black professionals who served as role models for her when she was a student at Chaney State Teachers' College, a black school in Pennsylvania. Ragsdale recalled the "marvelous years" she spent there and stated she would have been a "different product" without the experience. In Phoenix she suffered severe harassment but continued to work with her husband and other black leaders for civil rights. Active in church work and in numerous voluntary associations, she marched, picketed, and called for fairness.[29]

Women were as involved in the civil rights movement in Phoenix as men. Another black woman, Madge Copeland, arrived in the city from Louisiana with her husband, Clarence, in 1919. Widowed in 1929, she operated a black beauty shop in her home for twenty-five years. She also worked for the Democratic party during the Great Depression because it "helped poor people." Adept at registering voters and campaigning for Democratic candidates for office, she was eventually appointed the first permanent deputy county recorder, a position she held from 1947 to 1961. During the 1940s and 1950s, Copeland fought against segregation and discrimination at every opportunity. She marched, picketed, and participated in sit-ins, often in a leadership role. At the same time, she remained active in her church and other black community organizations. Like Eleanor Ragsdale and other active black women, she served as a strong role model; her dedication and skills helped bring about change.

When Copeland arrived in Phoenix, she was not impressed. The city was "very prejudiced," and the attitudes and actions of local whites did not improve sufficiently with time. Blacks were relegated to south Phoenix, and most of them worked in manual jobs. There were "very few opportunities," and "minorities always got less than anyone else," although some minorities received more than other minorities. Copeland later declared: "The Mexicans were segregated just like the Negroes. Of course, some of them got jobs because they could speak Spanish, and they wanted the Spanish trade . . . that was the cause of so many being hired long before the Negroes. So, for that reason, they got a number of jobs." [30]

In time, due in part to the efforts of activists like Ragsdale and Copeland, gains were made. The civil rights struggle finally brought change. Asked in 1981 if discrimination still existed in Phoenix, Copeland answered: "It does very much. It has abated, you know, it's quieted, but it's still there. I think it will always be here until the Lord turns everything to heaven as He said He would. I think it will always be here, but we don't have anything like as much as we used to have. Not anything like it." [31]

New housing opportunities for African Americans evolved in Phoenix following World War II, but they were limited and largely confined to south Phoenix. Beginning in 1946, the Progressive Builders' Association, a black construction firm headed by J. S. Jones and D. W. Williams, built attractive homes on tracts of land extending from Sixteenth to Fortieth streets, between Broadway and Roeser Road. In 1956, Park South, another attractive subdivision at south Sixteenth Street and Roeser Road, began attracting black buyers of new, affordable homes. Under the direction of J. S. Jones, Travis Williams, and Clyde Webb, the Williams and Jones Construction Company built Park South homes into the 1960s. The low income of blacks, however, remained an obstacle; according to developer Webb, "Most blacks were too poor to qualify to buy homes." [32]

The churches continued to play a strong role in African American community affairs. Clergymen and other civil rights activists often met at the churches and organized protests. The Tanner Chapel African Methodist Episcopal Church and the First Institutional Baptist Church (named the First Colored Baptist Church until 1951) provided financial aid and leadership training. Many members of the churches served as officers in the NAACP, the Urban League, and other organizations. Dr. Robert B. Phillips and his wife, Louise, for example, members of the First Institutional Baptist Church, worked hard as leaders for the NAACP, especially in the campaigns for decent housing for minorities and the integration of Phoenix Union High School.

The Reverend George Brooks, pastor of the Southminster Presbyterian Church, organized in south Phoenix in 1953, also served as a catalyst. In the 1950s and 1960s, Brooks labored diligently to integrate the Phoenix work force and met with some success; he and Lincoln Ragsdale, for example, as members and officers of the local NAACP, persuaded the president of the Valley National Bank to integrate the bank's employees. Brooks and other black and white members of the clergy approached many Phoenix employers and urged them to hire blacks, but not all co-operated; Motorola, with three plants in the Phoenix metropolitan area, resisted, finally hiring its first black in 1962. Brooks detested segregation in all its forms. "No doubt about it," he declared, "segregation has made the Negro poor. It's forced him into the slum areas, into bad schools, it's cut him off from better jobs. . . . Segregation has built a wall of poverty around the Negro." And "psychologically it's done worse than that," Brooks continued:

> There's hardly any mixing of the two races in Phoenix. In most parts of the city, a white boy can get into his early teens before he sees many Negroes. Then the ones he sees are likely to be busboys, janitors, street sweepers. He never sees educated Negroes holding responsible jobs. He isn't going to like any talk about social equality. This is bad for the Caucasian, no matter what the bigots say, but it's even worse for the Negro. He grows up in a segregated or near-segregated neighborhood. That's all he knows: segregation. He accepts it, takes it for granted in housing, employment, schools. He's conditioned to it, and for a lot of Negroes, it's a crutch, a defense against the world.[33]

By 1960, Phoenix African Americans were openly protesting their plight. With city officials and business leaders rejecting urban renewal and other federal assistance programs, and unsuccessfully urging "private industry to do it," black neighborhoods continued to deteriorate. Frustrated black residents increasingly joined with white sympathizers to press for their civil rights. In the early years of the decade, sit-in demonstrations and mass picketing conducted under the direction of the Phoenix Interdenominational Ministerial Alliance and the NAACP, including its Youth Council, brought results at places like Citrus Drugs and Woolworth's. A participant, Irene King, later recalled that "they just didn't serve you." The tactics employed proved successful, and during the remainder of the 1960s they were employed to break discriminatory practices and secure open-door policies in Phoenix establishments. The *Arizona Sun* declared in 1962, "If anyone doubts that there is discrimination against Negroes in Phoenix, he must be deaf, dumb, and blind."

When civil rights legislation failed to pass at the local and state level, the local press often cheered. As the *Arizona Republic* asserted in 1956, "The way to the abolition of discriminating practices is not through law." Civil rights legislation continued to be defeated time and again in Phoenix and Arizona. In 1961 a *Republic* editorial stated, "If there is a state in the union that doesn't need civil rights legislation, it is Arizona." Marches, picketing, and sit-in demonstrations infuriated those who resisted change; finally, increasing pressure from civil rights activists brought forth positive legislation from the city, state, and nation.

In the meantime, many owners of Phoenix establishments voluntarily adopted antidiscrimination policies once they understood what was at stake. A few white leaders helped. William P. Reilly, for example, an influential Phoenix utility executive, convinced some reluctant white restaurant owners to open their establishments to blacks. In 1959 the Hotel Adams allowed baseball star Willie Mays and his black teammates to stay at that hostelry, but only after New York Giants manager Leo Durocher raised hell. He threatened to pull his fifty-member team out of spring training in the Valley of the Sun. A little prodding helped. "Phoenix has made some progress in civil rights," asserted local writer Joseph Stocker in 1962, "but it has been agonizingly slow." In the 1960s and 1970s, the Southwest urban center would continue to advance slowly in the civil rights march.[34]

Critics often expressed their disappointment that Phoenicians did not possess a greater social conscience. The failure of city influentials to recognize and do something about negative conditions in parts of south Phoenix led outsiders to point to pockets of poverty in that section of the city that "could match misery for misery and squalor for squalor" with any city in America. The administration of city affairs won plaudits from the majority of Phoenix residents, especially those residing on the north side, but as a small minority of critics pointed out, not everybody was suitably represented. One observer noted that in Phoenix "the only areas being developed are ones where councilmen are interested. Look south of the tracks. Nothing's being done there." The people there were not represented on the city council.

In the early 1960s there were deliberate attempts by some groups to prevent African Americans from voting. According to Madge Copeland and other black civil rights workers, members of the Young Republicans sought to keep blacks from the ballot box by intimidating them outside polling places. The Reverend George Brooks later recalled how local attorney William Rehnquist, future United States Supreme Court justice, asked black voters arriving at the polls in Brooks's church to read from the Constitution. If they were unable or unwilling to do so, Rehnquist insisted they not be allowed to vote. Observed by witnesses, Brooks, who served as an election officer, confronted the lawyer. "I told him that he was interfering with the people's right of franchise, and I was going to call the sheriff and have him arrested." Rehnquist reluctantly left. African Americans finally won representation on the Phoenix City Council in

1965 when Dr. Morrison Warren, a respected educator, won election on the Charter Government ticket; in 1973 another African American, accountant Calvin Goode, was elected to the council. Morrison and Goode represented the African American community, but they faced difficult odds. Especially depressing was the continued presence of slums in the southern parts of the city.[35]

Following World War II, critical housing shortages in Phoenix encouraged efforts to provide for returning veterans and new settlers. Private real estate interests, in conjunction with federal housing loan policies, helped ease the situation over the years, but unlike many other cities, Phoenix did little to eradicate slums. For those familiar with the situation, the "city slums outranked the cotton camps for hovels, filth, and disease." As Dr. H. L. McMartin, director of the city-county health unit, declared in March 1946, "You don't have to go out to the cotton camps to find bad conditions." There are "appalling slum conditions still existing within the city limits and in a vast area immediately contiguous thereto." He pleaded with Phoenicians to deal with the "old, old problem of the slums 'south of the tracks.' "

Conditions on the south side disturbed Dr. McMartin, but he belonged to a minority of concerned citizens who realized that most residents of the north side were either unable or unwilling to see the "other Phoenix." He observed that

> Phoenicians from comfortable houses in the city's northern section, who seldom see anything but nice lawns and flower gardens, neat houses and paved streets, have but to step to a car and drive southward from the tracks for a few moments to learn how the other half of the city lives. In areas both in and out of the city, they will—to their amazement—see row after row of open backyard toilets, smelling to high heaven. They will see block upon block of shacks and hovels, squalid and depressing to an almost incredible extent. They will see dust-blanketed, littered streets and even dirtier alleys. They will see small children—white and black alike—playing in the midst of squalor that a hog raiser wouldn't tolerate in his pens.

Dr. McMartin emphasized that the slums were "not the result of war or the current housing shortage," for they existed long before the war. He noted that Phoenix had made a start toward slum clearance prior to the war with the building of the Marcos de Niza, Matthew Henson, and Frank Luke, Jr. housing projects. Federal aid had made them possible, and Dr. McMartin hoped that federal aid might once again meet the "urgent need for a much broader program of slum clearance." He blamed those Phoenicians who considered "slum property a good financial investment" for being "partly responsible for difficulties encountered in cleaning up blighted areas." His frustration evident, the doctor exclaimed that "some of our good people from the north side who own those things [slum area property] are the ones who ought to be blasted between the eyes."[36]

There was little support in north Phoenix for slum clearance. As Father McLoughlin lamented in the summer of 1946: "The northern half of Phoenix doesn't know how the southern half lives. The average Phoenician is interested only in his home, job, and recreation." During the next decade some progress was made; the three existing housing projects underwent expansion, and several new low-income units appeared. Opposition from the Phoenix Real Estate Board, the Phoenix Chamber of Commerce, and other local organizations retarded the development of public housing units in the city. Private interests considered government projects a threat to their businesses and their way of life. They gained widespread support from the local press, the general population, and city officials. In 1959, when the federal government informed the city that its housing code failed to meet federal standards, Phoenix officials refused to cooperate with federal authorities and thus deprived the city of federal funds. The federal government was particularly displeased with the housing code provision that allowed the landlords of slum dwellings to refuse admittance to inspectors.

The elected officials of Phoenix felt pressure from the *Republic* and the *Gazette,* as well as much of the population, including rabid right-wing groups such as the Stay American Committee and the John Birch Society, which managed to come up with eleven thousand signatures on petitions to repeal the housing code. In January 1961 city officials defiantly revoked the city's housing code and disbanded its urban renewal department. Urban renewal was dead in Phoenix and its opponents rejoiced, for to them it was "a scheme hatched by Communists." A few critics called the action reprehensible, but the Reverend Audrey L. Moore, head of the Stay American Committee and a vociferous opponent of the federal government's involvement in local affairs, reflected the thinking of many Phoenix residents when he warned that such schemes would lead the city, the state, and the nation "down the road to socialism."

The residential building boom made possible by Federal Housing Administration and Veterans Administration housing loans for individual families enabled the Phoenix metropolitan area to be ranked among the top ten areas of the nation in new-dwelling construction by 1960, but housing for low-income groups had by that year been effectively constrained. As a result of Phoenix's policy, a national journal observed a few years later that the city was left with "no urban renewal, no housing code to enforce even minimum standards in deteriorating buildings, and no serious plan to do anything about its slums." The bemused reporter concluded by noting that the local press was currently sponsoring a "City Beautiful" drive emphasizing the removal of unsightly signs and trash, a movement "that doesn't require any interference whatsoever from the federal government."[37]

9 PROGRESS AND PROBLEMS, 1960–1992

In 1960, Phoenix contained the largest African American population in Arizona, and while individuals from that minority group made meaningful advances in the next twenty years, progress for African Americans in general proved to be slow. Problems such as high unemployment, poor housing, and lack of education plagued the black neighborhoods of Phoenix. In 1980, for example, in the two areas of Phoenix with the heaviest black concentration, 36 percent in one area and 26 percent in the other had less than a grade school education. In the summer of that year, following the black uprising in Miami, Florida, black leaders in the Arizona capital were asked if they thought that the ingredients for a race riot were present in the city. In reply, spokesman Art Hamilton declared that "all the circumstances, the hopelessness, the helplessness exist in Phoenix."

In February 1962 the long-standing problems of high unemployment, poor housing, and lack of education and attainment were brought up at a U.S. Civil Rights Commission hearing in Phoenix. African American leaders representing the NAACP, Urban League, and other organizations testified that black unemployment and underemployment in both the private and public sectors far exceeded that of whites. In addition, both private and public housing units were occupied along racial lines in Phoenix, with more than 90 percent of the African American population residing south of Van Buren. Real estate interests continued to keep blacks from buying homes north of Van Buren. De facto school segregation still existed, and school districts north of Van Buren did not hire African American teachers.[1]

In the early 1960s young blacks increasingly demonstrated in protest. Sit-ins and marches on city hall and the state capitol were utilized by blacks to make metropolitan Phoenix aware of their plight. The young protesters joined the Congress of Racial Equality (CORE) and other new groups and offered new leadership to older groups such as the NAACP and the Urban League. Jim Williams, Austin Coleman, Cloves Campbell, Lincoln Ragsdale, the Reverend George Brooks, and others became spokesmen for blacks seeking civil rights. Sit-ins and marches helped secure a public accommodations ordinance from the city of Phoenix in July 1964 and a civil rights law from the state of Arizona in January 1965. These laws forbade discrimination in employment, housing, voting, and public accommodations.[2]

The passage of municipal and state civil rights laws, along with the coming of federal legislation, helped break down the barriers of discrimination. Blacks benefited, but the "white problem" remained. As a white Phoenix business executive put it in 1965:

> You ask about the Negro problem in Phoenix. Understand now, if you want to know what I really think, I can't be quoted. I can't have the company I work for associated with what I say. If you're going to use my name, then I'll repeat the standard line—civil rights, education, tolerance, the whole bit. But as a businessman and a taxpayer, I think there's a real problem. We've got all those people down there [South Phoenix] and let's be honest about it, most of them are costing the rest of us money.
>
> They're uneducated, unskilled. You can't hire or use half of them. Their crime rate is way up. They can't pay any taxes. I'm not anti-Negro, but you wanted my opinion. Just from the standpoint of simple economics, the city would be better off without them.
>
> Another thing, with all this civil rights marching and demonstrating, how long is it going to be before some half-educated crackpot gets those people all excited and we have a first-class race riot on our hands? This has nothing to do with prejudice; I'm talking straight economics and the city's image. I don't think there's any question about it; Phoenix would be better off if they weren't here.[3]

City and state discrimination laws were weakly enforced, and de facto segregation remained in the neighborhoods and in the schools. The issue of jobs became critical. The coming of federal antipoverty programs helped, but job-training projects proved limited and brought complaints. Following the civil rights hearings in Phoenix in 1962, private groups and city officials moved to meet the problems. The Greater Phoenix Council for Civic Unity and other civil rights organizations wanted substantial change. Peaceful change was the goal; the Reverend Martin Luther King, Jr., visited the city in March 1962 and June 1964, each time urging continued nonviolent action. On each occasion King delivered a message of brotherhood, calling upon his listeners to join in the struggle for justice and equality.

Community surveys, graphically detailing the depth and nature of poverty in Phoenix and pointing out the need for a "program of equal opportunity for all in employment, public accommodations and housing," encouraged the city council to create the Phoenix Human Rights Commission in July 1963. Chaired by William P. Reilly, who championed the development of more job opportunities for African Americans, it secured pledges from more than three hundred businesses to hire "without regard to race, color or creed." In 1967, Reilly, along with black activists Augustus Shaw, Carl Craig, Robert Nesby, George Brooks, and others, helped establish in Phoenix an affiliate of the Opportunities Industrialization Center (OIC), based in Philadelphia. A self-help job-training program supported by government funds, it would endure, for jobs and job training remained major issues.

Out of the Phoenix Human Rights Commission grew Operation LEAP (Leadership and Education for the Advancement of Phoenix), a public-private sector partnership agency established to combat poverty in the city. LEAP became a city department in January 1966, involved in federal War on Poverty programs, and some progress was made. A number of government-sponsored programs created new opportunities in education and employment. Mayor Milton Graham and the city council supported LEAP, and target-area neighborhood residents participated in its projects. Critics, however, remained dissatisfied; the situation had improved, but it needed more attention.[4]

Dissatisfaction centered on limited job training and the lack of minority hiring. There were complaints of the War on Poverty in Phoenix being "a day late and a dollar short." In May 1967, for example, a reporter declared that despite $15 million in new services, the "LEAP target area is more impoverished than in 1965." Despite all of LEAP's efforts, he continued, "people are still not working because they lack the ability to compete for work in the labor market." Another critic lamented, "The fact is that agency workers have been foundering in a sea of uncoordinated, limited programs that lead nowhere," and "all efforts have had a temporary Band-Aid effect." A LEAP report in July 1967 noted only "52 job placements out of 250 contacts in Phoenix." At the same time, Arizona continued to pay its welfare recipients considerably less than the national average; indeed, wrote one observer, "for the poor Arizona is a tough state." In addition, more and more poor blacks from Phoenix were being drafted to fight and die in Vietnam.

The 21.2-square-mile LEAP target area contained most of the African Americans and many of the Mexican Americans in the city, and within its boundaries could be found some of the worst slums west of the Mississippi River. Unemployment in the area in July 1967 was exceptionally high, and close to 30 percent of the residents lived on less than three thousand dollars a year. One observer asserted that the area "might be fairly termed a human disaster area in an affluent metropolis." It certainly pointed out that the boom in Phoenix benefited whites in the suburbs more than it did minority group members in core neighborhoods.[5]

In similar neighborhoods around the country, blacks and other minority groups were rioting, and on July 25, 1967, Phoenix experienced a violent confrontation when fire bombs were thrown and guns were fired at a police wagon on East Van Buren. Other disturbances occurred, and eventually a crowd of angry blacks gathered at the Sidney P. Osborn Project, a public housing facility located between Seventeenth and Eighteenth streets from Van Buren to Washington. Police sent to the scene were met with "fierce hostility," but the rioting subsided. At a meeting at Eastlake Park the next day, Mayor Graham emphasized that he would not tolerate "stoning, gunfire and disorder in the streets," but he also reiterated the city's intention to work toward racial justice. Young black leaders presented a list of grievances, noting especially the need for more job training and more jobs.

That evening rioting again erupted near the Osborn Project. Mayor Graham imposed a curfew and ordered police to enforce it. Arrests followed. About 280 people, including 38 juveniles, were taken into custody. A total of 376 Phoenix police officers were on duty at various times in the troubled area, while their duties elsewhere in the city were taken over by 190 state highway patrolmen, 148 sheriff's deputies, and 64 Phoenix firefighters. Isolated incidents continued to occur, but the curfew was lifted on July 30, and on that date Mayor Graham, preferring to call the recent disorder a "serious civil disobedience" rather than a "riot," announced that Phoenix intended to provide more job training and jobs for minority groups. Also, to counter charges of police harassment in Phoenix, he promised a city effort to make "community relations" a vital function of the police force.

The city seemed intent on fulfilling its promises, but skeptics called for more police to enforce law and order. Blacks as well as whites opposed the violence. Many black parents objected to the "riot" and criticized the young participants. Moreover, declared one of them, "Eighty percent of all the kids who were making all the noise wouldn't take a job if you offered it to them—or if they did, they wouldn't work. They want to get paid, that's all." Others blamed the outburst on previous riots in Los Angeles, Detroit, and other urban centers, which were vividly covered on national television; Phoenix blacks, it was said, were merely conforming to the prevailing pattern.[6]

African Americans led the way in protesting minority conditions in Phoenix and Arizona in the 1950s and 1960s. Few Mexican Americans joined blacks in local sit-ins and marches; in fact, Mexican American leaders persuaded their followers not to march with blacks. They declared that "even though they sympathized with the plight of the blacks, that the black problem was a black problem." The *Arizona Sun* reported on the dilemma, noting that the "divide and conquer" approach employed by Anglo Americans in the city gave each group a little, but not much. Each group struggled for what was made available, but neither group made substantial gains. "We made a great mistake not to work together for the benefits of both," the paper declared as early as 1957. The lack of cooperation encouraged deterioration and distrust in the relationship between the two groups. Those few Mexican Americans who marched in Phoenix in the early 1960s endeared themselves to blacks, but generally during the period the relationship declined.[7]

During the 1960s, as federal, state, and local governments responded to the protests of African Americans by establishing agencies and programs to create more opportunities for them, Mexican Americans developed "problems." In the LEAP program, for example, blacks initially received the top positions; Mexican Americans began pointing out that they had "the same problems" and wanted some of the new appointments. Chicanos and blacks more than ever became "rivals for goodies."

The lack of cooperation extended to other areas as well. Not only were Chicanos "white" when blacks needed help, but some Mexican American establishments refused to serve blacks. African Americans were so outraged when the proprietor of the El Rey Cafe on south Central Avenue refused them admittance, they threatened to burn it down; as a result, the owner changed her mind.

Out of the 1960s emerged a resurgence of African American benevolence and pride. The Urban League, NAACP, CORE, OIC, and other African American–led organizations provided leadership and inspiration and offered economic and legal assistance. Much-needed social services and cultural offerings came into being. The Broadway House apartments, sponsored by the First Institutional Baptist Church, and the Tanner Chapel Manor nursing home, sponsored by the Tanner Chapel African Methodist Episcopal Church, were established, and community medical centers opened with the support of African American leaders, including former Olympic champion Jessie Owens, who had retired in Phoenix. Joe Black, former Brooklyn Dodger pitcher and vice president of Greyhound Lines, a Phoenix corporation, and other prominent African Americans helped establish youth programs. Prominent black artist Eugene Grigsby taught many Phoenix youth the beauty of African art, while members of Richard H. Hamilton American Legion Post 65 (named after a Phoenix World War II black serviceman) taught them about the patriotism and valor of African American servicemen past and present. Civil rights advances and a new appreciation of black history gave new importance to Juneteenth and other traditional holidays.

African American women as well as men participated. Dedicated teacher Arlena E. Seneca won Phoenix Woman of the Year honors. Vernell Coleman, despite personal health problems, worked diligently to organize Juneteenth celebrations and Black History Month. Helen Mason worked equally hard to make a success of the Phoenix Black Theater Troupe. African American churches and other voluntary associations continued to contribute to community life in both spiritual and secular ways; a favorite activity was the awarding of scholarships to deserving college students. For example, a major social event was the annual debutante cotillion sponsored by the traditional Links chapter in Phoenix, an organization of middle-class black women who promoted community projects, especially educational opportunities for black youth.

Problems remained in 1980, but progress was evident. National and local civil rights legislation along with antipoverty programs helped make black organizations such as the NAACP and the Urban League more influential forces in the community. In 1980, for example, the Phoenix Urban League, under the able direction of Junius A. Bowman, had a staff of more than one hundred and operated programs that dealt extensively with job training, housing, education, health, and cultural enrichment. Administering a variety of projects from Head Start to Urban League Manor—a residence for the elderly and disabled—it proved to be one of the city's most respected professional social service agencies. It was especially adept at securing the support of white influentials and convincing many large companies to establish affirmative action or fair employment offices. Individuals as well as organizations made progress in the private as well as the public sector, but especially in the latter; Doeg Nelson, for example, advanced to assistant chief of the Phoenix Police Department, William Bell served as assistant city manager, and Hayzel B. Daniels became the first black municipal judge in Phoenix history.[8]

Both African American and Mexican American incomes remained higher in Phoenix than in rural Arizona. More qualified members of both groups experienced better opportunities for advancement in Phoenix and other Southwestern cities. At the same time, the Arizona capital in 1970 contained several African American and Mexican American neighborhoods that tended to have incomes below the median level of the city, high levels of crowded, substandard housing, and many impoverished families. The neighborhoods with high African American and Mexican American concentrations dramatically differed from the neighborhoods of the total Phoenix population (see Table 9.1).[9]

During the 1980s the African American population remained at 5 percent of the total Phoenix population. The number of blacks reached 51,053 in 1990, up from 37,672 in 1980 and 27,896 in 1970. At the same time, more African Americans, many of them professional and business people, moved into the middle class. The positive effects of civil rights awareness and of economic growth and prosperity made it easier for individual blacks to benefit from new economic and political opportunities, but progress for them as a group within the larger Phoenix population remained slow.

Educational and employment gains for individuals were noted during the decade, and structural changes in the city's political system allowed for more minority group representation. After the change to the district system in 1983, south Phoenix and much of west Phoenix elected minority group members to the city council. Mary Rose Garrido Wilcox represented District 7, predominated by Mexican Americans, and Calvin Goode represented District 8, where large numbers of both Mexican Americans and African Americans lived. Mexican American and African American members of the Arizona Legislature from south and west Phoenix, including Alfredo Gutierrez and Art Hamilton, continued to serve their constituents well.[10]

During the decade members of minority groups who could afford it dispersed throughout the city, but not without difficulty. Mexican Americans found it easier than blacks to relocate in predominantly Anglo neighborhoods; for blacks it often remained frustrating. "Racism is not as overt, not as blatant as it was," Phoenix television reporter Evelyn Thompson noted in 1982. "When I first came here in 1971, a real estate

Table 9.1. Housing and Income Indicators in African American and
Mexican American High-Concentration Neighborhoods
in Phoenix, 1970

	Median Value of Housing	Moder- ately Crowded Housing	Severely Crowded Housing	Families with Public Assistance Income	Families with Social Security Income
Phoenix African American and Mexican American high-concentration	$18,582	6.9%	2.1%	3.2%	20.2%
neighborhoods	$ 8,991	12.3%	8.6%	16.0%	20.6%

	Income Less Than 50% of Poverty Level	Income 50–100% Poverty Level	Income Two—Three Times Poverty Level	Income Three Times Poverty Level
Phoenix African American and Mexican American high-concentration	3.5%	5.4%	43.0%	48.1%
neighborhoods	12.3%	14.5%	54.1%	17.0%

SOURCE: John E. Crow, *Mexican Americans in Contemporary Arizona: A Social Demographic View* (San Francisco: R and E Research, 1975), 69.

agent said to me, 'Blacks don't live north of Thomas Road. I'm not going to show you any apartments in that area because nobody will rent to you.'" Unfortunately, the practice of steering blacks to "appropriate" neighborhoods persisted throughout the 1980s. In 1987, according to a study by the Equal Opportunity Department of the city of Phoenix, housing discrimination remained a problem and continued to encourage segregated living patterns (see Map 9.1).[11]

More African Americans entered Arizona State University in the 1980s, but racial incidents caused concern. Both the school and the city

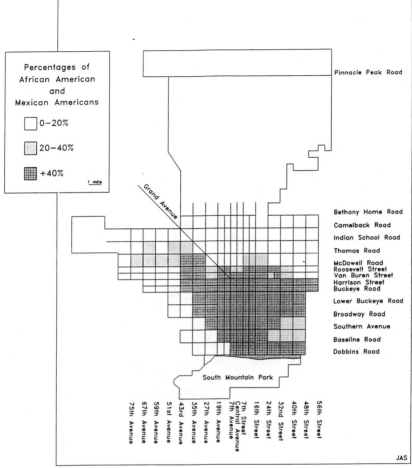

Percentages of
African American
and
Mexican Americans

☐ 0–20%

▦ 20–40%

▦ +40%

1 mile

Grand Avenue

Pinnacle Peak Road

Bethany Home Road

Camelback Road

Indian School Road

Thomas Road

McDowell Road
Roosevelt Street
Van Buren Street
Harrison Street
Buckeye Road

Lower Buckeye Road

Broadway Road

Southern Avenue

Baseline Road

Dobbins Road

South Mountain Park

75th Avenue
67th Avenue
59th Avenue
51st Avenue
43rd Avenue
35th Avenue
27th Avenue
19th Avenue
7th Avenue
Central Avenue
7th Street
16th Street
24th Street
32nd Street
40th Street
48th Street
56th Street

JAS

Source: The Phoenix Gazette, 1983

MAP 9.1 Minority Neighborhoods in Phoenix, 1983

of Tempe, a suburb of Phoenix and home to the university, celebrated a
Martin Luther King, Jr., holiday on the third Monday in January in spite
of the absence of a King holiday for the state. To eradicate racism and
promote racial harmony on campus, ASU created a variety of programs,
including courses dealing with cultural awareness and cultural diversity.
The rise in racial stereotyping and racial conflict evident in the nation's
colleges and universities at the time did not escape ASU. Conscientious

members of the university community tried to improve the racial situation, but opposition lingered and racial tension continued into the next decade. Critics complained that ASU still lagged in the recruitment of minority students, faculty, and administrators.

Subtle discrimination in many aspects of life pervaded Phoenix during the 1980s. "Racism is still a significant factor in the lives of blacks in Phoenix," asserted Brenda Smith, a state government worker, in 1982. But "discrimination and barriers are more subtle than they used to be, and the perception of them is defined by the individual's own attitudes and personal experiences, but it is still here." Phoenix, of course, remained largely white; indeed, as local columnist E. J. Montini wrote in early 1987, "Phoenix is, by far, the whitest big city in America."

A number of white residents failed to appreciate Montini's characterization of Phoenix as "the polyester suit of cities, the white bread, the fox trot, the Pat Boone of cities." One letter writer declared, "Wake up white man! You and the rag you work for are what is wrong with America. You probably want to speak Spanish, too, you nigger-loving son of a . . . . Racism is alive and well in Arizona as well as the entire country. Don't ever forget it." [12]

Although some American-born blacks appreciated newcomers from Africa, most had reservations. "The perception is that any immigrant steps over the black American, that any immigrant is always another layer on top of the black community," noted a Nigeria-born Phoenix resident in 1991. "For the individual who is struggling to survive, we are seen as rivals." However, some African and African American businessmen and professionals who could afford it lived in middle- and upper-middle-class neighborhoods in Phoenix, bound to them by class, if not by race. Although aware that prejudice against blacks existed, successful Africans and African Americans could find color-blind enclaves. "I am treated very well," remarked a Liberia-born college professor in 1991, "but I suppose it is my level of education."

The First Institutional Baptist Church in Phoenix exhibited a friendly attitude toward Africans and African culture. The Reverend Warren Stewart, pastor of the church, directed a preservation of African culture committee that included Africans and African Americans and aimed at bridging the gap between the two groups. "The criticism of African Americans is that we don't reach out to Africans," Stewart asserted in 1991. "African Americans are taught to look down on Africans because they think they come to America for economic reasons. On the other hand, the Africans think we are materialistic and have lost touch with our heritage." Bridging the gap, more private schools opened to blacks who wished to learn about their roots. The Saturday School in Phoenix, for example, in 1991 offered a program in African and African American history.

Some African Americans in Phoenix, as elsewhere in the nation, celebrated Kwanzaa, a seven-day holiday honoring their cultural heritage. Bessie Ealim and her family, who operated an African American bookstore and taught African American history classes, saw it as a much-needed opportunity. "When we were in school, we always thought our history started with a slave ship. But Kwanzaa tells us there was an existence before the slave ships," noted Ealim's daughter, Dorothy Ealim-Cole, in December 1991. "In a place like Arizona, where our children are always faced with negative images of Africa and being black, it's an ongoing challenge to present them with positive images."[13]

African American history and tradition also inspired the development of a black cultural center in Phoenix, to be housed in the former all-black George Washington Carver High School, named a state historical landmark in 1991. African Americans in Phoenix, according to one supporter, wanted "to give the youth a better understanding of our history." A good example of that history continued to be celebrated at one of the city's "major festivals," Juneteenth, an annual event usually held at Eastlake Park. Organizers noted that such celebrations called for more than "just fun." As coordinator Vernell Coleman explained, "They are to highlight black history and encourage youth to pursue a higher education." In 1987 the sponsors of Juneteenth awarded scholarships ranging from $100 to $500 to twenty-five inner-city high school and college students. "Our young people must stay in school and do their best," Coleman emphasized.

Blacks and other minority group members shared some of the prosperity in a booming Phoenix, especially individuals who took advantage of their opportunities and made gains in education, employment, and housing, but expectations often fell short. As one observer pointed out, "Educational opportunities for blacks in the Valley have improved considerably, but they still are not proportionately represented in the professional, scientific and technological areas of advanced studies." One area that showed considerable improvement was city government. One-third of Phoenix's employees were members of minority groups, although most of them held lower-level jobs. Some groups, of course, did better than others; black professional athletes held a privileged position in Phoenix, as elsewhere. As one of them declared in 1991, in Phoenix "most players feel they can reside in any neighborhood and send their kids to good schools, as well as dine out, shop and go about life's routines without incident."

Still Phoenix remained a segregated city. "Historically, the city of Phoenix has been a segregated city," the *Republic* reported in 1984, and "census and other data show that it is becoming more so." Living conditions in the predominantly minority neighborhoods continued to be less than desirable. The "majority of substandard housing units in Phoenix are found in an area bounded by Van Buren Street, Broadway Road, 35th Avenue and 48th Street—an area which is predominantly minority," noted the paper. At the same time, many middle-class minority neighborhoods containing attractive homes and yards existed in the southern part of the city.

Districts 7 and 8 not only continued to contain the majority of Mexican Americans and African Americans but also represented many of the poorer neighborhoods in Phoenix. District 7 covered most of southwest Phoenix south of McDowell Road and west of Central, while District 8 covered most of southeast Phoenix south of McDowell Road and east of Central. Table 9.2 illustrates the meaning of the statistics involved in the United States Census of 1980. Taken individually and collectively, they point out the socioeconomic condition of many Mexican Americans and African Americans in Phoenix at that time.

Those few African Americans in Phoenix who made it to the upper-income levels often moved to the suburbs, leaving those less fortunate financially behind in old neighborhoods rife with economic and social problems. Their departure worsened the plight of the African American neighborhoods, especially by depriving poor young people of successful role models. Observers applauded the rise of affluent blacks, but affluence remained less prevalent among blacks than whites. And for those wealthy enough to buy into expensive suburban neighborhoods, disappointment often ensued; for example, black millionaire entrepreneur Lincoln Ragsdale could live in fashionable Clearwater Hills in Paradise Valley, but he could not get into the local lily-white country club.

Over the years, exclusive Phoenix country clubs consistently turned down the few African Americans who requested membership. In 1987, for example, Ray Johnson, a successful black businessman, inquired about joining the Phoenix Country Club and was told he needed two sponsors. After finding them, he mailed in photographs of himself and his wife on request, and they visited the club with their sponsors. When told the membership fee would be $80,000, Johnson responded, "Where

Table 9.2. African American and Mexican American
            Demographic Data, 1980

	District 7	District 8	Total City
% minority	50.0	58.4	21.9
% female-head families, no husband present	18.0	21.4	13.9
% persons below poverty level	20.6	26.5	11.1
Median family income	$15,621	$14,247	$20,364
Employment (persons 16 years and older)			
% white collar occupations	16.5	19.6	28.0
% sales, clerical services	55.9	57.7	57.2
% blue collar occupations	27.6	22.7	14.8
% of males in labor force	79.0	74.5	82.8
% of females in labor force	55.9	55.6	61.0
Education (persons 25 years and older)			
% high school graduates	45.7	43.9	56.9
% of college graduates	7.3	9.1	16.5
Housing			
% renter occupied	39.6	46.0	35.9
% built since 1970	29.2	21.9	39.7
Median value, owner occupied	$39,278	$34,608	$56,291
Median rent, renter occupied	165	157	245
% substandard dwelling	55.7	77.1	31.1

SOURCE: Census of Population and Housing in *A Community Profile* (Phoenix, City of Phoenix Planning Department, 1985), 66–69.

do I send the check?" The nominating committee, however, quietly rejected him. "I was turned down and never given a reason why," he said. "Nobody would talk about it."

In the poorer neighborhoods, high unemployment, lack of education, and inadequate infrastructure persisted. The "welfare trap" took its toll as well, especially in the projects, and for many the future looked bleak and hopeless. Blight was everywhere, or so it seemed; one neighborhood at Twenty-fourth Street and Broadway Road was described as a war zone. Gangs, which provided a sense of belonging as well as economic gain for individual members, multiplied. Sales of crack cocaine and drive-by shootings increased; one resident of a deteriorating south Phoenix neighborhood declared, "You can't walk out your door without being afraid of getting hurt." Block Watch and other community involvement programs helped, and private and public efforts to improve conditions brought occasional progress in the 1980s, but turning around troubled neighborhoods proved difficult.

For the majority of African Americans who experienced upward mobility during the 1970s and 1980s, progress proved to be a reality. Gains were made in education, employment, and housing. Civil rights legislation, including affirmative action, and economic prosperity during most of the period helped. Public-service agencies and private black voluntary organizations offered a variety of programs benefiting the African American community, as did the many black churches in Phoenix.

African American leaders and organizations helped focus attention on the need for change. Cloves Campbell, the first African American to serve in the Arizona Senate (elected in 1970), observed that "job discrimination is not as open as it used to be in the Phoenix area, but it is still here." The change was brought about, he declared, not because of "any substantial change in the basic belief of white businessmen, but because of the efforts of such affirmative-action groups as the NAACP." With his brother Charles, Campbell published the *Arizona Informant*, the largest black newsweekly in the state. The paper, founded in 1968, covered both the progress and the problems of the African American community. Campbell blamed President Ronald Reagan, saying he had "sort of signaled the business community that 'hey, you can go slow. You don't have to worry about it as long as I'm here.'" Cutbacks in federal and local financial aid especially hurt. "A lot of programs that were begun during the Great Society have been cut back," stated Junius Bowman, head of the Phoenix Urban League in 1985. "There used to be a great and conscious promotion of economic development for blacks. Some of that is happening but not with such intensity as before." [14]

Moreover, race-related incidents continued to occur throughout the 1980s, retarding the development of positive racial relations and marking the road to success with doubts and fears. For example, some black leaders called the "overwhelmingly" white Phoenix Police Department "insensitive to blacks." Phoenix authorities claimed no pattern of police abuse, but critics doubted their conclusions. In other areas as well, reports documented abuses. According to a NAACP report issued in September 1991, that organization addressed "about 250 cases of discrimination each year in metropolitan Phoenix." The report noted "a continuing cycle in the Valley of people being discriminated against in housing and jobs."

Art Hamilton and other African American leaders often engaged in uphill battles. The population and the needs of the African American community were diverse. The gains made by middle-class African Americans increased the differences between them and the less fortunate classes, especially the so-called underclass left behind in the problem-plagued poorer neighborhoods. At times, African Americans who succeeded blamed the troubles of the poor on the poor; middle-class achievers understandably wished to dissociate themselves from the violent crime, drug trade, and other negative aspects of the underclass. Some observers wondered if it was too late for a unified effort. As one black reporter noted: "Recently a group of successful blacks were called together with the intent of alleviating the many severe problems of youth in the black community. Several good suggestions were offered. Unfortunately, 90 percent of those at the meeting did not live within the area where so-called black problems exist, and did not seem to understand problems in the black community."

Statistics indicated that during the 1980s poverty on the south side, particularly among African Americans and Hispanics, rose steadily while the citywide rate for Anglos declined. By 1990, 47 percent of African American children, 39 percent of Hispanic children, and 17 percent of Anglo children under age five lived in poverty. "The dichotomy of poverty in Phoenix is so drastic," declared one involved citizen in 1993, "it's not just that white people don't see it. Black people who are in a different economic group don't see it." The plight of poor minority neighborhoods should concern the more affluent, noted critics, for not only was it costly to tend, but it also encouraged the spread of crime throughout the city. It threatened the larger society.

Comparative data in Table 9.3 clearly point out the depressing situation for poor minority group members in Phoenix in 1991 in expanded Council Districts 7 and 8. The fact that Council Districts 1 and 2 in north Phoenix continued to be largely Anglo, while Council Districts 7 and 8 were still home to most African Americans and Hispanics in the city, once again illustrated persistent historical patterns.

Table 9.3. City Council Districts 1, 2, 7, and 8 Demographic
            Data, 1991

	Districts 1 and 2	Districts 7 and 8
Alcohol-related deaths	9	44
Suicides	31	47
Referrals to juvenile court for violent crimes	162	550
Births to unwed mothers	265	1,396
Referrals to juvenile court for drugs	74	263
High school dropouts	1,005	1,586
Percent of children living in two-parent household	77	53
Percent unemployed	6 and 7	14 and 20
Population	244,192	246,976

SOURCE: *Profile of City of Phoenix and Council Districts* (Phoenix: Data Network
for Human Services, 1992).

Class divisions contributed to the fragmentation of the African American community, as they did to other ethnic and racial groups, but some
common affronts and setbacks united it. Starting in 1982, for example,
Representative Hamilton repeatedly introduced legislation to establish
some form of official state observance in honor of Reverend Martin Luther King, Jr., but the Arizona Legislature repeatedly defeated his efforts.
In 1986, Governor Bruce Babbitt, who favored a paid holiday, created
one by executive order. In 1987 his successor, Evan Mecham, believing
Babbitt had exceeded his authority, rescinded the order, replacing it with
an unpaid holiday to be observed on the third Sunday in January, but
proponents of a paid holiday said King "deserved a paid holiday." The
Reverend Warren Stewart, pastor of the First Institutional Baptist Church
and a leading spokesman for a King holiday, led a march of 10,000 supporters on the state capitol. He called for recognition of King's vision of
a peaceful world without racial prejudice. "America is different because
of Dr. King, and we can't ever forget that," the black minister declared.
"He deserves his day and I'll fight for it as long as I live in this state."

The legislature, however, continued to defeat legislation that would establish a paid King holiday.

Finally, in 1989 the legislature approved the holiday, but not wanting to increase the number of paid holidays for state employees, it moved Columbus Day to a Sunday. Following complaints from Italian Americans, the Columbus Day holiday was restored and the King holiday also retained. In 1990, in a referendum-created statewide election, the King holiday met defeat by less than 1 percent of the vote. Although the vote made Mecham and his followers happy, it deeply disappointed and disturbed the African American population and its supporters and caused much unfavorable publicity about Arizona being a racist state. Critics began calling it "the Alabama of the Southwest." The state and its capital city also paid dearly in economic terms. Many groups and individuals boycotted Arizona, and the National Football League pulled the 1993 Super Bowl from the valley because of the divisive issue. The loss of revenue amounted to hundreds of millions of dollars, according to tourism and convention officials.

Many white Arizonans agreed that a paid King holiday should be a reality and continued to work with blacks to secure it. Supporters felt they had been denied an election victory because of confusion at the ballot boxes and the intervention of the National Football League. Arizona voters had a choice of two ballot propositions on the King holiday in the 1990 election, one creating a paid King holiday and another substituting a King holiday for Columbus Day. The yes vote split and the no vote did not; polls taken after the election showed that both propositions failed because the yes vote split. Polls also showed that many of those voting no did so because they changed their mind after the National Football League threatened to pull the Super Bowl out of the Valley of the Sun if voters failed to establish a King holiday in Arizona; they simply did not appreciate the NFL threatening them and voted accordingly. Other commentators cited the expense of adding a paid holiday, the rural vote, and doubts over King's morality and patriotism (some called him a womanizer, a Communist, a critic of United States involvement in Vietnam) as other reasons for the defeat.

Although the city of Phoenix quickly joined other cities, states, and the national government in establishing a paid King holiday, Arizona in 1991 remained the only state without any form of such a holiday. Yet another proposal for a King holiday was scheduled to be on the November 1992 ballot. If passed, it would establish a Martin Luther King, Jr./Civil Rights Day on the third Monday of January, matching the federal observance of the holiday. It would also combine the Washington and Lincoln state holidays in February into a single holiday, conforming to the national Presidents' Day holiday and ensuring that the number of paid state holidays remained constant. Stewart and countless other advocates looked forward to victory; opponents, of course, hoped it would fail. It passed.

The King day controversy reflected many of the problems faced by the African American community in the past in Phoenix, the rest of Arizona, and the nation. Problems continued to persist into the 1990s, but concerned observers also continued to be hopeful that the African American experience in Phoenix and Arizona would remain largely an advancing one. The passage of the King holiday in November 1992 seemed a good sign; if it had failed, however, the struggle for a positive outcome would have continued.

As Mayor Paul Johnson of Phoenix, a proponent of a paid King holiday in the state, declared at the time of Rosa Parks's visit to the city in January 1991, "I hope Arizona gets its King holiday in 1992, but if we don't we'll be back in 1994. If we don't get it then, we'll be back in 1996. . . . And every time, our resolve will get stronger." He echoed the determination of African American leaders. As the Reverend Henry Barnwell, pastor of the First New Life Missionary Baptist Church, promised, "We are not giving up until we celebrate in this state of ours a paid Martin Luther King, Jr., holiday." Representative Hamilton added, "If necessary, we will be back, and we will be back, and we will be back until we accomplish our goal."

With their goal accomplished, King holiday supporters looked to the future. In January 1993, Mayor Johnson noted that "creating the holiday was an important symbol, but now we need to move from symbol to substance." Concerned observers agreed; as one of them declared, that "substance" mentioned by Johnson meant "being a state in which the reality is equal rights and opportunities for all human beings."[15]

CONCLUSION THE PHOENIX EXPERIENCE

In Phoenix, as in many urban centers in the American West, Mexican Americans, Chinese Americans, and African Americans struggled heroically to survive and surmount inequities imposed by a white-dominated society. In the nineteenth and twentieth centuries the struggle and the difficulties proved to be continuous; progress was slow, and equity and parity were elusive. A complex and compelling endeavor, the struggle seemed endless but not fruitless, and concerned observers hoped that the experience of each group in the future would be positive.

Both Mexicans and Anglos helped establish Phoenix in the 1860s and 1870s. Both groups hoped to benefit from the commercial and agricultural development of the emerging town and its hinterland. Anglos soon outnumbered Mexicans, however, and dominated life in "American" Phoenix. Ethnocentric Anglos kept introducing American institutions and ideas in the Arizona town and applauded each time a new census report announced another drop in the percentage of Mexicans in the local population.

Largely shut out of the larger town, Mexicans created their own neighborhoods, or barrios, with their own residences, businesses, and cultural institutions. A small Mexican middle class emerged to serve the community. In Phoenix, as elsewhere, the Catholic Church, although partial to Anglo Catholics, played a considerable role in the lives of the Mexican faithful, providing a variety of spiritual and secular services. Other voluntary associations fulfilled particular functions, from the protective to the political to the patriotic. Social and cultural clubs never failed to remind the Mexican population of "home," that is, Mexico. Mexican merchants, artisans, and laborers enjoyed many Mexican holidays and fiestas and derived satisfaction from their cultural heritage. Most Mexicans in Phoenix came from the Mexican state of Sonora, located just across the border, and many of them considered themselves sojourners. Part of a chain migration, they found that a familiar neighborhood in Phoenix made their stay north of the border easier. Chain migration involved kinship and culture, and family and community concepts remained strong in Mexican neighborhoods, allowing inhabitants to preserve their traditions and cope with challenge. While a sense of ethnic identity and cultural awareness caused Mexicans to live together, discrimination and segregation also encouraged barrio development.

Similar situations evolved in other Southwestern communities. As Anglos became dominant, Mexican populations became less influential and more contained. Mexican economic and political power declined, and Mexican community life became increasingly confined. "Barriozation" of the Mexican population—the formation of physically and socially segregated barrios, or neighborhoods—became the norm. Insulated from hostile worlds, the barrios ensured the continuation of Mexican society. They allowed and promoted the development of ethnic consciousness and cultural identity. The Catholic Church functioned as a leading institution, and a variety of organizations served the community. Small groups of Mexican middle-class providers served and led Mexican populations. Close family ties persisted, Mexico remained home, and Mexican heritage was recognized and celebrated.[1]

At the same time, the subordinate political and economic status of Mexicans was established and encouraged by dominant Anglo populations. Mexicans experienced little political power outside the barrios, usually worked at unskilled or semiskilled jobs at the bottom of the occupational structure, and socially experienced second-class status in the larger community. Anglo attitudes and actions limited Mexican contact with Anglos.[2]

The attitudes and actions of the dominant Anglos in Phoenix and other urban centers directly influenced the ethnic emergence of the Mexican minority. Ethnic consciousness was motivated by economic, political, and cultural exclusion from the mainstream. Ethnic prejudice, stratification, segmentation, and exploitation isolated Mexicans as a subgroup. Barrio residents faced poverty and despair. The historical dynamics of segregation caused problems, especially geographic isolation from mainstream society and institutions. Despite problems, however, Mexicans and Mexican Americans not only survived but forged their own viable communities.[3]

At the same time they suffered discrimination and segregation, they developed an ethnic enclave and ethnic pride. Shared beliefs and experiences, along with ethnic institutions and organizations, contributed to group and community survival. For the Spanish-speaking, the barrio signified home, family, and friends. Positive forces of language, pride, culture, and community existed there. The family and family life served as a bedrock during good and difficult times. Spanish-language newspapers in Phoenix and other cities represented and defended the Mexican community and protested discrimination and oppression; they also reported on barrio institutional and associational life and printed news from Mexico. In an urban setting, the barrio offered a familiar surrounding where residents could identify with the traditions of their homeland while drawing on what the host society offered them within the constraints of institutionalized subordination.[4]

By 1920, Mexicans remained the largest minority group in Phoenix. During the following decade, Mexican community building increased. Unhappy with Anglo-dominated St. Mary's Catholic Church in Phoenix, Mexicans built their own religious edifices in the 1920s. A small middle class promoted the addition of more voluntary organizations to provide secular services to the population. Fraternal lodges, business organizations, political associations, and social and cultural clubs emerged to satisfy the needs and desires of the population; groups such as the Alianza Hispano Americana and the Liga Protectora Latina continued to lead the way. Such mutual-aid societies, or *mutualistas,* provided a variety of services, including low-cost life insurance and low-interest loans to Mexican-operated businesses. The organizations also promoted ethnic pride and civic involvement; they drew the community together and provided it with leadership. Individually and collectively, Mexican and Mexican American businessmen, professionals, artisans, and laborers contributed to the growth and development of Phoenix, but rarely were their contributions recognized outside their own community.

Mexican communities experienced the same result in other Southwestern urban centers. Individually and collectively, Mexicans and Mexican Americans created their own societies and helped define the boundaries of cultural and ethnic awareness. The Mexican way of life and Mexican patriotism were encouraged by a variety of organizations, including the *mutualistas.* Outside the barrios, however, little recognition was forthcoming. Mexicans and Mexican Americans remained largely outside mainstream Anglo society and culture. Unfair practices such as dual wage systems in the employment sector and dual support systems for schools and other public institutions persisted, helping to maintain second-class status for Mexicans and Mexican Americans in the Anglo-dominated cities. Despite continuing problems, such as political disenfranchisement, residential segregation, social discrimination, and labor segmentation, many of them persevered and progressed during the 1920s.[5]

The 1930s retarded community development. The Great Depression brought hard times and repatriation, but those Mexican Americans who survived the decade in Phoenix and other Southwestern cities found themselves on the verge of a new era. During the Depression years the struggle escalated as Anglos blamed their plight on the presence of Mexicans and Mexican Americans. The competition for jobs and aid was severe, and ugly incidents occurred; many Mexicans and Mexican Americans returned to Mexico voluntarily and involuntarily.

World War II brought economic relief and also proved to be a major turning point in Mexican American history. In Phoenix, as elsewhere, Mexican Americans joined in the war effort. Many joined the military service and fought valiantly, while others participated in war-related home front activities. Following the conflict, Mexican American veterans took advantage of the G.I. Bill and other benefits and determined to achieve first-class status in America. More America-oriented than ever, they wanted the American Dream, not the sojourner's dream of Mexico. Acculturated and educated, they wished to integrate into mainstream American society while retaining an appreciation of their Mexican heritage. Veterans' groups and other middle-class Mexican American organizations helped stimulate change, but not without a struggle. School desegregation and other gains in Phoenix and elsewhere in the 1950s made way for the Chicano era of the 1960s and 1970s.

In Phoenix and other Southwestern cities, the Mexican American era evolved from the 1920s to the 1950s. A generation of Mexican American leaders, bicultural in outlook, promoted the transition of themselves and others from Mexican to Mexican American. When immigration stopped and depopulation occurred during the 1930s, the development of a Mexican American mentality accelerated. The Mexican orientation of the past receded, giving way to a growing "spirit of Americanism," especially among the American-born middle class. During and after World War II, progress occurred in the historical struggle for justice and equity, and occasional economic, political, and social victories brought some satisfaction. Women as well as men were involved. Placida Garcia Smith and other spokeswomen for the Mexican American community in Phoenix learned the art of being assertive before the word was in vogue. Individually and collectively, women in Phoenix and other regional urban centers worked for positive change and helped motivate modest improvements. Such achievements, however, did not remove Mexican Americans from a subordinate position, nor did it settle their quest for identity. As a result, the struggle heightened with the arrival of the Chicano movement during the following two decades.[6]

Activist Chicano students at Arizona State University, inspired by their colleagues at educational institutions in California and other parts of the West, sought equity on campus and in the city of Phoenix. Forming Chicanos por la Causa and other organizations, the activists and their supporters brought new pressure to the struggle. Part of the national civil rights movement, they promoted justice and equality for all in society, as well as multicultural accommodation. More militant than previous leaders, they expressed their ideals and goals in no uncertain terms. They achieved considerable success in urban areas. In Phoenix and other Southwestern cities, upward mobility for Mexican Americans improved. Political activism, educational attainment, economic advancement, cultural awareness, and other positive factors made it easier for Chicanos to progress. More opportunities opened for prepared Chicanas as well as Chicanos. In urban areas Chicanas had always been present in the labor market, often gender oppressed, but the number participating increased during the Chicano era, and a greater degree of fairness evolved, although parity remained distant. As more married Chicanas entered the work force, some critics lamented the impact of Chicana employment on the "traditional" family, while others claimed that couples were more likely to have "egalitarian" values when wives worked. In their own way, Chicanos and Chicanas brought forward the struggle to achieve equality and opportunity in the United States.[7]

In the 1970s and 1980s, Chicanos continued to struggle and progress was recorded, but problems such as labor segmentation persisted. Anglos continued to dominate the higher-income occupations, while most Mexican Americans remained in lower-income jobs. Upward mobility allowed the Mexican American middle class to expand considerably, but the larger Mexican and Mexican American population in Phoenix and elsewhere experienced trouble achieving that status. Class and cultural differences created splits in the population, which lost much of its leadership to individual success and the American Dream. On occasion the Hispanic population united behind a particular goal, such as the election of Mexican American Ed Pastor to the U.S. House of Representatives in 1991, but generally diversity predominated in Phoenix. Those concerned called for a revitalization of the struggle for equality and opportunity for all, which they characterized as the "challenge of the 1990s."[8]

The Chinese who came to America in the last half of the nineteenth century often ended up in Western cities and towns. They began arriving in Phoenix in the 1870s, gradually increasing their population to 110 in 1880. Feeling unwelcome in white Phoenix, Chinese created their own community within the larger society. As a result of racial prejudice and discrimination, plus a desire to preserve their ethnic identity and perpetuate their cultural distinctiveness, they developed Chinatown. Led by the Ong clan, most Chinese in Phoenix, as elsewhere in the American West, were Cantonese from the province of Guangdong in southeastern China. Part of the chain-migration process, the Ongs and other Chinese considered themselves sojourners. Like early Mexican residents of Phoenix, they hoped to acquire enough money to eventually return home to China. Unlike the Mexicans, however, the Chinese were a long distance from home, although their dream was equally strong.

Anti-Chinese sentiment encouraged Chinese in Phoenix and elsewhere to avoid competing with others by working in occupations and businesses few others could or would do. Struggling to survive, they joined together in economic and social endeavors. Restaurants, groceries, laundries, and other business establishments also doubled as residences in Chinatown. Joss houses, Chinese specialty shops, and opium and gambling dens were among Phoenix Chinatown institutions catering to a variety of interests. Family associations, benevolent societies, and other organizations helped allow Chinese in Phoenix a sense of place and security. In Chinatown, Chinese language, food, music, and games were enjoyed, and topics of conversation ranged from past experiences in China to the difficulties of living in the American West. The concentrated Chinese community in Phoenix, much like Chinatowns in other frontier towns, served as a place of refuge in an alien world where residents could be among their own kind, communicate with them, and live a Chinese life as much as possible.

Concentrated in Chinatown, Phoenix Chinese resisted the dominant culture and retained their own. Being sojourners, they had no desire to become part of the larger community, and its negative attitudes and actions toward them only made them less appreciative of mainstream

America. Cultural distance was kept as socially isolated Chinatown provided its residents with a self-sufficient defense against the outside world. To the general population, the world of Phoenix Chinese seemed mysterious. Cries of "unassimilable and unscrupulous foreigners" and "the Chinese must go" were heard in Phoenix and elsewhere. Fewer in number in Arizona, the Chinese did not experience the violent treatment they suffered elsewhere in the American West, especially in California. In Arizona and Phoenix there was comparatively little discriminatory legislation and no riots or lynchings, but plenty of unofficial prejudice and oppression. Chinese were not only unwelcome but unwanted, for they represented a threat to American workers and the American culture, declared anti-Chinese spokesmen at the local and national levels. As a result, the anti-Chinese movement secured from Congress the passage of the Chinese exclusion acts limiting Chinese immigration into the country. Despite exemptions and illegal entries, the laws kept the Chinese population in the nation and in Arizona low.

White Americans considered Chinese and other people of color racially inferior and a threat to white people and white society. Anti-Chinese exclusionists viewed the "Chinese problem" as a social and cultural as well as an economic and political issue. As President Rutherford Hayes declared in 1879, the "present Chinese labor invasion is pernicious and should be discouraged. Our experience in dealing with weaker races is not encouraging. I would consider with favor any suitable measures to discourage the Chinese from coming to our shores." The racist Chinese Exclusion Act of 1882 clearly discriminated against Chinese because of "the color of their skin." The "heathen Chinee" threatened white workers and white America, warned the critics; the Chinese must be excluded. The Chinese community suffered racist attacks and negative images as paranoia fueled anti-Chinese sentiment and violence. At all levels the legal system reflected anti-Chinese sentiment. As one legal historian has put it, "As regards the Chinese, law in the Southwest was not colorblind."[9]

Internal quarrels as well as outside threats hurt the Phoenix Chinese community. Opium and gambling den quarrels, often involving violence, did not enhance Chinatown's image. Yet fines levied on the offenders helped to finance city government, and local authorities sought to extract as much money as possible from Chinese, especially those involved in the irregular economy. Chinese usually cooperated with local authorities, but they also united in the face of outside threats; for example, support for Chinese restaurants, laundries, and other businesses was forthcoming when the local press criticized them for engaging in "filthy practices" or being "public nuisances" or "Chinese monopolies." Chinese also united in celebrating traditional holidays, especially the popular Chinese New Year. The holiday was one of many attractions that drew curious numbers of the general population to Phoenix's Chinatown.

The scarcity of women in Chinese America meant that stable family life was missing in local Chinatowns. In Phoenix and other urban centers, Chinese residents maintained their ethnic awareness and cultural identity as best they could. A network of organizations substituted for the family life that was absent. Folk religion and festive celebrations helped hold communities together, while the Chinese-language press kept them interested and informed. Chinese stores played an essential role in community life, selling foods, herbs, and other goods from China. Places of rest and relaxation, the stores served as service and communication centers for Chinese. The Chinatown "bachelor society" offered the men mutual aid, a familiar culture, and protection from a hostile world. Few Chinese enjoyed the stability of family life, but the numerous associations served as substitute families. Despite the scarcity of women, a sense of community was forged.[10]

The majority of the Phoenix population wanted to rid the city of Chinese. Not being able to fulfill that wish, it rejoiced in the 1890s when Chinatown was moved to a new location outside the main business district. Phoenix leaders and their followers hoped that the Chinese would be less visible and bothersome in their new location. The new Chinatown was more viable and vibrant than its predecessor. A friendly, familiar neighborhood helped the Chinese survive an unfriendly, often vicious larger city, just as it did for other proscribed groups. Ong Louie, or "China Dick," leader of the Ong clan and unofficial mayor of Chinatown, presided over its physical and social structure and acted as spokesman for the Chinese community in its relations with the larger city. He ruled Chinatown with a firm hand and was admired and respected by leaders of the general population as well as members of the Chinese community.

Ong Louie and other Chinese residents of Phoenix were China-oriented and followed current events in their homeland. They supported the creation of the Chinese Republic early in the twentieth century; celebrating its founding became an established event in the Chinese community in Phoenix and elsewhere in the years to come. While Chinese tradition remained paramount in the Chinese population, which was still largely a bachelor society, signs of Americanization appeared. The various organizations remained integral to Chinese life, but some American-born children of Chinese families were speaking English and exploring the Christian religion. Individually and collectively, the Chinese increased their participation in American life. In World War I, Chinese American soldiers from Phoenix served overseas, and Chinese workers joined the war effort at home.

Chinese families and businesses had located outside Phoenix's Chinatown since the beginning. Much of Chinese life centered in Chinatown, but Chinese families increasingly lived and did business beyond its borders. Chinese businesses were never confined to Phoenix's Chinatowns, which were clusters of Chinese population. In the 1870s and 1880s, Chinese laundries, restaurants, and shops were scattered beyond the first Chinatown. The trend continued following the creation of the second Chinatown. City directories documented Chinese entrepreneurial efforts; by 1930 the number of Chinese business establishments in Phoenix exceeded fifty, up from fewer than twenty in 1900. Beginning in the twentieth century, there appeared to be fewer sojourners and more Chinese settlers in Phoenix. For a number of these early Chinese Americans, proprietorship meant a future in America for themselves and their families. Located throughout the city, Tang Shing and other entrepreneurs set examples for ambitious Chinese.

The women who were present played traditional roles. Chinese culture placed the female in a position subservient to the male; she was "to serve her father when young, serve her husband when married, and serve her son when widowed." Husbands, wives, and children worked in businesses, especially in groceries, laundries, and restaurants. As the lives of Lucy Tang and other Chinese women in Phoenix and other cities illustrated, home and work were often inseparable, and children were taught to respect and obey both parents. Women whose husbands did not operate their own businesses worked in the segmented labor market, helping as best they could to support the family. It was the mother's duty to pass Chinese tradition on to the children. Sons especially were encouraged to acquire an education, but the Chinese language and culture were also promoted. Daughters were expected to follow their mother's example.[11]

During the 1920s, despite racial prejudice and discrimination, success stories such as that of Tang Shing occurred in Phoenix, as they did throughout the nation. Also, older Chinese declined in number while younger Chinese and American-born Chinese became more numerous. They lessened their orientation toward China and became more America-oriented. More participation in the commercial and educational systems brought higher economic and social mobility for ambitious Chinese. No longer restricted by the sojourner outlook, Chinese young people studied English and received an American education in the Phoenix public schools during the day, and in the evening in Chinese homes and schools they learned to read, write, and speak Chinese. They also worked long hours helping out at home and in small family businesses. Education and hard work were viewed as keys to success in America and Phoenix. Young people retained Chinese ways but also became more Chinese American.

American-born children grew up exposed to American as well as Chinese culture. Public and private educational opportunities influenced them, but generational conflicts often developed when younger Chinese chose to emphasize their exposure to Americanization. Their elders lamented their lack of enthusiasm for traditional Chinese culture, if not Chinatown. Especially intense were conflicts over the tradition of parents choosing marriage partners for their children; progressive young Chinese often argued for the right to choose their own husband or wife. For young Chinese Americans who practiced American customs and mirrored American lifestyles, the American Dream became more magnetic. Yet obstacles remained; Chinese college graduates, for example, continued to have difficulty securing employment in their fields and were often passed over for white applicants. Limited job options in racist America frustrated and disappointed able and ambitious Chinese.[12]

The 1930s brought the problems of the Great Depression to the Phoenix Chinese community. The Chinese took care of their own to a large extent, but the economic competition for survival proved to be extremely intense. Numerous small Chinese grocery stores that had developed in Phoenix neighborhoods faced unprecedented competition in the 1930s from large food store chains, and some went out of business. Incidents of racial prejudice and charges of un-Americanism against the Chinese flared during the grocery wars, but the Chinese American community pulled together and survived the affront. Also, concerned about the bad image of Chinatown, Chinese American leaders and organizations began encouraging its dissolution; more Chinese Americans began moving and scattering to neighborhoods throughout the city.

Equal treatment for Chinese Americans proved elusive, however, as it did for other minority groups. Prejudice, isolation, segmentation, and exploitation reminded the Chinese community in Phoenix and elsewhere of its second-class status. Ethnic consciousness and ethnic subordination motivated Chinese to retain their ethnic identity while simultaneously working to break down barriers to opportunity created by the dominant larger society. The Chinese American Citizens Alliance and other organizations fought against discrimination and segregation and sought acceptance in American society through rectification of the situation. The lack of economic rights and civil rights for Chinese Americans brought protests; for example, attempts to drive the Chinese out of the grocery business in Phoenix and other Southwestern cities during the Great Depression failed because of their determined resistance.[13]

World War II and the postwar years helped motivate Phoenix Chinese to move away from Chinatown. China became an ally of the United States in the war, and many Chinese Americans joined the war effort both in the military service and at home. By the end of the conflict the federal government had repealed the Chinese exclusion laws and eliminated many obstacles to naturalization. Prejudice toward Chinese lessened, more occupational and residential mobility evolved, and Chinese Americans reached new plateaus of success. In the 1950s and 1960s, Wing Ong, Thomas Tang, and other successful individuals became role models for many young, educated, ambitious Chinese Americans. Chinese American associational life also continued to evolve in Phoenix; efforts to preserve and promote the Chinese community and Chinese culture occupied the time of a number of determined organizations.

Less active than other Phoenix minority groups in the civil rights movement, Chinese Americans nevertheless enjoyed its benefits. Their response to prejudice and discrimination emphasized entrepreneurial success and academic achievement. In the 1970s and 1980s, Phoenix's Chinese American middle class, made up largely of businessmen and professionals, lived throughout the city. Chinatown was a memory, and the American Dream a distinct possibility. Moreover, due in part to lenient immigration laws passed in 1965, a rapid influx of new immigrants from China and elsewhere in Asia flowed into Phoenix during the period. Many of them, educated and affluent, differed from the immigrants of the past. Class and cultural differences increased the diversity existing within the Chinese American and Asian American populations. Many of the newcomers, however, were poor and uneducated, and for them, as for their predecessors, the struggle remained. For those Chinese and other Asian Americans who succeeded in realizing the American Dream, recent anti-Asian attitudes and actions presented more obstacles to overcome.

The success of the Chinese American community attracted considerable attention from the media, which often distorted reality. Although middle-class Chinese took great pride in their achievements, they realized that reports of their progress had been exaggerated. The absence of Chinese Americans from top levels of management, for example, suggested "a glass ceiling," an invisible but impenetrable barrier to promotion, a common problem for all people of color. Also, like other groups, many Chinese Americans faced employment, housing, and health problems, as well as difficulties stemming from bicultural lifestyles. New immigrants pouring into Phoenix and other Southwestern cities introduced increasing diversity, which created further class and cultural differences, fragmenting the Asian community. In the 1990s critics continued to question promoters of the "model minority" image for their failure to recognize problems existing in the Chinese American population. Bipolar employment patterns, pockets of poverty in major urban centers, the rise of youth gangs, and the need for health care for the elderly remained among the more important issues calling for serious consideration.

As the image of the "model minority" gained attention, other racial minority groups often resented it. Antagonisms between various people of color not only continued but reached new levels of violence. The troubled relations of Chinese Americans, Hispanic Americans, and African Americans escalated in Phoenix as well as in New York, Chicago, and Los Angeles, making it difficult to achieve a feeling of optimism. Competition between ethnic and racial minorities worldwide in recent years divided them. Race-related incidents and riots in the United States reflected the ethnic and racial tension evident at home and jeopardized the future peace of urban America.[14]

The African American population in Phoenix reached 150 in 1900. By that year, an active, enterprising African American community had been forged. In the 1890s, as the black population rose, physical and institutional development took place. Black residences and businesses appeared, and Methodist and Baptist churches became centers of black spiritual and social life. A variety of voluntary associations emerged to foster black economic, political, cultural, and intellectual pursuits. Although most Phoenix African Americans made a living as service workers, laborers, and domestics, a small middle class composed of businessmen, ministers, and teachers directed black community life. Most blacks came from the South to Phoenix looking for a better life, but they could not escape racial prejudice and discrimination.

Racial prejudice and discrimination against the black population existed from the beginning in Phoenix. White newspapers in town took every opportunity to support segregation and second-class status for people of color. Proscribed racial minority groups in Phoenix lived in their own neighborhoods not only because of segregation and discrimination, but also because they hoped to preserve a sense of ethnic identity and cultural awareness. School segregation, however, was legally imposed upon blacks; the "colored rooms" and "colored schools" for African Americans were ordered by law.

African American communities throughout the Northern and Western United States were forged during the late nineteenth and early twentieth centuries as unprecedented numbers of Southern blacks migrated. New York, Detroit, Cleveland, Chicago, Los Angeles, San Francisco, and other major urban centers gained the most population and often set the pace for smaller cities. Blacks in the larger places organized communities in which they sought to take care of themselves and their own. Churches and other institutions offered spiritual and secular support to residents. A variety of economic, political, social, and cultural associations tried to meet new demands and improve the quality of life in the growing neighborhoods of urban African Americans. Racial prejudice and racial exclusion confined blacks to their own communities, where they worked to overcome educational barriers, labor segmentation, and social stratification. At the same time, within their own communities, although class conscious themselves, they retained and developed African American racial and cultural identity. Second-class status remained the rule outside the black neighborhoods, but black life flourished within their boundaries.[15]

Holidays and other special occasions provided welcome relief for members of the Phoenix African American community. When Booker T. Washington and other nationally known black leaders visited the city, blacks turned out to welcome them. William P. Crump and other local black leaders were familiar with African American history and leadership, and they worked diligently to protect and promote the welfare of the black population. With the support of the black press in Phoenix, black leaders and organizations protested unfair laws and unfair treatment. Despite military service in World War I and contributions to the war effort at home, obstacles to first-class acceptance in America and Phoenix remained. At times there was violence; in the early 1920s, for example, the Ku Klux Klan used force in Phoenix, as it did elsewhere. Although African Americans were always few in number compared to the Anglo population and hardly posed a threat to its domination, they and other minority group members experienced inequity.

Like the Mexican Americans and the Chinese Americans, African Americans were left out of the larger, racist white society in Phoenix and developed their own community. By the 1920s black men and women were utilizing their own south-side neighborhoods, businesses, churches, schools, and voluntary associations. They had their own park, hotel, and hospital. Separate sections at local theaters and separate nights and days at local dance halls and swimming pools imposed humiliating restrictions on African Americans in white Phoenix, but black community life offered a refuge. It also offered fine examples of black pride and progress.

As elsewhere, whites considered themselves superior to other racial and ethnic groups. Individually and collectively, racists did their utmost to keep "undesirable" racial and ethnic groups in their "proper place." The persistence of racist attitudes and actions reflected the strong racial ideology that had existed in the United States since slavery. As one historian later declared, "Most whites believed that blacks were innately inferior, that racial antagonism could not be overcome, and that blacks, at best, must remain a subservient group in white society." Those who held these beliefs looked to the "science" of race, along with "popular knowledge," as proof that they were the truth. Such beliefs encouraged whites to assign, legally and illegally, second-class status to blacks in Phoenix and other American cities. Such beliefs, an observer noted, "confined the race to squalid housing, decrepit schools, and menial jobs." Institutional racism denied equality to blacks in housing, education, employment, and the justice system. In the face of racial discrimination and segregation, however, black populations in Phoenix and elsewhere struggled to overcome white racist-imposed barriers. External forces hindered black progress, but internal forces often provided the strength needed to go on; as one historian has put it, "Where possible, blacks established institutions to serve their needs, supplement the family's role, and bind black people into a community of shared disadvantage."[16]

Exclusion, however, took its toll on the black population. The Great Depression also played havoc with African Americans in Phoenix, as it did in other cities. Economic downturns often hit racial minority groups first. Being at the lower end of the economic scale in Phoenix, black workers and businesses experienced fewer opportunities in the 1930s. Often the last hired and the first fired, blacks suffered more than any other minority group during the depression period. At the same time, members of the Phoenix black community worked hard to alleviate the suffering; they utilized old and new organizations to combat the problems of the 1930s. They also supported Franklin D. Roosevelt and his

New Deal. Despite difficult circumstances, black leaders during the decade encouraged celebrations of black history and black holidays. Emancipation Day and other important occasions reminded blacks of their past struggles and injected them with pride and inspiration, enabling them to better fight current problems. Black churches, acting to meet spiritual and secular needs, especially served as rallying points during trying times.

For African Americans, as well as Mexican Americans and Chinese Americans in Phoenix, World War II worked as a catalyst. Serving bravely in the armed forces and joining the war effort at home, they were determined to secure more economic opportunities and civil rights during and after the war. Having fought a war to defeat racism, they felt it was time for them to be treated equitably as first-class American citizens. Some gains occurred in Phoenix and elsewhere, but the struggle continued. African American veterans, like others, benefited from the G.I. Bill and other postwar rewards. Also, local chapters of the National Urban League and the National Association for the Advancement of Colored People called for change, and the drive for justice and equality escalated, but resistance made change difficult to realize.

Many white Americans, despite the Nazi experience and the work of respected scholars who challenged the notion of racial superiority, remained racists. Another great migration of Southern blacks to Northern and Western urban centers occurred during and after World War II, causing considerable interracial tension and conflict. Political, economic, and social justice for blacks remained elusive during the postwar years, and the attainment of first-class citizenship proved to be slow. Race restrictions kept blacks from living where they wanted, for example. While whites moved to the suburbs, the great majority of blacks remained in the inner cities. Blacks wanted the suburban dream, but they were ineligible; as one observer declared, regarding black housing opportunities, "Negro buyers, regardless of affluence, education, or credit rating, would be refused and discouraged if they should attempt to purchase a home in the new developments which cater to the white market."[17]

In the 1950s and 1960s, despite ongoing racial prejudice and discrimination, improvements followed more militant protests. Successful national and local legal moves to desegregate the schools and end discrimination in employment, housing, public accommodations, and voting were celebrated. In Phoenix and elsewhere, national and local civil rights legislation brought more economic, political, and social opportunities to members of the black community, especially to those members equipped and prepared to benefit from them most. For many, the struggle persisted. "Both Blacks and Spanish have a disproportionate share of the overcrowded population as well as a disproportionate share of families with incomes under $7,000," noted a study of housing in Phoenix. The lack of education and the high unemployment rate among both groups disturbed housing officials, who lamented the presence of Phoenix minority group members living in the "dilapidated housing" concentrated south of Van Buren and north of Broadway between Twenty-seventh Avenue and Forty-eighth Street.

Racial minority groups in Phoenix rarely joined together in pursuit of common goals, but each gained as a result of the general effort put forth by all groups. Progress persisted into the 1970s and 1980s, and the African American middle class expanded, experiencing to some degree the same success as the Mexican American and Chinese American middle classes, particularly in areas such as occupational mobility and residential mobility. Historically, however, the failure of minority groups to unite in the struggle to conquer common problems, and their traditional tendency to dislike each other and to see each other as rivals, proved debilitating.

Increased Hispanic immigration in the 1980s and 1990s impacted the African American community. Black neighborhoods felt the pressure of encroaching Hispanics (largely Mexicans), which caused friction and resentment between both groups. "African Americans complain that Hispanics are taking a bigger piece of that tiny slice of economic pie left for minorities," noted a 1993 report. "It's the same piece African Americans say they have fought for generations to get." Leaders of the larger Hispanic population responded that African Americans "don't have an exclusive on the legacy of suffering, and that civil rights in this country—through programs like Affirmative Action—have favored African Americans." As in the past, Hispanics and blacks competed for limited resources, and as the number of Hispanics multiplied, conflict increased between the groups. New Hispanic economic and political power threatened to increase discontent among adversely affected groups in the minority population, and observers warned of the danger; other critics remembered the past and asserted that there were those in Phoenix "who would rather see the Hispanics and blacks divide and fight against themselves."

Class divisions had always existed among blacks in Phoenix and other urban centers, as they did in other minority groups, but never to the extent they reached in the 1980s and 1990s. In urban America, the black middle class became larger, wealthier, and more dispersed, while the black underclass also grew larger, poorer, and more concentrated in the inner cities. Considering these developments, some observers declared that "class had become more important than race in determining black life-chances." For the underclass left behind, it was said, the future looked bleak.[18]

At the same time, there were successful blacks who took the time to help those less fortunate than themselves. For example, the Black Women's Task Force, established in Phoenix in 1983, hoped to help the city's African American poor work their way out of poverty. "I remember what Rev. King told us, that we're not really free unless we bring all our brothers and sisters up with us," declared Lynette Myles Gibbs, a leader of the organization. "I came from the very bottom and I'm real sensitive about helping others," she added. "I had someone who helped me. Unless we have friends take us by the hand and show us there is another life, we may get lost."[19]

While the African American community welcomed improvements and the rise of successful middle-class members, problems remained. Those who gained entry into the middle class reflected the upward mobility possible in Phoenix and in the nation. For others, however, educational, employment, and housing opportunities were elusive, and parity with white Americans seemed unlikely in the near future. In addition, the economic recession of the late 1980s persisted into the 1990s, making it more difficult for many unprepared African Americans and other minority group members, as well as many Anglos, to progress. The principal problem confronting the growing black underclass remained economic depression. The labor market closed for many young uneducated black males, while the number of black families headed by single women rose. The percentage of such families among blacks increased much faster than the percentage for whites. Lower educational levels, lower wage levels, and racial and gender discrimination put black women at greater disadvantage in the labor market and made them more dependent on welfare. Like other women of color, they suffered from multiple oppressions. Responsible for small children and unable to work or to find work, they often depended upon public assistance for survival.

Better jobs and wages would, according to observers, change the dismal trends. In addition, more job opportunities had to be created in the inner cities because the "deindustrialization of America" and the movement of plants and offices to the suburbs had impacted unemployment rates. In Phoenix and other urban centers, most blacks and other people of color remained in the central city. For example, only 21 percent of

African American households and 31 percent of Mexican American households in the Phoenix metropolitan area in 1980 lived outside the central city of Phoenix. In contrast, 49 percent of Anglo households lived in the suburbs.[20]

For many African Americans the struggle continued. In the early 1990s the progress and prosperity of the black middle class increased the differences between it and the black lower classes in Phoenix and in America. Class and cultural divisions appeared to be diffusing any attempt at community unity. The Phoenix African American community could unify behind an issue as important as a holiday for Martin Luther King, Jr., but it remained fragmented as various individuals and groups pursued their own agendas. In this respect, it resembled the diverse Mexican American and Asian American communities in Phoenix, and elsewhere, not to mention the diverse Anglo American community.

All told, historians considering the multiracial, multicultural course of American history cannot deny the heroic struggle for equity and parity in American society participated in by all three minority groups. Despite problems, it resulted in substantial progress for many Mexican Americans, Chinese Americans, and African Americans in Phoenix and other cities of the American West. As the struggle persisted into the 1990s, concerned observers hoped that it would continue to bear positive results, but fewer problems. Fewer problems are a precondition to a better Phoenix and a better America. The challenges are imposing, but considering the gains made in the past, the future holds hope for even more progress.

NOTES

INTRODUCTION

1. Bradford Luckingham, *Phoenix: The History of a Southwestern Metropolis* (Tucson: University of Arizona Press, 1989). In this study, Anglos are defined as white people of non-Hispanic descent.

2. Alex M. Saragoza, "The Significance of Recent Chicano-related Historical Writings: An Appraisal," *Ethnic Affairs* 1 (Fall 1987), 24–62; Thomas E. Sheridan, *Los Tucsonenses: The Mexican Community in Tucson, 1854–1941* (Tucson: University of Arizona Press, 1986); Francisco A. Rosales, "The Mexican Immigrant Experience in Chicago, Houston, and Tucson: Comparisons and Contrasts," in Francisco A. Rosales and Barry J. Kaplan, eds., *Houston: A Twentieth Century Urban Frontier* (Port Washington: Associated Faculty Press, 1983), 58–77; Shih-shan Henry Tsai, *The Chinese Experience in America* (Bloomington: Indiana University Press, 1986); Ronald Takaki, *Strangers From a Distant Shore: A History of Asian Americans* (New York: Penguin Books, 1989); Kenneth L. Kusmer, "The Black Urban Experience in American History," in Darlene Clark Hine, ed., *The State of Afro-American History: Past, Present, and Future* (Baton Rouge: Louisiana State University Press, 1986), 91–122; Quintard Taylor, "Black Urban Development—Another View: Seattle's Central District, 1910–1940," *Pacific Historical Review* 58 (December 1989), 429–48. See also Patricia Nelson Limerick, *The Legacy of Conquest: The Unbroken Past of the American West* (New York: W.W. Norton & Company, 1987); Michael P. Malone and Richard W. Etulain, *The American West: A Twentieth Century History* (Lincoln: University of Nebraska Press, 1989); Richard White, *"It's Your Misfortune and None of My Own": A New History of the American West* (Norman: University of Oklahoma Press, 1991).

3. Bradford Luckingham, *The Urban Southwest: A Profile History of Al-*

buquerque, El Paso, Phoenix and Tucson (El Paso: Texas Western Press, University of Texas, El Paso, 1982); Mario T. Garcia, *Desert Immigrants: The Mexicans of El Paso, 1880–1920* (New Haven: Yale University Press, 1981); Albert Camarillo, *Chicanos in a Changing Society: From Mexican Pueblos to American Barrios in Santa Barbara and Southern California, 1848–1930* (Cambridge: Harvard University Press, 1979); Richard Griswold del Castillo, *The Los Angeles Barrio, 1850–1890: A Social History* (Berkeley: University of California Press, 1979); Ricardo Romo, *East Los Angeles: History of a Barrio* (Austin: University of Texas Press, 1983); Sheridan, *Los Tucsonenses;* Arnoldo DeLeón, *Ethnicity in the Sunbelt: A History of Mexican Americans in Houston* (Houston: Mexican American Studies, University of Houston, 1989); Ricardo Romo, "Mexican Americans in the New West," in Gerald D. Nash and Richard W. Etulain, eds., *The Twentieth Century West: Historical Interpretations* (Albuquerque: University of New Mexico Press, 1989), 123–45; Lawrence A. Cardoso, *Mexican Emigration to the United States, 1897–1931* (Tucson, University of Arizona Press, 1980).

4. Luckingham, *The Urban Southwest;* Garcia, *Desert Immigrants;* Camarillo, *Chicanos in a Changing Society;* Griswold del Castillo, *Los Angeles Barrio;* Romo, *East Los Angeles;* Sheridan, *Los Tucsonenses;* DeLeón, *Houston;* Carlos E. Cortes, "Mexicans," in Stephen Thernstrom, ed., *Harvard Encyclopedia of American Ethnic Groups* (Cambridge: Harvard University Press, 1980), 217–34; Romo, "Mexican Americans in the New West," 123–45; Richard Griswold del Castillo, *La Familia: Chicano Families in the Urban Southwest, 1848 to the Present* (Notre Dame: University of Notre Dame Press, 1984); Jose Amaro Hernandez, *Mutual Aid for Survival: The Case of the Mexican American* (Malabar, Florida: Robert E. Krieger Publishing Company, 1983).

5. Rodolpho Alvarez, "The Psycho-Historical and Socioeconomic Development of the Chicano Community in the United States," *Social Science Quarterly* 53 (March 1973), 920–42; Mario T. Garcia, *Mexican Americans: Leadership, Ideology & Identity, 1930–1960* (New Haven: Yale University Press, 1989); Richard A. Garcia, *Rise of the Mexican American Middle Class: San Antonio, 1929–1941* (College Station: Texas A & M University Press, 1991); F. Arturo Rosales, "Mexicans in Houston: The Struggle to Survive, 1908–1975," *Houston Review* 3 (Summer 1981), 224–48; Cortes, "Mexicans," 217–34; Romo, "Mexican Americans in the New West," 123–45; Abraham Hoffman, *Unwanted Mexican Americans in the Great Depression: Repatriation Pressures, 1929–1939* (Tucson: University of Arizona Press, 1974).

6. Garcia, *Mexican Americans;* Garcia, *Mexican American Middle Class;* Gerald D. Nash, *The American West Transformed: The Impact of the Second World War* (Bloomington: Indiana University Press, 1985); Raul Morin, *Among the Valiant: Mexican Americans in World War II and Korea* (Alhambra, CA: Borden Publishing Company, 1966); David Montejano, *Anglos and Mexicans in*

the Making of Texas, 1836–1986 (Austin: University of Texas Press, 1987); Romo, "Mexican Americans in the New West," 123–45; Cortes, "Mexicans," 217–34; Alvarez, "Chicano Community," 931–36; Saragoza, "The Significance of Recent Chicano-related Historical Writings: An Appraisal," 24–62.

7. Romo, "Mexican Americans in the New West," 123–45; Saragoza, "Historical Writings," 41–62; Garcia, *Mexican Americans;* Garcia, *Mexican American Middle Class;* DeLeón, *Houston;* Oscar J. Martinez, *The Chicanos of El Paso: An Assessment of Progress* (El Paso: Texas Western Press, University of Texas, El Paso, 1980); Cortes, "Mexicans," 217–34; Albert Camarillo, *Chicanos in California: A History of Mexican Americans in California* (San Francisco: Boyd and Fraser Publishing Company, 1984); Hispanic Policy Development Project, *A More Perfect Union: Achieving Hispanic Parity by the Year 2000* (New York: Hispanic Policy Development Project, 1990).

8. June Mei, "Socioeconomic Origins of Emigration: Guangdong to California, 1850–1882," in Lucie Cheng and Edna Bonacich, eds., *Labor Immigration Under Captitalism: Asian Workers in the United States Before World War II* (Berkeley: University of California Press, 1984), 219–47; Ronald Takaki, *History of Asian Americans;* Tsai, *The Chinese Experience;* Roger Daniels, *Asian America: Chinese and Japanese in the United States Since 1850* (Seattle: University of Washington Press, 1988); Gunther Barth, *Bitter Strength: A History of the Chinese in the United States, 1850–1870* (Cambridge: Harvard University Press, 1964).

9. Stanford M. Lyman, *The Asian in the West* (Reno: University of Nevada Press, 1970); Him Mark Lai, "Chinese," in Stephen Thernstrom, ed., *Harvard Encyclopedia of American Ethnic Groups* (Cambridge: Harvard University Press, 1980), 217–34; Takaki, *A History of Asian Americans;* Tsai, *The Chinese Experience;* Daniels, *Asian America;* Barth, *Bitter Strength.*

10. Roger Daniels, "American Historians and East Asian Immigrants," *Pacific Historical Review* 43 (November 1974), 449–72; Elmer C. Sandmeyer, *The Anti-Chinese Movement in California* (Urbana: University of Illinois Press, 1973); Stuart Creighton Miller, *The Unwelcome Immigrant: The American Image of the Chinese, 1785–1882* (Berkeley: University of California Press, 1969); Lai, "Chinese," 217–34; Takaki, *A History of Asian Americans;* Tsai, *The Chinese Experience;* Daniels, *Asian America.*

11. Donald Dale Jackson, " 'Behave like your actions reflect all Chinese,' " *Smithsonian* 21 (April 1990), 115–25; John Wunder, "Chinese in Trouble: Criminal Law and Race on the Trans-Mississippi Frontier," *Western Historical Quarterly* 17 (January 1986), 25–41; Daniels, "East Asian Immigrants," 449–72; Tsai, *The Chinese Experience;* Daniels, *Asian America;* Takaki, *A History of Asian Americans.*

12. Lyman, *Asian in the West;* Lyman, "Conflict and the Web of Group Affiliation in San Francisco's Chinatown, 1850–1910," *Pacific Historical Review*

43 (November 1974), 473–99; Lai, "Chinese," 217–34; Rose Hum Lee, *The Chinese in the United States of America* (Hong Kong: Cathay Press, 1960); Daniels, *Asian America;* Tsai, *The Chinese Experience;* Takaki, *A History of Asian Americans.*

13. Ivan H. Light, *Ethnic Enterprise in America: Business and Welfare Among Chinese, Japanese and Blacks* (Berkeley: University of California Press, 1972); Lai, "Chinese," 217–34; Tsai, *The Chinese Experience;* Takaki, *A History of Asian Americans;* Daniels, *Asian America.*

14. Lai, "Chinese," 217–34; Tsai, *The Chinese Experience;* Takaki, *A History of Asian Americans;* Daniels, *Asian America.*

15. Laurence B. de Graaf, "Recognition, Racism and Reflections on the Writing of Western Black History," *Pacific Historical Review* 44 (February 1975), 22–51; Laurence B. de Graaf, "Race, Sex, and Region: Black Women in the American West, 1850–1920," *Pacific Historical Review* 49 (May 1980), 285–314; Quintard Taylor, "The Emergence of Black Communities in the Pacific Northwest, 1856–1910," *Journal of Negro History* 64 (Fall 1979), 342–51; Douglas Henry Daniels, *Pioneer Urbanites: A Social History of Black San Francisco* (Philadelphia: Temple University Press, 1980); Alwyn Barr, "Blacks in Southwestern Cities," *Red River Valley Historical Review* 6 (Spring 1981), 5–7; Luckingham, *The Urban Southwest.*

16. Albert Broussard, "Organizing the Black Community in the San Francisco Bay Area, 1915–1930," *Arizona and the West* 23 (Winter 1981), 335–54; Laurence B. de Graaf, "The City of Black Angels: Emergence of the Los Angeles Ghetto, 1890–1930," *Pacific Historical Review* 39 (August 1970), 323–52; Taylor, "Black Urban Development," 429–48; Daniels, *Pioneer Urbanites;* Luckingham, *The Urban Southwest.*

17. Stephen J. Leonard, "Black-White Relations in Denver, 1930s–1970s," *The Midwest Review* 12 (December 1990), 56–64; Rudolph M. Lapp, *Afro-Americans in California,* 2nd ed. (San Francisco: Boyd and Fraser, 1987); Nash, *The American West Transformed;* Gerald D. Nash, *The American West in The Twentieth Century: A Short History of an Urban Oasis* (Englewood Cliffs: Prentice Hall, 1973); Quintard Taylor, "The Great Migration: The Afro-American Communities of Seattle and Portland During the 1940s," *Arizona and the West* 23 (Summer 1981), 109–26; Luckingham, *Phoenix.*

18. Reynolds Farley and Walter R. Allen, *The Color Line and the Quality of Life in America* (New York: Oxford University Press, 1989); William Julius Wilson, *The Declining Significance of Race: Blacks and Changing American Institutions* (Chicago: University of Chicago Press, 1978); William Julius Wilson, *The Truly Disadvantaged: The Inner City, the Underclass, and Public Policy* (Chicago: University of Chicago Press, 1987); Alphonso Pinkney, *The Myth of Black Progress* (Cambridge: Harvard University Press, 1984); James O. and Lois E. Horton, "Race and Class," *American Quarterly* 35 (Spring-Summer 1983), 155–68; Lapp, *Afro-Americans in California;* Shelby Steele, *The Content of Our*

Character: A New Vision of Race in America (New York: St. Martin's, 1990); Nicholas Lemann, "Healing the Ghettos: A Vision of the Possible in Race Relations," *Atlantic* 203 (March 1991), 22–24.

CHAPTER 1

1. Bradford Luckingham, *The Urban Southwest: A Profile History of Albuquerque, El Paso, Phoenix and Tucson* (El Paso: Texas Western Press, The University of Texas, El Paso, 1982), 1–2. See also C. L. Sonnichsen, *Pass of the North: Four Centuries on the Rio Grande* (El Paso: Texas Western Press, University of Texas, El Paso, 1968).

2. Luckingham, *The Urban Southwest,* 1–16; Bradford Luckingham, "The American Southwest: An Urban View," *Western Historical Quarterly* 15 (July 1984), 261–80. See also Albert Camarillo, *Chicanos in a Changing Society: From Mexican Pueblos to American Barrios in Santa Barbara and Southern California, 1848–1930* (Cambridge: Harvard University Press, 1979); Thomas E. Sheridan, *Los Tucsonenses: The Mexican Community in Tucson, 1854–1941* (Tucson: University of Arizona Press, 1989); Richard Griswold del Castillo, *The Los Angeles Barrio, 1850–1890: A Social History* (Berkeley: University of California Press, 1980).

3. Herbert R. Patrick, *The Ancient Canal Systems and Pueblos of the Salt River, Arizona* (Phoenix: Phoenix Printing Company, 1903); Jeffrey Cook, "Patterns of Desert Urbanization: The Evolution of Metropolitan Phoenix," in Gideon Golaney, ed., *Urban Planning for Arid Zones: American Experiences and Directions* (New York: Praeger, 1978), 205–08; Geoffrey P. Mawn, "Phoenix, Arizona: Central City of the Southwest, 1870–1920," (Ph.D. dissertation, Arizona State University, 1979), 2–3; Michael H. Bartlett, Thomas M. Kolaz, and David A. Gregory, *Archaeology in the City: A Hohokam Village in Phoenix, Arizona* (Tucson: University of Arizona Press, 1986), 17–34.

4. John Francis Bannon, *The Spanish Borderlands Frontier, 1513–1821* (New York: Holt, Rinehart and Winston, 1970); David J. Weber, *The Mexican Frontier, 1821–1846: The American Southwest Under Mexico* (Albuquerque: University of New Mexico Press, 1982); Luckingham, *The Urban Southwest;* Camarillo, *Chicanos in a Changing Society;* Griswold del Castillo, *The Los Angeles Barrio.*

5. Bradford Luckingham, *Phoenix: The History of a Southwestern Metropolis* (Tucson: University of Arizona Press, 1989), 13; Geoffrey P. Mawn, "Promoters, Speculators and the Selection of the Phoenix Townsite," *Arizona and the West* 19 (Fall 1977), 214–15.

6. Luckingham, *Phoenix,* 13–16; Mawn, "Promoters," 215–18; Pete Rey Dimas, "Perspectives on Progress and a Mexican American Community's Struggle for Existence," (Ph.D. dissertation, Arizona State University, 1991), 31–37.

7. (Prescott) *Weekly Arizona Miner,* January 20, April 27, 1872, December 2, 1876, April 20, 1877; Patricia Adank Canode, "Hispanics in the Early Phoenix Community" (Geoffrey P. Mawn files, Arizona Historical Foundation, Hayden Library, Arizona State University); Dimas, "Struggle for Existence," 32–37.

8. *Weekly Arizona Miner,* May 13, 1871; *Phoenix Herald,* August 17, 1883; *Phoenix Daily Herald,* May 8, 1896; Adank, "Early Phoenix," 6–7; Thomas Edwin Farish, *History of Arizona,* vol. II (San Francisco: Filmer Brothers Electrotype Company, 1915), 101.

9. *Weekly Arizona Miner,* April 27, June 1, November 30, 1872, July 12, September 6, 13, 1873, April 30, 1877.

10. *Weekly Arizona Miner,* April 13, 1872; *San Diego Union,* March 5, 1872; *Arizona Enterprise,* March 20, 1878; *Territorial Expositor,* June 25, 1880; U.S. Federal Census, Arizona Territory, 1870, 1880.

11. *Salt River Herald,* June 1, 1878; *Territorial Expositor,* May 9, 1879; *Phoenix Herald,* October 23, 1879; *Arizona Gazette,* May 9, 1883, March 14, 1884; Karen Lynn Smith, "From Town to City: A History of Phoenix, 1870–1912," (M.A. thesis, University of California, Santa Barbara, 1978), 24–25; Patrick Hamilton, *The Resources of Arizona* (San Francisco: Meyer, 1884), 80–84; Luckingham, *The Urban Southwest,* 18–19.

12. *Territorial Expositor,* May 9, 1879; *Phoenix Herald,* September 13, October 2, 1880, June 24, 1881; Smith, "History of Phoenix," 23–24.

13. *Phoenix Herald,* September 13, October 2, 4, December 13, 1880, January 13, 1881, September 16, 1887; *Phoenix Daily Herald,* September 23, 1880, September 17, 1881, September 12, 1885, May 21, August 13, 1886, October 17, 1887; *Arizona Gazette,* December 21, 1881.

14. *Salt River Herald,* June 6, 1877, August 3, December 28, 1878, May 7, 1879, February 1, 1881; *Phoenix Daily Herald,* July 14, 29, 1888, August 2, 1889, June 2, 1897.

15. *Arizona Gazette,* November 3, 1884; *Phoenix Daily Herald,* May 12, June 12, December 5, 1888, October 16, 1889, October 15, November 5, 9, 1894.

16. *Phoenix Herald,* October 3, 1887; *Arizona Gazette,* July 6, 1890; *Phoenix Daily Herald,* March 27, 1888, May 5, 14, 20, 22, 31, June 20, 1889, January 29, 1891, March 16, 23, October 14, 1893.

17. *Phoenix Daily Herald,* January 22, 1894, September 16, 1985, April 28, 29, 1898; *Arizona Republican,* March 31, 1899.

18. *Arizona Republican,* June 23, 1900.

19. *Arizona Republican,* June 6, July 2, September 22, 1900, March 7, 21, 1902, September 27, 1903.

20. *Arizona Republican,* May 5, 1902, September 17, 1903, January 14, September 14, 15, 16, 1905, February 15, May 6, 1908.

21. Luckingham, *Phoenix,* 33–34; Bradford Luckingham, "The Southwest-

ern Urban Frontier, 1880–1930," *Journal of the West* 18 (July 1979), 46–48; Phoenix Chamber of Commerce, *Resources of the Salt River Valley* (Phoenix: Phoenix Directory Company, 1891); Shirley J. Roberts, "Minority Group Poverty in Phoenix: A Socio-Economic Survey," *Journal of Arizona History* 14 (Winter 1973), 349–51.

22. Luckingham, *Phoenix*, 59–60; A. D. Beasley, *Phoenix, Arizona, Maricopa County* (Phoenix: Union Label, 1910), 14; Oscar J. Martinez, "On the Size of the Chicano Population: New Estimates, 1850–1900," *AZTLAN: International Journal of Chicano Studies Research* 6 (Spring 1975), 43–67; Lawrence A. Cardoso, *Mexican Immigration to the United States, 1897–1921* (Tucson: University of Arizona Press, 1980), 36–37; Camarillo, *Chicanos in a Changing Society*, 117.

23. *Arizona Republican*, October 12, 13, 1913; *Arizona Gazette*, February 3, 1914; Luckingham, *Phoenix*, 67.

24. *Arizona Republican*, September 17, October 11, 1912, April 25, 1914, August 25, September 16, 1915.

25. *Arizona Republican*, February 10, 11, 27, March 24, May 17, 29, 1915, May 21, 1916; *Arizona Gazette*, June 6, November 25, 1919; James McBride, "The Liga Protectora Latina: A Mexican American Benevolent Society in Arizona," *Journal of the West* 19 (October 1975), 82–90.

26. *Arizona Republican*, June 26, 29, 30, July 21, 22, 29, August 8, 12, September 6, 1915, December 24, 1916; *Arizona Gazette*, July 20, 1928; *Phoenix City and Salt River Valley Directory, 1928* (Phoenix: Arizona Directory Company, 1928), 217; Dimas, "Struggle for Existence," 55–59; Michael J. Kotlanger, "Phoenix, Arizona, 1920–1940" (Ph.D. dissertation, Arizona State University, 1983), 433–34, 475; Julie A. Corley, "St. Mary's Parish, Phoenix, Arizona," (M.A. thesis, Arizona State University, 1992); Adam Diaz interview (Phoenix History Project, Arizona State Historical Society, 1976).

27. *Arizona Gazette*, May 25, 29, 1918; *Arizona Republican*, May 10, 1919.

28. *Arizona Republican*, May 19, September 5, 1917, March 17, 1918, February 20, August 7, 1920; Bradford Luckingham, "Urban Development in Arizona: The Rise of Phoenix," *Journal of Arizona History* 22 (Summer 1981), 203–04; Kotlanger, "Phoenix, 1920–1940," 425–27; Herbert B. Peterson, "A Twentieth Century Journey to Cibola: Tragedy of the Bracero in Maricopa County, 1917–1921" (M.A. thesis, Arizona State University, 1975), passim; Herbert B. Peterson, "Twentieth Century Search for Cibola: Post–World War I Mexican Labor Exploitation in Arizona," in Manuel P. Servin, ed., *An Awakened Minority: The Mexican Americans* (Beverly Hills: Glencoe Press, 1974), 113–132.

29. *Arizona Republican*, August 7, 1920, January 14, 15, February 10, 23, June 12, 15, 1921; Dimas, "Struggle for Existence," 39–52; Peterson, "Journey to Cibola," passim; Peterson, "Post–World War I Labor Exploitation in Arizona," 113–32; Mark Reisler, *By The Sweat of Their Brow: Mexican Immigrant*

Labor in the United States, 1900–1940 (Westport: Greenwood Press, 1976), 49–50.

30. *Arizona Republican,* November 25, 1919, September 16, 1920; Luckingham, *Phoenix,* 95–96; Kotlanger, "Phoenix, 1920–1940," 443; *Phoenix City and Salt River Valley Directory, 1930* (Phoenix: Arizona Directory Company, 1930); 224; Adam Diaz interview (Arizona Collection, Hayden Library, Arizona State University, October 25, 1977).

31. *Arizona Republican,* April 10, June 10, 1918, January 22, 26, 1920, March 16, 1921, July 8, 1922; Mary Ruth Titcomb, "Americanization and Mexicans in the Southwest: A History of Phoenix's Friendly House, 1920–1983," (M.A. thesis, University of California, Santa Barbara, 1983), 6–41.

32. Titcomb, "Americanization," 6–41, passim.

33. Bradford Luckingham, *Epidemic in the Southwest, 1918–1919* (El Paso: Texas Western Press, University of Texas, El Paso, 1984), 46–47.

34. *Arizona Republican,* May 26, September 5, 1917, October 10, 15–20, 22, 1918, September 15, November 20, 1919; *Arizona Gazette,* October 10, 15, 19, 22, 1918; Titcomb, "Americanization," 20–22.

35. Frederick Simpich, "Arizona Comes of Age," *The National Geographic Magazine* 55 (January 1929), 47.

36. *Arizona Republican,* June 19, August 26, 1919, September 21, 1929; *Phoenix Gazette,* September 21, 1929; W. D. Chesterfield to Joseph S. Jenkes, "Report, November 14, 1935" (Typescript, Fred Wilson Papers, Arizona Collection, Hayden Library, Arizona State University), 1–23.

37. *Arizona Republican,* September 21, 1929; *Phoenix Gazette,* September 21, 1929.

CHAPTER 2

1. *U.S. Census of Population, 1930–1940;* Shirley J. Roberts, "Minority Group Poverty in Phoenix: A Socio-Economic Survey," *Journal of Arizona History* 14 (Winter 1973), 355–58; Michael J. Kotlanger, "Phoenix, Arizona, 1920–1940" (Ph.D. dissertation, Arizona State University, 1983), 444–48.

2. *Arizona Republican,* August 4, 1935; Roberts, "Minority Group Poverty," 358–59; Pete Rey Dimas, "Perspectives on Progress and a Mexican American Community's Struggle for Existence" (Ph.D. dissertation, Arizona State University, 1991), 97–99; Kotlanger, "Phoenix, 1920–1940," 403–06.

3. *Arizona Republican,* August 4, 1935; Roberts, "Minority Group Poverty," 358–59; Dimas, "Struggle for Existence," 97–99; Kotlanger, "Phoenix, 1920–1940," 403–06; Val Cordova interview (Phoenix History Project, Arizona Historical Society, 1976); Richard Barnett and Joseph Garai, *Where the States Stand on Civil Rights* (New York, 1962), 18–20.

4. Emmett McLoughlin, *People's Padre: An Autobiography* (Boston: Beacon Press, 1959), 40–58.

5. *Phoenix Gazette,* July 31, 1933; Mary Ruth Titcomb, "Americanization and Mexicans in the Southwest: A History of Phoenix's Friendly House, 1920–1983" (M.A. thesis, University of California, Santa Barbara, 1983), 41–57.

6. *Arizona Republican,* September 17, 1935; Titcomb, "Americanization," 42–47; Dimas, "Struggle for Existence," 103. See also Abraham Hoffman, *Unwanted Mexican Americans in the Great Depression: Repatriation Measures, 1929–1939* (Tucson: University of Arizona Press, 1974).

7. *Arizona Republic,* October 26, 1933, October 19, 1937; Office of Government Reports, Statistical Section Report No. 10, Volume I–County Data: "Arizona" (Washington, D.C.: U.S. Government Printing Office, 1940); Malcolm Brown and Orin Cassmore, *Migratory Cotton Pickers in Arizona* (Washington, D.C., U.S. Government Printing Office, 1939), xi–xxi, 5–10, 49–79; Richard Lowitt, *The New Deal and the West* (Bloomington: Indiana University Press, 1984), 16–21; Richard Lowitt and Maurine Beasley, eds., *One Third of a Nation: Lorena Hickok Reports on the Great Depression* (Urbana: University of Illinois Press, 1981), 238–42. See also Marsha L. Weisiger, "Mythic Fields of Plenty: The Plight of Depression-Era Oklahoma Migrants in Arizona," *Journal of Arizona History* 32 (Autumn 1991), 241–266.

8. *Arizona Republic,* September 16, 1933, August 1, September 17, October 13, 1939, September 16, 1942; Dimas, "Struggle for Existence," 107–08; Kotlanger, "Phoenix 1920–1940," 431–33; Titcomb, "Americanization," 54–55.

9. *Arizona Republic,* August 1, September 17, October 13, 1939.

10. *Arizona Republic,* June 20, 1934, August 15, 1935, July 23, 1936, September 16, 1938, August 1, 1940; *Phoenix Gazette,* July 20, 1940; Adam Diaz interview (Phoenix History Project, Arizona Historical Society, 1976); Dimas, "Struggle for Existence," 107–08; Titcomb, "Americanization," 54–55; Joe Alvarado interview (Phoenix History Project, Arizona Historical Society, Phoenix, 1978); Val Cordova interview; Carlos Morales interview (Phoenix History Project, Arizona Historical Society, Phoenix, 1977); Edward F. Orduna interview (Phoenix History Project, Arizona Historical Society, Phoenix, 1977).

11. Titcomb, "Americanization," 54–55.

12. Christine Marin, "Patriotism Abroad and Repression at Home: Mexican Americans in World War II" (Typescript, Arizona Collection, Hayden Library, Arizona State University, 1977), 13–27; Christine Marin, "Mexican Americans on the Home Front: Community Organizations in Arizona During World War II" (Typescript, Arizona Collection, Hayden Library, Arizona State University), 3–15. See also Raul Morin, *Among the Valiant: Mexican Americans in World War II and Korea* (Alhambra, CA: Borden Publishing Co., 1966).

13. Michael Konig, "Toward Metropolis Status: Charter Government and the Rise of Phoenix, 1945–1960" (Ph.D dissertation, Arizona State University, 1983), 166–68, 186–89; Raymond Johnson Flores, "The Socio-Economic Status Trends of the Mexican People Residing in Arizona" (M.A. thesis, Arizona

State University, 1951), 42–54; Roy B. Yanez interview (Phoenix History Project, Arizona Historical Society, Phoenix, 1977).

14. Flores, "The Socio-Economic Status Trends of the Mexican People Residing in Arizona," 42–59, 69–95.

15. Roy B. Yanez interview; Konig, "Toward Metropolis Status," 166–68, 186–89.

16. *Arizona Republic,* November 13, 1933, November 21, 1947, January 12, 1991; James Officer, *Arizona's Hispanic Perspective* (Phoenix: Arizona Academy, 1981), 111–12; *Hearings Before the United States Commission on Civil Rights, Phoenix, Arizona, February 3, 1962* (Washington, D.C., U.S. Government Printing Office, 1962), 36–42, 67–79, 86–95, passim; Konig, "Toward Metropolis Status," 166–168, 186–189; Flores, "The Socio-Economic Status Trends of the Mexican People Residing in Arizona," 42–54; Joe Alvarado interview; Roy B. Yanez interview; Adam Diaz interview.

17. Barry Edward Lamb, "The Making of a Chicano Civil Rights Activist: Ralph Estrada of Arizona" (M.A. thesis, Arizona State University, 1988), 82–117, passim; Alicia Morado, "Gonzalez v. Sheely: The First Desegregation Case in the State of Arizona" (Typescript, Chicano Collection, Hayden Library, Arizona State University, 1988), 1–15.

18. *Hearings,* 67–79, 86–95; Flores, "The Socio-Economic Status Trends of the Mexican People Residing in Arizona," 42–59; 69–95.

19. *Hearings,* 67–79, 86–95.

20. *El Sol,* September 15, 1942, April 2, 1944, May 4, September 6, 1945; *Arizona Republic,* March 11, 1956, February 4, 1973; Mary Franco French interview (Phoenix History Project, Arizona Historical Society, Phoenix, 1978); Adam Diaz interview; Flores, "The Socio-Economic Status Trends of the Mexican People Residing in Arizona," 42–59, 69–95; Jose Amaro Fernandez, *Mutual Aid for Survival: The Case of the Mexican American* (Malabar, FL: Krieger, 1983), 49–51; Greater Phoenix Council for Civic Unity, ed., *To Secure These Rights* (Phoenix: Phoenix Sun Publishing Company, 1961), 14–16, 62–65, passim.

21. Eugene Marin interview (Phoenix History Project, Arizona Historical Society, Phoenix, 1976).

22. *Hearings,* 67–79, 86–95; Adam Diaz interview; Flores, "The Socio-Economic Status Trends of the Mexican People Residing in Arizona," 42–59, 69–95; Eugene Marin interview.

23. *Arizona Republic,* November 21, 1947; Officer, *Arizona's Hispanic Perspective,* 111–12; Flores, "The Socio-Economic Status Trends of the Mexican People Residing in Arizona," 42–59, 69–95; Greater Phoenix Council for Civic Unity, ed., *To Secure These Rights,* 14–16, 62–65, passim.

24. *Phoenix Gazette,* February 26, 1962; Adam Diaz interview; Titcomb, "Americanization," 54–74.

25. Placida Garcia Smith interview (Phoenix History Project, Arizona His-

torical Society, Phoenix, 1975); Mary Melcher, "Madge Copeland and Placida Garcia Smith: Community Organizers, Phoenix, Arizona, 1930–1960" (Unpublished manuscript, Women's Studies, Arizona State University, 1987), 10–20.

26. Joe Alvarado interview; Val Cordova interview; Charles Lama, Jr., interview (Phoenix History Project, Arizona Historical Society, Phoenix, 1977).

CHAPTER 3

1. *El Sol,* January 11, 1974, September 12, 1975, April 30, 1976; *New Times,* June 11–17, 1986; Joe Alvarado interview (Phoenix History Project, Arizona Historical Society, Phoenix, 1978); Val Cordova interview (Phoenix History Project, Arizona Historical Society, Phoenix, 1976); Charles Lama, Jr., interview (Phoenix History Project, Arizona Historical Society, Phoenix, 1977); Bradford Luckingham, *The Urban Southwest: A Profile History of Albuquerque, El Paso, Phoenix and Tucson* (El Paso: Texas Western Press, The University of Texas, El Paso, 1982), passim; John E. Crow, *Mexican Americans in Contemporary Arizona: A Social and Demographic View* (San Francisco: R and E Research Associates, 1975), 62–80; Mary Melcher, "Madge Copeland and Placida Garcia Smith: Community Organizers, Phoenix, Arizona, 1930–1960" (Unpublished manuscript, Women's Studies, Arizona State University, 1987), 10–20; *Hearings Before the United States Commission on Civil Rights, Phoenix, Arizona, February 3, 1962* (Washington, D.C., U.S. Government Printing Office, 1962), passim; James Officer, *Arizona's Hispanic Perspective* (Phoenix: Arizona Academy, 1981), 143–61, passim; Patricia A. Adank, "Chicano Activism in Maricopa County—Two Incidents in Retrospect," in Manuel P. Servin, ed., *An Awakened Minority: The Mexican Americans* (Beverly Hills: Sage, 1974), 246–65.

2. Crow, *Mexican Americans in Contemporary Arizona,* 62–80.

3. *El Sol,* January 11, 1974, September 12, 1975, April 30, 1976; *New Times,* June 11–17, 1986; Joe Alvarado interview; Val Cordova interview; Charles Lama, Jr., interview; Crow, *Mexican Americans in Contemporary Arizona,* 62–80; Officer, *Arizona's Hispanic Perspective,* 143–61; Adank, "Chicano Activism in Maricopa County," 246–65.

4. Adank, "Chicano Activism in Maricopa County," 246–65; *New Times,* June 11–17, 1986.

5. *Arizona Republic,* October 9, December 2, 1970; *Phoenix Gazette,* October 7, December 3, 1970, January 13, 16, February 2, 1971; "Furors on a High School Campus," *Arizona* (November 20, 1970), 6–11; Robert Donohoe letter to LULAC, April 11, 1969 (Robert Donohoe Papers, Arizona Collection, Hayden Library, Arizona State University); Yvonne Garrett, "Chicano Politics in the Phoenix Metropolitan Area" (Typescript, Chicano Collection, Hayden Library, Arizona State University, 1973), 1–17; Adank, "Chicano Activism in Maricopa County," 246–65.

6. Mary Ruth Titcomb, "Americanization and Mexicans in the Southwest:

A History of Phoenix's Friendly House, 1920–1983" (M.A. thesis, University of California, Santa Barbara, 1983), 73–95, 102–104; Garrett, "Chicano Politics," 1–17.

7. *Arizona Republic*, November 15, 1960, November 26, 1966, June 18, 1967, January 7, 1971, June 25, 1973, May 26, July 1, May 19, 1975, May 17, 1976; Jose Amaro Hernandez, *Mutual Aid for Survival: The Case of the Mexican American* (Malabar, Florida: Robert E. Krieger Publishing Company, 1983), 56–59; Barry Edward Lamb, "The Making of a Chicano Civil Rights Activist: Ralph Estrada of Arizona" (M.A. thesis, Arizona State University, 1988), 122–60; Titcomb, "Americanization," 73–95, 102–104; Officer, *Arizona's Hispanic Perspective*, 153–61; Garrett, "Chicano Politics," 1–17; Arabella Martinez and David B. Carlson, "Developing Leadership in Minority Communities (Typescript, Chicanos por la Causa, 1983), 81–87; Carl Craig interview (Phoenix History Project, Arizona Historical Society, 1976).

8. Officer, *Arizona's Hispanic Perspective*, 113–61; Franklin J. James et al., *Minorities in the Sunbelt* (New Brunswick, NJ: Rutgers University Press, 1984), 135–39; Pam Hait, "South Phoenix," *Phoenix* 9 (August 1974), 54, 119.

9. Joe Kullman, "The Youth Gang Controversy," *Phoenix* 14 (August 1979), 152–57; Pete Garcia interview (Phoenix History Project, Arizona Historical Society, Phoenix, 1978).

10. Susan Schultz, "Illegal Aliens: Today's Underground Railroad," *Phoenix* 14 (September 1979), 71–75, 112–13, 129.

11. *Arizona Republic*, December 13, 1981, October 6, 1983, October 31, 1986; *New Times*, December 19–25, 1984, May 1–7, 1985; Vicki Hay, "Calvin Goode: South Phoenix Survivor," *Phoenix* 19 (April 1984), 57–58; Whitney Drake, "The 50 Most Influential People in Arizona," *Arizona Living* 17 (July 1986), 32–41, 49.

12. *Arizona Republic*, December 13, 1981, June 13, 1982, October 6, 1983, October 31, 1986, January 8, May 16, 1987; *Phoenix Gazette*, December 18, 1984, September 30, 1985, April 8, 1986, January 5, 26, 1987; *New Times*, December 19–25, 1984, May 1–7, 1985; Hay, "Calvin Goode," 57–58; Data Network for Human Services, *Demographic Trends in Maricopa County: Cities, Towns and Places, 1980–1990* (Phoenix: Data Network for Human Services, 1992).

13. *Arizona Republic*, January 8, May 16, 1987, October 22, 26, 1991; *Phoenix Gazette*, January 8, 26, May 4, 1987.

14. *Phoenix Gazette*, January 19, April 23, 1983; *Arizona Republic*, October 26, 1983.

15. *Phoenix Gazette*, January 19, April 23, 1983, May 25, June 21, 1984, March 29, 1986, January 7, 1987, April 22, December 26, 1991, January 28, 1992; *Arizona Republic*, November 9, 1982, October 26, 1983, July 14, 1985, January 1, 1987, June 6, 9, 1991; *New Times*, December 19–25, 1984, September 16–22, 1987.

16. Peggy DeMarco, Sam LaTana, Rennie A. Null, Claude C. Vallieres, "The West Approach Land Acquisition Project; A Post-Relocation Study" (M.S.W. thesis, Arizona State University, 1979), 5–36, passim; Pete Rey Dimas, "Perspectives on Progress and a Mexican American Community's Struggle for Existence" (Ph.D. dissertation, Arizona State University, 1991), 157–256, passim; *Phoenix Gazette,* March 29, 1986.

17. *Arizona Republic,* December 29, 1983, March 1, 1984, April 29, June 16, 1985, July 22, November 27, 1990, June 6, July 8, November 12, 1991; *Phoenix Gazette,* January 19, 1983, March 9, 1984, March 16, 1986, January 26, April 6, 1987; *New Times,* December 31, 1986, January 6, 1987; Crow, *Mexican Americans in Contemporary Arizona,* 78–79, 83–84.

18. *Arizona Republic,* December 19, 1983, March 1, 1984, April 29, June 16, 1985; *Phoenix Gazette,* March 9, 1986; *New Times,* December 31, 1986, January 6, 1987; Ad Hoc Committee on Human Relations, "The Phoenix Commission on Human Relations: A Promise Unfulfilled" (Typescript, City of Phoenix, September 12, 1984), 1–5, 47–58, passim; "Partnership in Fair Housing Conference" (Typescript, City of Phoenix, May 21, 1986), 8–9; James et al., *Minorities in the Sunbelt,* 62–81, 135–39, passim; Leonard Gordon and Albert J. Mayer, "The Housing Segregation and Housing Conditions of Hispanics in Phoenix, With Comparisons With Other Southwest Cities," in Elizabeth Huttman and Winn Blauw, eds., *Urban Housing Segregation of Minorities in the United States and Western Europe* (Durham: Duke University Press, 1990), 12.

19. *Phoenix Gazette,* May 4, 1983; *Arizona Republic,* December 29, 1983.

20. *El Sol,* January 18, February 1, April 12, July 5, 12, August 2, 16, 30, 1991; *Phoenix Gazette,* May 4, 1983, June 14, 1984, January 21, 1985, November 7, 1986, January 1, 2, February 3, March 9, 26, 1987, May 3, 10, June 2, 15, 1990, March 29, April 1, 22, February 28, March 29, September 13, 30, November 11, 1991; *Arizona Republic,* December 20, 1983, May 17, 1986, January 4, 17, 25, March 27, April 12, 1987, August 30, 1990, January 17, September 25, 1991; January 27, 1992; *New Times,* January 30–February 5, May 4–10, 1985, May 21–27, 1986; *Greater Phoenix Business Journal,* March 30, 1987; *Arizona Informant,* September 19, October 8, 1990, April 3, 10, June 5, August 7, November 28, December 25, 1991; Titcomb, "Americanization," 95–97; Kris Aron, "Chicanos por la Causa: Developing Leadership for the Future," *Phoenix* 19 (December 1984), 101–02, 130–35.

CHAPTER 4

1. Shih-shan Henry Tsai, *The Chinese Experience in America* (Bloomington: Indiana University Press, 1986), 2–10; Ronald Takaki, *Strangers From A Different Shore: A History of Asian Americans* (New York: Penguin Books, 1989), 29–78; Roger Daniels, *Asian America: Chinese and Japanese in the United States Since 1850* (Seattle: University of Washington Press, 1988), 9–28; June

Mei, "Socioeconomic Origins of Emigration: Guangdong to California, 1850–1882," in Lucie Cheng and Edna Bonacich, eds., *Labor Immigration Under Capitalism: Asian Workers in the United States Before World War II* (Berkeley: University of California Press, 1984), 219–47.

2. Daniels, *Asian America*, 29–66; Takaki, *A History of Asian Americans*, 79–131; Tsai, *The Chinese Experience*, 28–89; Gunther Barth, *Bitter Strength: A History of the Chinese in the United States, 1850–1870* (Cambridge: Harvard University Press, 1964), passim.

3. *Salt River Herald*, August 10, 1878; (Prescott) *Weekly Arizona Miner*, October 3, 1879; Laurence Michael Fong, "Sojourners and Settlers: The Chinese Experience in Arizona," *Journal of Arizona History* 21 (Fall 1980), 227–56; Florence C. Lister and Robert H. Lister, "Chinese Sojourners in Territorial Prescott," *Journal of the Southwest* 31 (Spring 1989), 1–76; John Wunder, "Chinese in Trouble: Criminal Law and Race on the Trans-Mississippi West Frontier," *Western Historical Quarterly* 17 (January 1986), 25–41.

4. Tsai, *The Chinese Experience*, 28–50; Takaki, *A History of Asian Americans*, 230–256; Fong, "Sojourners and Settlers," 227–56; Florence C. Lister and Robert H. Lister, *The Chinese of Early Tucson: Historic Archaeology from the Tucson Urban Renewal Project* (Tucson: University of Arizona Press, 1989), 1–15; U.S. Federal Census, Arizona Territory, 1880.

5. *Weekly Arizona Miner*, September 5, 1879; Fong, "Sojourners and Settlers," 248–50; Lister, "Chinese Sojourners," 20.

6. Fong, "Sojourners and Settlers," 248–53; Roger D. Hardaway, "Unlawful Love: A History of Arizona's Miscegenation Law," *Journal of Arizona History* 27 (Autumn 1986), 377–390.

7. Fong, "Sojourners and Settlers," 227–56; U.S. Federal Census, Arizona Territory, 1870.

8. *Arizona Gazette*, February 26, 1886; Daniels, *Asian America*, 29–66; Tsai, *The Chinese Experience*, 56–89.

9. *Salt River Herald*, June 11, 1878; *Territorial Expositor*, July 16, 1880.

10. *Weekly Arizona Miner*, July 13, 1872, February 20, 1874; *Salt River Herald*, September 14, 1878; *Phoenix Herald*, September 15, 1880, August 2, 1882; *Phoenix Daily Herald*, September 12, 1891; *Arizona Republican*, July 21, 1900; James M. Barney, "The Business Progress of Phoenix in 1892" (Barney Collection, Arizona Historical Foundation, Hayden Library, Arizona State University, 1950), 42–43; Gary P. Tipton, "Men Out of China," *Journal of Arizona History* 18 (Autumn 1977), 346.

11. *Salt River Herald*, February 5, 15, 1879; *Territorial Expositor*, August 13, 1880.

12. *Arizona Gazette*, April 5, 1886.

13. *Phoenix Herald*, March 8, 1880.

14. *Phoenix Herald*, June 14, August 13, 16, 1879; *Phoenix Daily Herald*, April 21, July 10, September 21, 1885.

15. *Phoenix Daily Herald,* September 11, 21, 25, 1885; *Arizona Gazette,* October 13, 1885.

16. Tsai, *The Chinese Experience,* 56–89, 110–132; Daniels, *Asian America,* 29–67, 186–199; Fong, "Sojourners and Settlers," 227–56; Takaki, *A History of Asian Americans,* 231–39; Donald Dale Jackson, "'Behave like your actions reflect all Chinese,'" *Smithsonian* 21 (April 1990), 115–25; Vivian Wei Chiang, "The Chinese Community in Phoenix Arizona: A Study of Acculturation and Assimilation" (M.A. thesis, Arizona State University, 1970), 27–43; Beverly Hall, "Hey Chinamen, Do You Speak English?" (Typescript, Hayden Library, Arizona State University, 1980), 1–11; Clifford Alan Perkins, "Recollections of a Chinese-Immigration Inspector," in Anne Hughes Morgan and Rennard Strickland, eds., *Arizona Memories* (Tucson: University of Arizona Press, 1984), 217–31.

17. *Phoenix Herald,* October 29, 1879.

18. *Arizona Gazette,* February 10, March 14, April 13, 1883, January 28, July 26, 1884, April 8, 1886; *Phoenix Herald,* October 29, 1879; *Phoenix Daily Herald,* January 28, 1888.

19. *Salt River Herald,* February 5, 1879; *Arizona Gazette,* November 11, 14, 1881, September 12, 1882, March 12, 1884, May 8, 10, 1886, September 9, 1887, October 16, 1889; *Phoenix Daily Herald,* December 29, 1885, April 14, 1886.

20. *Weekly Arizona Miner,* February 20, 1874; *Territorial Expositor,* December 30, 1879; *Phoenix Herald,* January 28, 29, 1881; *Phoenix Daily Herald,* February 8, 1888, February 16, 1893, January 1, 1895; *Arizona Gazette,* May 10, 1889; *Arizona Daily Gazette,* February 7, 9, 1891.

21. *Phoenix Daily Herald,* May 10, 1889, April 27, 1891; *Arizona Republican,* December 10, 1893; Tsai, *The Chinese Experience,* 33–36; Takaki, *A History of Asian Americans,* 230–69; Beverly Hall, "Hey Chinamen, Do you Speak English?" 1–11; Leigh Dana Johnson, "Equal Rights and the Heathen Chinee: Black Activism in San Francisco, 1865–1875," *Western Historical Quarterly* 11 (January 1980), 57–68; Arnold Shankman, "Black on Yellow: African Americans View Chinese Americans, 1850–1935," *Phylon* 39 (Spring 1978), 1–17; Arnold Shankman, "The Image of Mexico and Mexican Americans in the Black Press, 1890–1935," *Journal of Ethnic Studies* 3 (Summer 1975), 43–56.

22. *Phoenix Herald,* July 6, 1880; *Arizona Republican,* June 23, 1890.

23. *Phoenix Daily Herald,* July 28, August 11, September 4, 22, 27, 1895.

24. *Phoenix Daily Herald,* September 22, October 25, December 6, 1895.

25. *Phoenix Daily Herald, Arizona Republican,* June 23, 1890, *Phoenix Daily Herald,* December 6, 1895; *The Arizona Directory Company's Phoenix Directory of the Year 1895* (Phoenix: The Arizona Directory Company, 1895), 2.

26. Tsai, *The Chinese Experience,* 28–55; Takaki, *A History of Asian Americans,* 79–131, 230–69; Daniels, *Asian America,* 67–99; Stanford M. Lyman, *The Asian in the West* (Reno: University of Nevada Press, 1970), 9–46;

Tipton, "Men Out of China," 346; County Records and Deed Index, Maricopa County, 1878–1921; Robert Ong Hing interview (Phoenix History Project, Arizona Historical Society, Phoenix, 1978); Yee Sing interview (Phoenix History Project, Arizona Historical Society, Phoenix, 1977); Frank Yee interview (Phoenix History Project, Arizona Historical Society, Phoenix, 1976).

27. *Territorial Expositor,* September 3, 1879; *Phoenix Daily Herald,* August 17, 1880, October 7, 1892; *Arizona Republican,* December 5, 1899, April 13, May 15, 1917, July 11, 1917, May 26, 1925; *New Times,* February 13–19, 1991; Michael J. Kotlanger, "Phoenix, Arizona, 1920–1940" (Ph.D. dissertation, Arizona State University, 1983), 411–470; Ivan H. Light, *Ethnic Enterprise in America: Business and Welfare Among Chinese, Japanese and Blacks* (Berkeley: University of California Press, 1972), 4–8, 19–27, passim; Robert Ong Hing interview; Yee Sing interview; Violet Toy interview (Phoenix History Project, Arizona Historical Society, Phoenix, 1976).

28. *Arizona Gazette,* April 23, 1889; *Phoenix Daily Herald,* August 1, 1890; *Arizona Republican,* November 6, 1911.

29. *Arizona Republican,* June 23, 1890, March 9, 11, 1910; Tipton, "Men Out of China," 345–56; Booker T. Washington, "The Race Problem in Arizona," *The Independent* 71 (October 1911), 909–13.

30. *Phoenix Daily Herald,* April 28, September 14, 1893; *Arizona Republican,* June 30, 1902, December 3, 1908, July 15, 1910, August 16, 1920; Daniels, *Asian America,* 57–58.

31. Chiang, "Chinese Community in Phoenix," 54–57; Chiu Thai Yen, "The Chinese in Phoenix," *Phoenix* 5 (January 1970), 38–40, 95–96.

32. *Phoenix Gazette,* January 23, 1929; *Arizona Republican,* January 23, 1929.

33. *Arizona Republican,* February 27, 1902, February 20, 1905, February 13, 1907, August 16, 1920.

34. *Arizona Republican,* March 9, 10, 1910, March 10, 1911, December 12, 1919, June 6, August 15, 1920, February 23, 1922, March 17, August 26, 1923; Kotlanger, "Phoenix, Arizona, 1920–1940," 414–19.

35. *Arizona Gazette,* March 25, 28, 1926; *Arizona Republican,* February 26, 1926, September 11, 1930.

36. *Arizona Republican,* September 20, November 5, 1911, June 7, 1916, November 29, 1922, January 21, 1923; *Phoenix and Salt River Valley Directory, 1923* (Phoenix: Arizona Directory Company, 1923), 125; Kotlanger, "Phoenix, Arizona, 1920–1940," 411–12.

37. *Arizona Republican,* February 9, 1923; Tsai, *The Chinese Experience,* 98; Chiang, "Chinese Community in Phoenix," 37–41; Fong, "Sojourners and Settlers," 250–51; Yee Sing interview; Sing Yee, Jr., interview (Phoenix History Project, Arizona Historical Society, Phoenix, 1977); Tipton, "Men Out of China," 353–56. Traditional Chinese family names are listed first, a reverse order

from the Anglo tradition, but many have been transposed over the years. In Phoenix, for example, this accounts for the transposition of the names of Yee Sing and his son Sing Yee, Jr. Yee is the family name. Some families reversed the order of names and gave their children distinctly Anglo first names; in Phoenix, for example, immigrant Tang Shing's son is Judge Thomas Tang. In this work the author has followed the sources in his use of names.

38. *Phoenix Daily Herald,* January 10, July 26, November 10, 1887; *Arizona Gazette,* June 21, 1918; *Arizona Republican,* May 26, 1901, November 11, 1917, January 25, July 5, 1918, May 10, 1919, April 20, 1920, July 4, 1922.

39. *Arizona Republican,* April 9, 1929; *Phoenix City and Salt River Valley Directory, 1926,* 127; Tipton, "Men Out of China," 354–55; D. H. Toy interview (Phoenix History Project, Arizona Historical Society, Phoenix, 1976); Lucy Tang interview (Phoenix History Project, Arizona Historical Society, Phoenix, 1976); Thomas Tang interview (Phoenix History Project, Arizona Historical Society, Phoenix, 1976).

40. Tsai, *The Chinese Experience,* 90–114; Daniels, *Asian America,* 230–69; Tipton, "Men Out of China," 347–55; Fong, "Settlers and Sojourners," 253–54; *New Times,* February 13–19, 1991; Burt Smith, *What Happened to the Vacant Lots?* (Phoenix: Trails West Publishing Company, 1973), 89–91; Frank Yee interview; Sing Yee interview; Robert Ong Hing interview.

CHAPTER 5

1. *Arizona Republic,* January 13, 1938, July 2, 1939; Richard Nagasawa, *Summer Wind: The Story of an Immigrant Chinese Politician* (Tucson: Westernlore Press, 1986), 84–86; *Phoenix City and Salt River Valley Directory, 1929* (Phoenix: Arizona Directory Company, 1929), passim; *Phoenix City and Salt River Valley Directory, 1930* (Phoenix: Arizona Directory Company, 1930), 222–24, passim; Walter Ong interview (Phoenix History Project, Arizona Historical Society, Phoenix, 1978).

2. Susie Sato, "Before Pearl Harbor: Early Japanese Settlers in Arizona," *Journal of Arizona History* 14 (Winter 1973), 317–34; Yoshiju Kimura, *Arizona Sunset* (Phoenix, Published by the Author, 1980), passim.

3. Sato, "Before Pearl Harbor," 317–34; Jack August, "The Anti-Japanese Crusade in Arizona's Salt River Valley, 1934–35," *Arizona and the West* 21 (Summer 1979), 113–36; Kimura, *Arizona Sunset,* passim.

4. *Arizona Republic,* March 8, November 1, 1934, June 19, 1936, February 24, April 9, 1938; Gary P. Tipton, "Men Out of China," *Journal of Arizona History* 18 (Autumn 1977), 353–56; Vivian Wei Chiang, "The Chinese Community in Phoenix Arizona: A Study of Acculturation and Assimilation" (M.A. thesis, Arizona State University, 1970), 44–45; Michael J. Kotlanger, "Phoenix, Arizona, 1920–1940" (Ph.D. dissertation, Arizona State University, 1983), 419–

20; Michael H. Bernstein, "Geographical Perspectives on Skid Row in Phoenix, Arizona" (M.A. thesis, Arizona State University, 1972), 60–61; Shirley J. Roberts, "Minority Group Poverty in Phoenix: A Socio-Economic Survey," *Journal of Arizona History* 14 (Winter 1973), 358; Richard Nagasawa and Paul Leung, "Geographic Distribution of Chinese in Phoenix, Arizona," *Research Review* 1 (January 1982), 6–8; D. H. Toy interview (Phoenix History Project, Arizona Historical Society, Phoenix, 1976).

5. *Phoenix Gazette,* April 4, 1942; Shih-shan Henry Tsai, *The Chinese Experience in America* (Bloomington: Indiana University Press, 1986), 114–18; Ronald Takaki, *Strangers From A Different Shore: A History of Asian Americans* (New York: Penguin Books, 1989), 371–79; Roger Daniels, *Asian America: Chinese and Japanese in the United States Since 1850* (Seattle: University of Washington Press, 1988), 186–99; The Phoenix Chinatown Archaeology Project, *Table Summarizing Review of City of Phoenix Directories, 1917–1982* (Phoenix: Dames & Moore, 1991); D. H. Toy interview.

6. Tsai, *The Chinese Experience,* 114–18; Takaki, *A History of Asian Americans,* 371–79; Daniels, *Asian America,* 186–99; Walter Ong interview; Robert Ong Hing interview (Phoenix History Project, Arizona Historical Society, Phoenix, 1978); Thomas Tang interview (Phoenix History Project, Arizona Historical Society, Phoenix, 1976).

7. Kimura, *Arizona Sunset,* 59–82; Shelly C. Dudley, "Japanese Relocation: Local Attitudes and Reactions," *History Forum* 3 (Spring 1981), 5–20; Samuel T. Caruso, "After Pearl Harbor: Arizona's Response to the Gila River Relocation Center," *Journal of Arizona History* 14 (Winter 1973), 335–45; Paul Bailey, *City of the Sun: The Japanese Concentration Camp at Poston, Arizona* (Los Angeles, Westernlore Press, 1970), passim; Roger Daniels, *Concentration Camps USA: Japanese Americans and World War II* (New York: Holt, Rinehart & Winston, 1971), 83–84.

8. Kimura, *Arizona Sunset,* 59–82; Dudley, "Japanese Relocation," 5–20.

9. *Phoenix Gazette,* November 8, 1948.

10. *New Times,* February 13–19, 1991; Nagasawa, *Summer Wind,* passim.

11. *New Times,* February 13–19, 1991.

12. *New Times,* February 13–19, 1991.

13. *New Times,* February 13–19, 1991; *Arizona Republic,* October 15, 1948; Nagasawa, *Summer Wind,* 22–34.

14. *Arizona Sun,* August 18, September 1, 8, 15, 22, 1950; *New Times,* February 13–19, 1991; Nagasawa, *Summer Wind,* 64–73, passim.

15. *New Times,* February 13–19, 1991; Nagasawa, *Summer Wind,* 64–73, passim.

16. *Phoenix Gazette,* April 4, 1942, October 27, 1948, October 10, 1950; Nagasawa, *Summer Wind,* 89–99; Walter Ong interview; Robert Ong Hing interview.

17. Chiang, "Chinese Community in Phoenix," 43; Nagasawa, *Summer*

Wind, 24–26, passim; *Hearings Before the United States Commission on Civil Rights, Arizona, February 3, 1962* (Washington, D.C.: U.S. Government Printing Office, 1962), 125–27.

   18. Walter Ong interview, 1978.

CHAPTER 6

   1. *Phoenix Gazette,* July 30, 1982; *Hearings Before the United States Commission on Civil Rights, Arizona, February 3, 1962* (Washington, D.C.: U.S. Government Printing Office, 1962), 125–27.

   2. *Arizona Republic,* February 19, 1985; Walter Ong interview (Phoenix History Project, Arizona Historical Society, Phoenix, 1978).

   3. Shih-shan Henry Tsai, *The Chinese Experience in America* (Bloomington: Indiana University Press, 1986), 157–61; Vivian Wei Chiang, "The Chinese Community in Phoenix Arizona: A Study of Acculturation and Assimilation" (M.A. thesis, Arizona State University, 1970), 36–57, 102–115.

   4. Chiang, "Chinese Community in Phoenix," 36–57, 102–115, passim; Susie Ling, "The Mountain Movers: Asian American Women's Movement in Los Angeles," *Amerasia Journal* 15 (Spring 1989), 51–67.

   5. Tsai, *The Chinese Experience,* 187–92; Roger Daniels, *Asian America: Chinese and Japanese in the United States Since 1850* (Seattle: University of Washington Press, 1988), 317–28, 341–44; Ronald Takaki, *Strangers From A Different Shore: A History of Asian Americans* (New York: Penguin Books, 1989), 473–84; Ling, "The Mountain Movers: Asian American Women's Movement in Los Angeles," 51–67.

   6. *Arizona Chinese Times,* November 1, 1990; *New Times,* February 13–19, 1991; Chiang, "Chinese Community in Phoenix," 51–59; Richard Nagasawa and Paul Leung, "Geographic Distribution of Chinese in Phoenix, Arizona," *Research Review* 1 (January 1982), 608.

   7. *Phoenix Gazette,* March 23, 1991.

   8. *Phoenix Gazette,* March 23, 1991; *New Times,* February 13–19, 1991.

   9. *Phoenix Gazette,* March 23, 1991; *New Times,* February 13–19, 1991; Takaki, *A History of Asian Americans,* 479–84; Daniels, *Asian America,* 341–44.

   10. *Phoenix Gazette,* March 23, 1991; *New Times,* February 13–19, 1991.

   11. *Arizona Chinese Times,* November 1, 1990; *Arizona Republic,* January 1, April 9, August 23, October 15, December 23, 1990, January 21, 1991; *Phoenix Gazette,* July 31, 1980, April 9, September 14, 1990, January 22, 1991; *New Times,* April 22–28, 1987.

   12. *Arizona Chinese Times,* November 1, 1990; *Arizona Republic,* January 1, April 9, August 23, October 15, December 23, 1990, January 21, 1991; *Phoenix Gazette,* July 31, 1980, April 9, September 14, 1990, January 22, 1991; *New Times,* April 22–28, 1987; Data Network for Human Services, *Demo-*

graphic Trends in Maricopa County: Cities, Towns and Places, 1980–1990 (Phoenix: Data Network for Human Services, 1992).

13. Robert Ong Hing interview (Phoenix History Project, Arizona Historical Society, Phoenix, 1975).

14. *Phoenix Gazette*, November 8, 1985, August 17, 1990; Robert Ong Hing interview. See also Richard Nagasawa et al., *The Elderly Chinese: A Forgotten Minority* (Tempe, Arizona State University, 1980).

15. *Arizona Chinese Times*, June 1, November 1, December 1, 1990, February 5, March 1, 1991; *Arizona Republic*, October 10, 1990.

16. *Arizona Chinese Times*, June 1, November 1, December 1, 1990, February 5, March 1, 1991.

17. Tsai, *Chinese Experience in America*, 34–35.

CHAPTER 7

1. Lawrence B. DeGraff, "The City of Black Angels: Emergence of the Los Angeles Ghetto, 1890–1930," *Pacific Historical Review* 39 (August 1970), 323–70; Quintard Taylor, "The Emergence of Black Communities in the Pacific Northwest, 1865–1910," *Journal of Negro History* 64 (Fall 1979), 342–54; Rudolph M. Lapp, *Blacks in Gold Rush California* (New Haven: Yale University Press, 1937); Douglas Henry Daniels, *Pioneer Urbanites: A Social and Cultural History of Black San Francisco* (Philadelphia: Temple University Press, 1980); Alwyn Barr, "Blacks in Southwestern Cities," *Red River Valley Historical Review* 6 (Spring 1981), 5–7; Bradford Luckingham, *The Urban Southwest: A Profile History of Albuquerque, El Paso, Phoenix and Tucson* (El Paso: Texas Western Press, 1982). See also Kenneth L. Kusmer, "The Black Urban Experience in American History," in Darlene Clark Hine, ed., *The State of Afro-American History: Past, Present, and Future* (Baton Rouge: Louisiana State University Press, 1986), 91–122.

2. *Salt River Herald*, May 11, 1878; *Arizona Republican*, July 21, November 27, 1899; "History of Blacks in Phoenix Notes" (Geoffrey P. Mawn files, Arizona Historical Foundation, Hayden Library, Arizona State University); Richard E. Harris, "First Families," *Black Heritage in Arizona* 1 (November 1976), 1–5; U.S. Federal Census, Arizona Territory, 1880, 1900.

3. Harris, "First Families," 1–5.

4. *Phoenix Daily Herald*, January 30, 1890; *Arizona Republican*, October 13, 1899, March 9, October 6, 1890, September 15, 1904, January 13, February 14, 1908; William and Valida Smith, *A History of the First Institutional Baptist Church* (Phoenix: First Institutional Baptist Church, 1985), 10–11; "Blacks in Phoenix Notes" (Mawn files); Harris, "First Families," 1–5.

5. *Phoenix Daily Herald*, September 30, October 14, 1896, April 22, 1897, June 27, 1899; *Arizona Republican*, November 14, 1891, April 3, 1894, September 23, 1898, March 15, 1899, January 18, June 1, August 8, September 6, 9,

19, October 20, November 2, 1900, June 19, 1908, September 22, 1909, March 3, April 7, 1910.

   6. *Phoenix Daily Herald,* October 21, 1890, September 30, 1896, November 17, December 16, 1897, May 5, 1898, February 21, April 6, 1899; *Arizona Republican,* August 22, 1905, September 5, 1906, April 17, 1910; "Blacks in Phoenix Notes" (Mawn files); U.S. Federal Census, Arizona Territory, 1910.

   7. "Blacks in Phoenix Notes" (Mawn files).

   8. *Arizona Republican,* February 25, 1906, March 31, 1910, January 3, March 12, 1911, February 25, March 4, 7, 10, 1912, August 24, 1915; A. De Beano, *Directory of the Colored Population of Phoenix, Arizona, 1915–1916* (Phoenix: Arizona Supply Company, 1916), passim.

   9. *Arizona Republican,* January 8, February 1, March 31, April 3, 7, June 18, July 2, September 18, 19, 20, 23, December 23, 1910, July 16, 1912; Emily Williams interview (Phoenix History Project, Arizona Historical Society, Phoenix, 1975); Mary E. Gill and John S. Goff, "Joseph H. Kibbey and School Segregation in Arizona," *Journal of Arizona History* 21 (Winter 1980), 411–22; Harris, "First Families," 3–5; "Blacks in Phoenix Notes" (Mawn files).

   10. Geoffrey P. Mawn, "Phoenix, Arizona: Central City of the Southwest, 1870–1920 (Ph.D. dissertation, Arizona State University, 1979), 411–12; Thomas A. Hvidsten, "Prostitution in Phoenix, 1889–1920" (Typescript, Hayden Library, Arizona State University, 1973), 5–13.

   11. *Arizona Republican,* September 21, 23, 24, October 19, 1911; Booker T. Washington, "The Race Problem in Arizona," *The Independent* 71 (October 1911), 909–13.

   12. *Arizona Republican,* January 25, February 17, March 6, April 14, 19, May 20, June 4, 1913.

   13. *Arizona Republican,* October 12, 13, 1913; *Arizona Gazette,* February 3, 1914; Bradford Luckingham, *Phoenix: The History of a Southwestern Metropolis* (Tucson: University of Arizona Press, 1989), 67.

   14. *Arizona Republican,* June 4, 5, 6, 1915; "Blacks in Phoenix Notes" (Mawn files).

   15. *Arizona Republican,* March 3, April 19, 24, 1916; "Blacks in Phoenix Notes" (Mawn files).

   16. (Phoenix) *Independent,* July 20, 1922; *Phoenix Tribune,* July 22, 29, August 14, October 14, 1922; Emily Williams interview; Sue Wilson Abbey, "The Ku Klux Klan in Arizona, 1921–1925," *Journal of Arizona History* 14 (Spring 1973), 10–30. For the national experience of the Ku Klux Klan in the city, see Kenneth T. Jackson, *The Ku Klux Klan in the City, 1915–1930* (New York: Oxford University Press, 1967).

   17. *Phoenix Tribune,* June 4, 1913, August 3, 31, September 17, 23, 1918; *Arizona Republican,* May 10, 1919; Emily Williams interview.

   18. J. Morris Richard, *Birth of Arizona* (Phoenix: Arizona Books, 1940), 24; Michael J. Kotlanger, "Phoenix Arizona, 1920–1940" (Ph.D. dissertation,

Arizona State University, 1983), 296–97; W. A. Robinson, "The Progress of Integration in the Public Schools," *Journal of Negro Education* 25 (Fall 1956), 371–72; W. A. Robinson, "Segregation and Integration in Our Public Schools," in Greater Phoenix Council for Civic Unity, ed., *To Secure These Rights* (Phoenix: Phoenix Sun Publishing Company, 1961), 19–25; Richard E. Harris, *The First 100 Years: A History of Arizona's Blacks* (Apache Junction: Relmo, 1983), 51.

19. *Arizona Republican,* June 30, August 15, September 7, 13, December 25, 27, 1915, December 25, 1927; *Phoenix Tribune,* November 12, 1921; *Phoenix City and Salt River Valley Directory, 1928* (Phoenix: Arizona Directory Company, 1928), passim; Kotlanger, "Phoenix Arizona, 1920–1940," 450–52, 457–64; Harris, *The First 100 Years,* 51; "Blacks in Phoenix Notes" (Mawn files); Smith, *First Institutional Baptist Church,* 11–16.

20. *Phoenix Tribune,* September 21, 28, 1918, March 29, April 19, November 22, 1919, April 3, 1920, April 18, December 14, 1925; *Arizona Republican,* December 27, 1929; Harris, "First Families," 6; Harris, *The First 100 Years,* 51.

21. *Phoenix Tribune,* July 21, 26, 1921, August 4, 18, 1925; *Arizona Republican,* July 30, 1921; Earl Zarbin, *All the Time a Newspaper: The First 100 Years of the Arizona Republic* (Phoenix: The Arizona Republic, 1990), 114–15.

22. *Arizona Republican,* June 19, 1920, June 21, 1921, June 19, 1924, June 19, 1926, June 19, 1938; *Phoenix Gazette,* November 20, 1928; Smith, *First Institutional Baptist Church,* 15.

CHAPTER 8

1. Richard E. Harris, *The First 100 Years: A History of Arizona's Blacks* (Apache Junction: Relmo, 1983), 53–57; Alton Thomas, "Minority Housing in Phoenix," in Greater Phoenix Council for Civic Unity, ed., *To Secure These Rights* (Phoenix: Phoenix Sun Publishing Company, 1961), 9; Shirley J. Roberts, "Minority Group Poverty in Phoenix: A Socio-Economic Survey," *Journal of Arizona History* 14 (Winter 1973), 357–58; Michael J. Kotlanger, "Phoenix Arizona, 1920–1940" (Ph.D. dissertation, Arizona State University, 1983), 447–48; Mattie Hackett, "A Survey of Living Conditions of Girls in the Negro Schools of Phoenix, Arizona" (M.A. thesis, Arizona State University, 1939), 17, 43.

2. *Phoenix Gazette,* November 20, 1928; *Arizona Republican,* April 17, 1931; *Phoenix City and Salt River Valley Directory, 1930* (Phoenix: Arizona Directory Company, 1930), 223; Harris, *The First 100 Years,* 56–57; Kotlanger, "Phoenix, 1920–1940," 449–55, 462–63.

3. Roberts, "Minority Group Poverty," 349–58; Kotlanger, "Phoenix, 1920–1940," 444–48; Harris, *The First 100 Years,* 53–57; Thomas, "Minority Housing," 9; Hackett, "A Survey of Living Conditions," 17, 43; *Arizona Repub-*

lican, June 19, 1920, June 21, 1921, June 19, 1924, June 19, 1926, June 19, 1938; Smith, *First Institutional Baptist Church,* 15.

4. Arthur G. Horton, *An Economic, Political and Social Survey of Phoenix and the Valley of the Sun* (Tempe: Southside Progress, 1941), 183; The Citizens Survey Committee of Metropolitan Phoenix, *Community Survey of Family and Child Welfare, Health, Recreation, and Community Organizations in Metropolitan Phoenix* (Phoenix: City of Phoenix, 1946), 3; Emmett McLoughlin, *People's Padre: An Autobiography* (Boston: Beacon Press, 1954), 40–41.

5. *Phoenix Gazette,* January 11, February 11, 15, 1939; McLoughlin, *People's Padre,* 40–42; Mary Bennett, "Recording the History of Phoenix Memorial Hospital" (Typescript, Bennett Collection, Arizona Collection, Hayden Library, Arizona State University), 3–6.

6. McLoughlin, *People's Padre,* 3–13, 35–42; Bennett, "History of Phoenix Memorial Hospital," 2.

7. McLoughlin, *People's Padre,* 42–43; Julie A. Corley, "St. Mary's Parish, Phoenix, Arizona" (M.A. thesis, Arizona State University, 1992), 72.

8. McLoughlin, *People's Padre,* 43–44.

9. McLoughlin, *People's Padre,* 47–51; Joseph Stocker, "The Ball and the Cross," *The Catholic World* 165 (June 1947), 260–64.

10. McLoughlin, *People's Padre,* 53–54. For the *Gazette* series, see *Phoenix Gazette,* January 9–February 28, 1939.

11. McLoughlin, *People's Padre,* 54–55; *Phoenix Gazette,* March 10, 13, 1939.

12. *Phoenix Gazette,* January 10, 11, 18, 19, 31, February 2, 3, 7, 16, 25, 28, March 10, 13, 1939; *Arizona Republic,* September 17, 1935; McLoughlin, *People's Padre,* 55–58.

13. *Arizona Republic,* March 23, 1947, September 5, 1948; *Phoenix Gazette,* May 23, 1947; McLoughlin, *People's Padre,* 58, 101–14, 127–81; Stocker, "Ball and Cross," 260–64; Barbara Lambesis, "Memorial Hospital History," *Arizona Medicine* 33 (July 1976), 592–97; "Too Material," *Time Magazine* (December 13, 1948), 65–67.

14. *Arizona Sun,* April 7, 1950; *Arizona Republic,* September 7, 1961, September 1, 1964, March 6, 1969, October 10, 1970; *Phoenix Gazette,* May 23, 1947, June 17, 1963; Bennett, "History of Phoenix Memorial Hospital," 19–67.

15. *Arizona Republic,* September 8, 1932, July 26, 1949.

16. Irene King interview (Arizona Collection, Hayden Library, Arizona State University, 1981); *Arizona Republic,* November 27, 28, 30, 1942, February 26, 1943, December 3, 1978; *Arizona Sun,* February 1, 8, 16, 23, 1951.

17. *Arizona Sun,* February 5, May 17, June 2, July 5, November 22, 1946; February 2, 1947.

18. Lincoln Ragsdale interview (Arizona Historical Foundation, Hayden Library, Arizona State University, 1990).

19. *Arizona Sun,* May 17, September 13, October 17, 20, 1946, February 2, 21, March 2, June 20, October 24, 1947, April 2, August 27, September 24, November 5, 1948, February 20, April 15, 1949, September 19, 1952, February 27, 1953; *Arizona Republic,* January 20, 1946; *Phoenix Gazette,* October 13, 1947, February 28, 1993; Hackett, "A Survey of Living Conditions," 43–50, 102; William P. Mahoney, Jr., interview (Arizona Collection, Hayden Library, Arizona State University, 1976); Lincoln Ragsdale interview; Emily Williams interview (Phoenix History Project, Arizona Historical Society, Phoenix, 1975); Irene King interview; Bernard Black interview ((Phoenix History Project, Arizona Historical Society, Phoenix, 1978); Curtis O. Greenfield interview (Phoenix History Project, Arizona Historical Society, Phoenix, 1977); Harris, *The First 100 Years,* 69–74, 81–98, 138–141, passim.

20. William P. Mahoney, Jr., interview.

21. William P. Mahoney, Jr., interview. Greater Phoenix Council for Civic Unity, ed., *To Secure These Rights,* 9–13, 17–46; Mary Melcher, "Blacks and Whites Together: Interracial Leadership in the Phoenix Civil Rights Movement," *Journal of Arizona History* 32 (Summer 1991), 195–216.

22. W. A. Robinson, "The Progress of Integration in the Public Schools," *Journal of Negro Education* 25 (Fall 1956), 371–79.

23. Robinson, "The Progress of Integration in the Public Schools," 371–79; Harris, *The First 100 Years,* 69–74, 81–98, 138–41, passim.

24. *Arizona Sun,* October 26, 1951, February 13, 1953, May 13, 1955; *Phoenix Gazette,* February 10, 1953, December 1, 1960; Mahoney interview; Carl E. Craig interview (Phoenix History Project, Arizona Historical Society, Phoenix, 1978); Lincoln Ragsdale interview; Curtis O. Greenfield interview; Eleanor Ragsdale interview (Arizona Collection, Hayden Library, Arizona State University, 1991); Hayzel Burton Daniels, "A Black Magistrate's Struggles," in Anne Hodges Morgan and Rennard Strickland, eds., *Arizona Memories* (Tucson: University of Arizona Press, 1984), 335–338; Greater Phoenix Council for Civic Unity, ed., *To Serve These Rights,* 9–13, 17–46; Harris, *The First 100 Years,* 69–74, 81–98, 138–141, passim; Melcher, "Phoenix Civil Rights Movement," 195–216.

25. *Arizona Republic,* September 19, 23, 26, 1952.

26. *Phoenix Gazette,* December 1, 1960; *Hearings Before the United States Commission on Civil Rights, Phoenix, Arizona, February 3, 1962* (Washington, D.C.: U.S. Government Printing Office, 1962), 16–26, 34–68, 101–139, passim; Harris, *The First 100 Years,* 69–74, 81–98, 138–41.

27. Lincoln Ragsdale interview.

28. Lincoln Ragsdale interview.

29. Eleanor Ragsdale interview.

30. Madge Copeland interview (Arizona Collection, Hayden Library, Arizona State University, 1985); Mary Melcher, "Madge Copeland and Placida Garcia Smith: Community Organizers, Phoenix, Arizona, 1930–1960" (Unpub-

lished manuscript, Arizona State University, Women's Studies, 1987).

31. Madge Copeland interview; Melcher, "Madge Copeland"; Melcher, "Phoenix Civil Rights Movement," 195–216.

32. Harris, *The First 100 Years*, 69–74, 81–98, 138–46; Clyde Webb interview (Phoenix History Project, Arizona Historical Society, Phoenix, 1978).

33. George Brooks interview (Arizona Historical Foundation, Hayden Library, Arizona State University, 1990); Lincoln Ragsdale interview; Melcher, "Phoenix Civil Rights Movement," 195–216.

34. *Arizona Sun*, May 17, 1946, November 14, 1947, October 10, 1952, April 19, December 7, 1956, January 29, September 1, 1960, April 6, 1961, February 1, July 19, 1962; Travis Williams interview (Phoenix History Project, Arizona Historical Society, Phoenix, 1978); George Brooks interview; Irene King interview; *Phoenix Gazette*, February 28, 1993; Harris, *The First 100 Years*, 69–74, 81–98, 138–146, passim; *Hearings*, 16–26, 34–68, 101–139, passim; Melcher, "Phoenix Civil Rights Movement," 195–216.

35. *Arizona Sun*, November 8, 1962; *Arizona Informant*, November 18, December 2, 1971; *Arizona Republic*, February 23, 1952; Milton Mackaye, "Phoenix," *Saturday Evening Post* (October 18, 1947), 37, 88–95; Roberts, "Minority Group Poverty," 355–360; Bradford Luckingham, "Urban Development in Arizona: The Rise of Phoenix," *Journal of Arizona History* 22 (Summer 1981), 227–228; Brooks interview; Morrison Warren interview (Arizona Collection, Hayden Library, Arizona State University, 1987); Madge Copeland interview (Arizona Historical Foundation, Hayden Library, Arizona State University, 1990); Melcher, "Phoenix Civil Rights Movement," 208–209.

36. *Arizona Republic*, March 1, 1946. Michael Konig, "Toward Metropolis Status: Charter Government and the Rise of Phoenix, 1945–1960" (Ph.D dissertation, Arizona State University, 1983), 170–71.

37. Michael H. Bernstein, "Geographical Perspectives on Skid Row in Phoenix, Arizona" (M.A. thesis, Arizona State University, 1972), passim; Robert Calvin Hird II, "Property Tax Assessment Bias in the Phoenix Area" (D.B.A. dissertation, Arizona State University, 1970), 211–258; Michael Konig, "Toward Metropolis Status: Charter Government and the Rise of Phoenix, Arizona, 1945–1960" (Ph.D. dissertation, Arizona State University, 1983), 123–83; C. S. Brosnahan, "How Phoenix Lost Its Housing Code," *Arizona Frontiers* (November 1961), 7–8; Robert Blair Piser, "A Climate of Opinion: The John Birch Society in Phoenix," *Arizona Frontiers* (February 1962), 20–22; Richard L. Gilbert, "Phoenix Unreborn," *The Reporter* 29 (November 21, 1963), 48–49; Melcher, "Phoenix Civil Rights Movement," 209.

CHAPTER 9

1. Bradford Luckingham, *The Urban Southwest: A Profile History of Albuquerque, El Paso, Phoenix and Tucson* (El Paso: Texas Western Press, 1982),

117–18, 124; Richard E. Harris, *The First 100 Years: A History of Arizona's Blacks* (Apache Junction: Relmo, 1983), 94–115; *Hearings Before the United States Commission on Civil Rights, Phoenix, Arizona, February 3, 1962* (Washington, D.C.: U.S. Government Printing Office, 1962), passim; Andrew Kopkind, "Modern Times in Phoenix," *The New Republic* (November 6, 1965), 14–16; John E. Crow, *Discrimination, Poverty and the Negro: Arizona in the National Context* (Tucson: University of Arizona Press, 1968), 1–49.

2. Harris, *The First 100 Years,* 95–115; Crow, *Negro,* 1–49; Mary Melcher, "Blacks and Whites Together: Interracial Leadership in the Phoenix Civil Rights Movement," *Journal of Arizona History* 32 (Summer 1991), 207–211.

3. Richard Newhall, "The Negro in Phoenix," *Phoenix Point West* 6 (September 1965), 15–18.

4. Newhall, "The Negro in Phoenix," 15–18; Lois Broyles, "A Look at the Problem Through the Eyes of the Negro," *Arizona* (June 2, 1968), 5–10; Gary A. Stallings, "Phoenix and the National Press: A Crooked Image," *Phoenix Point West* 7 (March 1966), 14–27; Melcher, "Phoenix Civil Rights Movement," 207.

5. *Arizona Republic,* July 18, 26, 31, 1967; National Urban League, *Economic and Cultural Progress of the Negro: Phoenix, Arizona* (New York: Urban League, 1965), passim; The University of Arizona, *Civil Disorders, Lawlessness, and Their Roots* (Tucson: University of Arizona Press, 1969), 50–74.

6. *Arizona Republic,* September 27, October 27, 1965, July 18, 26, 31, 1967, August 24, 1969; Crow, *Negro,* 1–17; National Urban League, *Economic and Cultural Progress of the Negro: Phoenix, Arizona,* passim; The University of Arizona, *Civil Disorders, Lawlessness, and Their Roots,* 50–74; City of Phoenix, *Chronological History of LEAP* (Phoenix: City of Phoenix, 1967), 1–16; John Preston, "Look Who's Fighting 'Police Harassment,'" *Arizona* (May 3, 1970), 7–9.

7. *Arizona Sun,* May 9, 1957; Carl E. Craig interview.

8. *Arizona Sun,* May 9, 1957; *Arizona Informant,* December 4, 1974, July 30, 1975; *Arizona Republic,* July 16, 17, 1967, April 28, 1986; Crow, *Negro,* passim; Harris, *The First 100 Years,* 102–138; Melcher, "Phoenix Civil Rights Movement," 195–216; "A Brief History of the Urban League in Phoenix" (Typescript, Phoenix Urban League, 1981), 10–11; Eugene Grigsby interview (Arizona Collection, Hayden Library, Arizona State University, 1990); Carl E. Craig interview; Franklin J. James et al., *Minorities in the Sunbelt* (New Brunswick: Rutgers University Press, 1984), 135–139, passim; John E. Crow, *Mexican Americans in Contemporary Arizona: A Social and Demographic View* (San Francisco: R and E Research Associates, 1975), 69.

9. Crow, *Mexican Americans in Contemporary Arizona,* 69.

10. *Arizona Republic,* March 1, 1984, June 16, 1985; *Phoenix Gazette,* January 19, 1983, March 9, 1984, March 16, 1986, April 6, 1987; *New Times,* December 31, 1986–January 6, 1987; Ad Hoc Committee on Human Relations,

"The Phoenix Commission on Human Relations: A Promise Unfulfilled" (Typescript, City of Phoenix, September 12, 1984), 1–5, 47–58, passim; "Partnership in Fair Housing Conference" (Typescript, City of Phoenix, May 21, 1986), 8–9; James et al., *Minorities in the Sunbelt*, 62–81, 135–139, passim; Data Network for Human Services, *Demographic Trends in Maricopa County: Cities, Towns and Places, 1980–1990* (Phoenix: Data Network for Human Services, 1992).

11. Boye De Mente, "Living Black in Phoenix," *Phoenix* 17 (September 1982), 102–105, 125–126; "Partnership in Fair Housing Conference," 8–9.

12. *Arizona Informant*, August 20, October 8, 1980, February 27, May 1, 1985; *Phoenix Gazette*, March 30, 31, 1983, April 1, June 15, July 3, 1984, March 13, 1986, March 24, June 17, 1987, July 17, 1989, March 16, June 28, August 3, 8, November 30, 1990, December 25, 1991; *Arizona Republic*, September 19, 1984, February 22, 27, 1985, March 24, May 31, June 12, 1987, May 5, 1988, April 30, June 12, August 20, 1989, January 13, April 2, 1990, August 8, October 27, December 10–13, 19, 20, 29, 1991, June 13, 1992; *New Times*, December 19–24, 1984, February 13–19, April 24–30, 1991; "Housing Discrimination in Phoenix" (Typescript, City of Phoenix, 1986), 1–2; De Mente, "Living Black in Phoenix," 102–105, 125–126; Joseph Stocker, "Are Blacks Losing Hard-Won Ground?" *Phoenix* 20 (May 1985), 24.

13. *Phoenix Gazette*, February 5, 7, May 15, August 8–15, 19, December 2, 1991; *Arizona Republic*, August 8, October 27, December 10–13, 19, 20, 29, 1991; *New Times*, April 24–30, 1991.

14. *Arizona Informant*, August 20, October 8, 1980, February 27, May 1, 1985; *Phoenix Gazette*, March 30, 31, 1983, April 1, June 15, July 3, 1984, March 13, 1986, March 24, June 17, 1987, July 17, 1989, March 16, June 28, August 3, 8, November 30, 1990, December 25, 1991; *Arizona Republic*, September 19, 1984, February 22, 27, 1985, March 24, May 31, June 12, 1987, May 5, 1988, April 30, June 12, August 20, 1989, January 13, April 2, 1990, August 8, October 27, December 10–13, 19, 20, 29, 1991, June 13, 1992; *New Times*, December 19–24, 1984, February 13–19, April 24–30, 1991.

15. *Arizona Informant*, February 4, 1976, January 16, 1985, April 11, July 25, October 3, November 14, 21, 1990, January 16, August 21, 1991; *Arizona Republic*, May 10, 1986, March 23, April 4, May 28, 1987, September 26, December 22, 1989, March 2, November 8, 15, 1990, January 22, May 15, September 13, November 3, 1991, January 17, 18, 19, 20, 21, 1992, January 1, 1993; *Phoenix Gazette*, May 19, November 7, 1986, March 30, May 17, 1990, February 5, 7, May 15, August 8–15, 19, December 2, 1991, June 6, 1993; *New Times*, May 26–April 1, 1986, May 24–30, 1989, May 25–31, November 14–20, 1990, February 27–March 4, April 24–30, 1991, November 4, 1992; Data Network for Human Services, *Profile of City of Phoenix and Council Districts* (Phoenix: Data Network for Human Services, 1992), 14–27, 60–71.

CONCLUSION

1. Albert Camarillo, *Chicanos in a Changing Society: From Mexican Pueblos to American Barrios in Santa Barbara and Southern California, 1898–1930* (Cambridge: Harvard University Press, 1979); Richard Griswold del Castillo, *The Los Angeles Barrio, 1850–1890: A Social History* (Berkeley: University of California Press, 1979); Mario T. Garcia, *Desert Immigrants: The Mexicans of El Paso, 1880–1920* (New Haven: Yale University Press, 1981); Thomas E. Sheridan, *Los Tucsonenses: The Mexican Community in Tucson, 1854–1941* (Tucson: University of Arizona Press, 1986); Arnoldo De León, *Ethnicity in the Sunbelt: A History of Mexican Americans in Houston* (Houston: Mexican American Studies, University of Houston, 1989); Richard Griswold del Castillo, *La Familia: Chicano Families in the Urban Southwest, 1848 to the Present* (Notre Dame: University of Notre Dame Press, 1984); Robert R. Alvarez, Jr., *Familia: Migration and Adaptations* (Berkeley: University of California Press, 1987).

2. Camarillo, *Chicanos in a Changing Society;* Griswold del Castillo, *Los Angeles Barrio;* Bradford Luckingham, *The Urban Southwest: A Profile History of Albuquerque, El Paso, Phoenix and Tucson* (Texas Western Press, University of Texas, El Paso, 1982); Ricardo Romo, *East Los Angeles: History of a Barrio* (Austin: University of Texas Press, 1983); De León, *Houston.*

3. Griswold del Castillo, *Los Angeles Barrio;* Romo, *East Los Angeles;* Camarillo, *Chicanos in a Changing Society;* Garcia, *Desert Immigrants;* Sheridan, *Los Tucsonenses;* De León, *Houston.*

4. Camarillo, *Chicanos in a Changing Society;* Garcia, *Desert Immigrants;* De León, *Houston;* Sheridan, *Los Tucsonenses;* Griswold del Castillo, *La Familia;* Alvarez, *Familia.*

5. Romo, *East Los Angeles;* Camarillo, *Chicanos in a Changing Society;* De León, *Houston;* Luckingham, *The Urban Southwest;* Guadalupe San Miguel, Sr., *"Let All of Them Take Heed": Mexican Americans and the Campaign for Equality in Texas, 1910–1981* (Austin: University of Texas Press, 1987); Ricardo Romo, "The Urbanization of Southwestern Chicanos in the Early Twentieth Century," *New Scholar* 6 (Spring 1977), 183–208; Gilbert G. Gonzalez, "Segregation of Mexican Children in a Southern California City: The Legacy of Expansionism and the American Southwest," *Western Historical Quarterly* 16 (January 1985), 55–76; Mario T. Garcia, "Americanization of the Mexican Immigrant, 1880–1930," *Journal of Ethnic Studies* 6 (Summer 1978), 19–32; Douglas Monroy, "The Swallows of the Old Mission: Mexicans and the Racial Politics of Growth in Los Angeles during the Interwar Period," *Western Historical Quarterly* 14 (October 1983), 435–458.

6. Mario T. Garcia, *Mexican Americans: Leadership, Ideology, & Identity, 1930–1960* (New Haven: Yale University Press, 1989); Richard A. Garcia, *Rise of the Mexican American Middle Class: San Antonio, 1929–1941* (College Station: Texas A & M University Press, 1991); Roberto R. Treviño, "Prensa

Y Patria: The Spanish-Language Press and the Biculturation of the Tejano Middle Class, 1920–1940," *Western Historical Quarterly* 22 (November 1991), 451–472.

7. Bradford Luckingham, *Phoenix: The History of a Southwestern Metropolis* (Tucson: University of Arizona Press, 1989); Mario T. Garcia, "Introduction: Chicano Studies in the 1980s," in Mario T. Garcia and Francisco Lomeli, eds., *History, Culture, and Society: Chicano Studies in the 1980s* (Ypsilanti, Mich.: Bilingual Press, 1983), 7–10; De León, *Houston;* David Montejano, *Anglos and Mexicans in the Making of Texas, 1836–1986* (Austin: University of Texas Press, 1987); Patricia Zavella, *Women's Work and Chicano Families* (Ithaca: Cornell University Press, 1987); Denise Segura, "Labor Market Stratification: The Chicana Experience," *Berkeley Journal of Sociology* 29 (Spring 1984), 57–80; Alfredo Mirandé and Evangelina Enriquez, *La Chicana: The Mexican American Woman* (Chicago: University of Chicago Press, 1979).

8. Garcia, *Mexican Americans;* Rudolfo Acuña, *Occupied America: A History of Chicanos,* 3rd Edition (New York: Harper & Row, 1988); Oscar J. Martinez, *The Chicanos of El Paso: An Assessment of Progress* (El Paso: Texas Western Press, University of Texas, El Paso, 1980); De León, *Houston;* Bert N. Corona, "Chicano Scholars and Public Issues in the United States in the Eighties," in Garcia and Lomeli, eds., *History, Culture, Society,* 11–14; Alex M. Saragoza, "The Significance of Recent Chicano-related Historical Writings: An Appraisal," *Ethnic Affairs* 1 (Fall 1987), 24–62; Albert Camarillo, *Chicanos in Calfornia: A History of Mexican Americans in California* (San Francisco: Boyd and Fraser Publishing Company, 1984); Ricardo Romo, "Mexican Americans in the New West," in Gerald D. Nash and Richard W. Etulain, eds., *The Twentieth Century West: Historical Interpretations* (Albuquerque: University of New Mexico Press, 1989).

9. Ronald Takaki, *Iron Cages: Race and Culture in 19th-Century America* (New York: Oxford University Press, 1990); Stanford M. Lyman, *The Asian in the West* (Reno: University of Nevada Press, 1970); Catherine L. Brown and Clifton W. Pannell, "The Chinese in America" in Jesse O. McKee, ed., *Ethnicity in Contemporary America: A Geographical Appraisal* (Dubuque: Kendall/Hunt Publishing Company, 1985), 195–216; Ching-Tsu Wu, ed., *"Chink"! A Documentary History of Anti Chinese Prejudice in America* (New York: World Publishers, 1972); John R. Wunder, "Chinese in Trouble: Criminal Law and Race on the Trans-Mississippi West Frontier," *Western Historical Quarterly* 17 (January 1986), 25–41; John R. Wunder, "Law and the Chinese on the Southwest Frontier, 1850s–1902," *Western Legal History* 2 (Summer/Fall, 1989), 139–158; Roger Daniels, ed., *Anti-Chinese Violence in North America* (New York: Arno Press, 1978).

10. Diane Mei Lin Mark and Ginger Chih, *A Place Called Chinese America* (Dubuque: Kendall/Hunt Publishing Company, 1982); June Mei, "Socioeconomic Developments among the Chinese in San Francisco, 1948–1906" in Lucie

Cheng and Edna Bonacich, eds., *Labor Immigration Under Capitalism: Asian Workers in the United States Before World War II* (Berkeley: University of California Press, 1989), 370–401.

11. Mark and Chih, *A Place Called Chinese America;* Ronald Takaki, *Strangers from a Different Shore: A History of Asian Americans* (New York: Penguin Books, 1989); Shih-shan Henry Tsai, *The Chinese Experience in America* (Bloomington: Indiana University Press, 1986).

12. Tsai, *The Chinese Experience;* Takaki, *A History of Asian Americans;* Mark and Chih, *A Place Called Chinese America;* Roger Daniels, *Asian America: Chinese and Japanese in the United States Since 1850* (Seattle: University of Washington Press, 1988); Ronald Takaki, "Reflections on Racial Patterns in America, An Historical Perspective," *Ethnicity and Public Policy* 1 (Summer 1982), 1–23.

13. Takaki, *A History of Asian Americans;* Mark and Chih, *A Place Called Chinese America;* Tsai, *The Chinese Experience.*

14. Takaki, *A History of Asian Americans;* Takaki, "Reflections on Racial Patterns," 1–23; Daniels, *Asian America;* Mark and Chih, *A Place Called Chinese America;* Chalsa Loo and Paul Ong, "Slaying Demons with a Sewing Needle: Feminist Issues for Chinatown's Women," *Berkeley Journal of Sociology* 27 (Fall 1982), 77–87.

15. George A. Davis and O. Fred Donaldson, *Blacks in the United States: A Geographic Perspective* (Boston: Houghton Mifflin, 1975); Gilbert Osofsky, *Harlem: The Making of a Ghetto,* 2nd Edition (New York: Harper & Row, 1971); David M. Katzman, *Before the Ghetto: Black Detroit in the Nineteenth Century* (Urbana: University of Illinois Press, 1975); Kenneth Kusmer, *A Ghetto Takes Shape: Black Cleveland, 1870–1930* (Urbana: University of Illinois Press, 1978); Allen H. Spear, *Black Chicago: The Making of a Negro Ghetto, 1890–1920* (Chicago: University of Chicago Press, 1967); Lawrence B. de Graaf, "The City of Black Angels: Emergence of the Los Angeles Ghetto, 1890–1930," *Pacific Historical Review* 39 (August 1970), 323–48; Douglas Henry Daniels, *Pioneer Urbanites: A Social History of Black San Francisco* (Philadelphia: Temple University Press, 1980); Raymond A. Mohl, *The New City: Urban America in the Industrial Age, 1865–1920* (Arlington Heights: Harlan Davidson, 1985); Glenn C. Altschuler, *Race, Ethnicity and Class in American Social Thought, 1865–1919* (Arlington Heights: Harland Davidson, 1982).

16. Ronald Takaki, *Iron Cages: Race and Culture in 19th-Century America;* Robert Blauner, *Racial Oppression in America* (New York: Harper & Row, 1972); Altschuler, *Race, Ethnicity and Class in American Social Thought;* Aldus Newby, *Jim Crow's Defense: Anti-Negro Thought in America* (Baton Rouge: Louisiana State University Press, 1965); George M. Fredrickson, *The Arrogance of Race: Historical Perspectives on Slavery, Racism, and Social Inequality* (Middletown: Wesleyan University Press, 1988); Glenda Riley, "American Daughters: Black Women in the West," *Montana: The Magazine of Western History* 38

(Spring 1988), 14–27; Kenneth Kusmer, "The Black Urban Experience in American History," in Darlene Clark Hine, ed., *The State of Afro-American History: Past, Present, and Future* (Baton Rouge: Louisiana State University Press, 1986), 91–222.

17. Richard Polenberg, *One Nation Divisible: Class, Race, and Ethnicity in the United States Since 1938* (New York: Viking Press, 1980); Nicholas Lemann, *The Promised Land: The Great Black Migration and How It Changed America* (New York: Random House, 1991); Gary A. Tobin, "Introduction: Housing Segregation in the 1980s," in Gary A. Tobin, ed., *Divided Neighborhoods: Changing Patterns of Racial Segregation* (Beverly Hills: Sage Publications, 1987), 8–14; Joe T. Darden, "Choosing Neighbors and Neighborhoods: The Role of Race in Housing Preference," in Tobin, ed., *Divided Neighborhoods,* 15–42.

18. Polenberg, *One Nation Divisible;* William Juluis Wilson, *The Declining Significance of Race: Blacks and Changing American Institutions* (Chicago: University of Chicago Press, 1975); City of Phoenix Commission on Housing, *Housing in Phoenix* (Phoenix: City of Phoenix, 1973), 70–74, 110–157; *Phoenix Gazette,* March 21, 1993.

19. *Phoenix Gazette,* February 11, 1993.

20. Reynolds Farley and Walter R. Allen, *The Color Line and the Quality of Life in America* (New York: Oxford University Press, 1989); Wilson, *The Declining Significance of Race;* William Julius Wilson, *The Truly Disadvantaged: The Inner City, the Underclass, and Public Policy* (Chicago: University of Chicago Press, 1987); Alphonse Pinkney, *The Myth of Black Progress* (Cambridge: Harvard University Press, 1984); Lemann, *The Promised Land;* Phyllis M. Palmer, "White Women/Black Women: The Dualism of Female Identity and Experience," *Feminist Studies* 9 (Winter 1983), 151–170; Bart Landry, *The New Black Middle Class* (Berkeley: University of California Press, 1987); Nicholas Lemann, "Healing the Ghettos: A Vision of the Possible in Race Relations," *Atlantic* 203 (March 1991), 22–24; Leonard Gordon and Albert J. Mayer, "Housing Segregation and Housing Conditions for Hispanics in Phoenix and Other Southwestern Cities," in Elizabeth D. Huttman, ed., *Urban Housing Segregation of Minorities in Western Europe and the United States* (Durham: Duke University Press, 1991), 285–300; *Phoenix Gazette,* February 11, 1993.

INDEX

ABOUT THE AUTHOR

Bradford Luckingham, professor of history at Arizona State University, Tempe, holds a B.S. degree from Northern Arizona University in Flagstaff; an M.A. degree from the University of Missouri, Columbia; and a Ph.D. from the University of California at Davis. Professor Luckingham is the author of *The Urban Southwest: A Profile History of Albuquerque, El Paso, Phoenix and Tucson* (1982), *Epidemic in the Southwest, 1918–1919* (1984), and the award-winning *Phoenix: The History of a Southwestern Metropolis* (1989). He also has published articles in numerous journals, among them *Southern California Quarterly, Journal of the West, Journal of Arizona History, Western Historical Quarterly, Journal of the Southwest,* and *Journal of Urban History.*